A Challenge to Love

A CHALLENGE TO LOVE

Gay and Lesbian Catholics in the Church

Edited by Robert Nugent

with an Introduction by
Bishop Walter F. Sullivan

CROSSROAD · NEW YORK

*To Jeannine Gramick and Jack Farnell,
friends for many years and people
with whom I can laugh and cry.*

1983

The Crossroad Publishing Company
575 Lexington Avenue, New York, N.Y. 10022

Printed in the United States of America

Library of Congress Cataloging in Publication Data

Main entry under title:
A Challenge to love.
1. Homosexuality—Religious aspects—Catholic
Church—Addresses, essays, lectures. 2. Church work
with homosexuals—United States—Addresses, essays,
lectures. 3. Catholic Church—United States—Addresses,
essays, lectures. I. Nugent, Robert, SDS.
BX1795.H66C46   1982   261.8'35766   82-19850
ISBN 0-8245-0518-2 (pbk.)

"The Church . . . is a big community within which there are different situations in the individual communities. There is no lack of people suffering oppression and persecution. In the whole Catholic community, in the individual local churches, there must be an increase in the sense of particular solidarity with these brothers and sisters in the faith. . . . Solidarity means above all a proper understanding and then proper action, not on the basis of what corresponds to the concept of the person offering help, but on the basis of what corresponds to the real needs of the person being helped, and what corresponds to his or her dignity."

JOHN PAUL II
Address to the College
of Cardinals
November 5, 1979

"The Church has always taught that due consideration should be given to the circumstances which may affect, even change, the moral value of human acts. In making the rules for morality for contemporary society those who really stray from traditional teachings of the Church are those who fail to take into account the current evolution of the world."

ARCHBISHOP JOSEPH PLOURDE
Ottawa, Canada
1981 Lenten Pastoral Letter
"Building Happy Families"

"I would today recommend to you one point which must always count as an essential characteristic of our Society. This is [its] universality. . . . Our task, the aim of our Society, the spirit of our Society is the *omnibus et ubique*. . . . The Society is not limited as regards the place nor it is restricted as to classes of people. We are to work among the learned and unlearned, among civilized and uncivilized people. No nation, no people, no class is excluded. . . . Do not try always to concentrate where there is the greater success. Everywhere where there are souls we must work. And this I should like to leave you as a legacy. Never depart from this."

FRANCIS MARY OF THE CROSS JORDAN
Founder of the Salvatorians

Contents

Acknowledgments

This collection of essays is the result of the collaborative efforts of many individuals. I am especially grateful to the contributors who have shared their original thoughts on a most sensitive and controversial topic and many for the first time in so public a forum. Their courage and labors are a great source of strength to all of us who are engaged in various forms of ministry to gay and lesbian Catholics.

I would also like especially to thank Bishop Walter Sullivan whose leadership in so many areas of contemporary Church life has made the diocese of Richmond, Virginia one of the most Spirit-filled communities in the whole American Catholic community. The faith and vitality of the church of Richmond are due in large part to the vision and trust of its chief shepherd, a man who always speaks honestly, courageously, and humbly from his heart.

My own religious community, the Society of the Divine Savior, has been most supportive of me over the past few years in a ministry that has not always been received with understanding, enthusiasm, or encouragement in some sectors of Church life.

I am also grateful to all my colleagues, both past and present, at New Ways Ministry, especially Jeannine Gramick, Thomas Hlas, Kevin McAnally, Rick Garcia, Joseph Orndorff, and Joseph Bekisz, for their help and encouragement in the editing of this book. Finally I want to express thanks to Cos Rubencamp, C.F.X., and Jay Pinkerton, O.F.M.

This book is dedicated to two individuals who have had a great impact both personally and ministerially, on my life: Jeannine Gramick of the School Sisters of Notre Dame who was instrumental in first involving me in gay ministry in 1971 through her own prophetic outreach and example in Philadelphia, and whose friendship and shared ministry have been sustaining and challenging in my life and ministry ever since; and to Jack Farnell who introduced me to three very happy years of working, along with himself, among the poor and needy at St. John's Hospice in the Philadelphia skid row section, and who remains to this day a treasured friend and loyal companion.

Robert Nugent
Washington, D.C.

Introduction

Few topics in society today arouse strong, personal feelings in the way occasioned by the subject of this book. Few other issues being discussed in the Catholic community are as difficult and complex from every conceivable angle as is the subject of this collection of essays.

Because of the problems surrounding the issue of homosexuality in our society and Church, there is a continuing interest in data from the empirical and social sciences, and an increasing need for balanced and sensitive pastoral responses from all religious denominations. Voices of homosexual Catholics and other Christians are being raised, sometimes in anger and protest, but most often with difficult but sincere questions and genuine, personal concerns about their stance before God, their place in the Church, and the quality of their relationships with others.

In 1976, the American Catholic bishops in their pastoral letter, *To Live in Christ Jesus*, articulated a concise, yet comprehensive and balanced view of homosexuality from a Catholic perspective when they wrote:

> Some persons find themselves, through no fault of their own, to have a homosexual orientation. Homosexuals, like everyone else, should not suffer from prejudice against their basic human rights. They have a right to respect, friendship and justice. They should have an active role in the Christian community. Homosexual activity, however, as distinguished from homosexual orientation, is morally wrong. Like heterosexual persons, homosexuals are called to give witness to chastity, avoiding, with God's grace, behavior which is wrong for them, just as non-marital sexual relations are wrong for heterosexuals. Nonetheless, because heterosexuals can usually look forward to marriage, and homosexuals, while their orientation continues, might not, the Christian community should provide them a special degree of pastoral understanding and care.

Since then, several individual bishops have issued pastoral statements on the topic of homosexuality, or have instituted official forms of ministry to "sexual minorities." In 1975, the *Declaration on Certain Questions Concerning Sexual Ethics* from the Sacred Congregation for the Doctrine of the Faith addressed the topic of homosexuality, and Pope John Paul II, during his visit to the United States, reaffirmed Church teaching and called upon the bishops to be "compassionate pastors." Several other national hierarchies have issued discussion documents and pastoral guidelines on homosexuality as well. These statements help us to understand the mind of the Church, which has to be taken seriously in any Catholic discussion on homosexuality. Central to this teaching is the fundamental distinction between homosexual *orientation* and homosexual *behavior*.

Yet, we cannot remain satisfied that, once we have clearly articulated the official Church position on homosexuality, nothing else remains to be done in the area of pastoral care for homosexual people and education on this topic for the larger human community, including the families and friends of homosexual people. This is especially true in those cases where the teaching of the Church itself has been presented in such a way that it has been the source or occasion of some of the pain and alienation that many homosexual Catholics experience. We cannot overlook those injustices, including rejection, hostility, or indifference on the part of Christians, that have resulted in a denial of respect or of full participation in the community for homosexual people. We must examine our own hearts and consciences and know that each of us stands in need of real conversion in this area.

While reaffirming its sincere conviction from revelation, tradition, and Christian experience on the meaning of human sexuality, the Church must also provide spiritual and pastoral assistance to those individuals who struggle to integrate a homosexual orientation into a Christian life of deep inner peace. In an age where the flagrant violation of the most basic forms of human rights is so common, we must be especially aware of the need to defend the rights and dignity of every human being, including homosexual people, because of our fundamental belief that each individual, regardless of sexual orientation, is precious in the sight of the Lord and must be no less in ours.

In his pastoral letter, *Who is My Neighbor?*, Rembert Weakland, O.S.B., archbishop of Milwaukee, urges all of us to engage in "more dialogue among the grassroot levels, our pastoral ministers and academic people in all fields so that all sides can contribute to a deeper understanding of this complex moral issue." It is my hope that *A Challenge to Love* will promote that kind of fruitful and life-giving dialogue of which Archbishop Weakland speaks.

Many voices from a wide variety of backgrounds, experiences, and values have been brought together in this effort. All of them come from the Catholic Christian tradition, although not all of them reach the same conclusion. It is vital that we try to listen to them as they attempt to speak to some central issues and to share with us their personal insights on the topic of homosexuality. It is not necessary that we agree with each of them completely, but it is important that we appreciate and respond to their openness, honesty, and courage in writing on this sensitive and often controversial subject from their respective academic disciplines and life experiences. This, in turn, will contribute to that ongoing dialogue that I believe to be so important in the life of the Church today not only on this issue but on so many others that we face as a community of followers of Jesus still on the road of life and truth.

Dialogue by its very nature implies a variety of views and positions: it means degrees of differences and mutual agreement; it may even involve some tension among the participants and at times an inability to reach complete agreement or resolution. Hopefully, mutual sharing will eventually determine whether the differences are real or apparent and whether minor differences can be put aside so that the real issues can be engaged and resolved. Healthy dialogue will ultimately uncover views that are not coherent and arguments that are not sound.

In his encyclical letter *Ecclesiam Suam,* Pope Paul VI wrote at some length about the specific characteristics of dialogue.

> It is an outpouring of thought; it is an invitation to the exercise of the highest powers. . . . This very claim would be enough to classify the dialogue among the best manifestations of human activity and culture. . . . A second characteristic of the dialogue is meekness. . . . The dialogue is not proud; it is not bitter; it is not offensive. Its authority is intrinsic to the truth it explains, to the charity it communicates, to the example it proposes. It is not a command; it is not an imposition; it is peaceful; it avoids violent methods; it is patient; it is generous. . . . In the dialogue, one discovers how different are the ways which lead to the light of faith, and how it is possible to make them converge on the same goal. Even if these ways are divergent, they can become complementary by forcing our reasoning process out of the worn paths and by obliging it to deepen its research, to find fresh expressions. The dialectic of this exercise of thought and patience will make us discover elements of truth also in the opinions of others; it will force us to express our teaching with great fairness; and it will reward us for the work of having explained it in accordance with the objectives of another or despite his slow assimilation of our teaching. The dialogue will make us wise.

I believe that many of the contributions to this book will prove helpful in engaging in that dialogue which will make us wise. This book will be particularly helpful to those individuals and groups who care about this issue or whose lives are touched by the human reality and experience of homosexuality. Parents and families, theologians and pastors, women and men religious, vocation and formation personnel, gay and lesbian Catholics will all find in these essays a rich source of stimulating and thought-provoking ideas from writers whose knowledge and experience are invaluable to the People of God. I hope that these essays will help all of us to clarify, revise, or develop our own thinking on the subject of homosexuality. *A Challenge to Love* is a challenge to the whole Church. Some voices challenge us to love and accept homosexual Catholics; some challenge our understanding of human sexuality; some challenge our pastoral approaches. All the voices challenge us, as Christian adults, to engage in the difficult task of providing for gay and lesbian Christians that "special degree of pastoral understanding and care" that we American bishops spoke of in 1976.

What we cannot afford is a failure to meet the challenge to move ahead in our common search for justice. We cannot allow ourselves to be paralyzed by a fear that prevents us from speaking and listening to each other actively, attentively, and respectfully, even at those times when we cannot agree with or accept fully what the other is saying.

The prophet Isaiah said of the Servant, "A bruised reed he shall not break, and a smoldering wick he shall not quench." Jesus never refused dialogue or interaction with any individual or group. He was supremely able to break through all the stereotypes and prejudices of his own age, which categorized and isolated individuals as "poor," "unlearned," "Pharisee," "unclean," "Gentile," "outside the law," and so forth. He was able to reach and touch all such persons with his own healing love, a love which often came in the form of a challenge to listen and hear the voice of God in their lives and respond to that call in even greater trust and fidelity to a loving God who counted the hairs of their head and cared for them as for the sparrows of the earth. As followers and ministers of that same Jesus, the Church today can do no less.

Walter F. Sullivan
Bishop of Richmond

I

SOCIETAL
PERSPECTIVES

JEANNINE GRAMICK

Prejudice, Religion, and Homosexual People

Negative and fearful attitudes and responses of lesbian and gay persons often cause them many social and personal difficulties. Early studies on homosexuality centered on these personal problems which homosexual people experienced in society. The individual lesbian or gay person was viewed as a source of the problem; recently, however, empirical research has focused on the attitudes and behavior of others in society who have labeled homosexuality as a deviance. Such labeling is a major factor contributing to the problems and difficulties that lesbian and gay persons encounter. "Victim analysis" alone is not sufficient to effectively change people's attitudes and practices (Williams 1971). The very system that produced the damage must also be closely examined and, hopefully, modified.

Sociologists are beginning to recognize that the difficulties minority groups experience can be more accurately attributed to certain definitions and characteristics of the majority which is discriminating against them (Herzog 1970). Previously, minority groups were studied in order to determine the deficiency within them which contributed to their inferior social status and consequent social discrimination. Observers now see certain characteristics in the majority that can offer more plausible explanations of people's prejudices and discriminatory practices.

The model which attempts to locate the problems as being rooted in the minority group itself is called the "organism deficiency" model; the model which considers the problem to be embedded in the attitudes and behavior of the majority who define deviancy from their own vantage point is called the "social deficiency" model. For the most part, this kind of research has been almost exclusively limited to the study of blacks (Billingsley 1970) and the poor (Herzog 1970; MacDonald 1973). The social deficiency model admits that some lack does in fact exist in the individuals of a particular minority group. However, it questions whether or not those inadequacies are the result of social discrimination rather than something inherent in the group itself.

In the case of homosexual persons, for instance, some researchers, despite repeated negative findings, continue to look for data to substantiate the belief that lesbian and gay people are abnormal, unhappy, or maladjusted. The need for such a search may lie in the values and needs of the researcher rather than in a commitment to objective scientific research.

The Shift to the Study of Homophobia

In keeping with the trend to analyze minority groups from the social deficiency model, sociologists in the last fifteen years have begun to discuss the social fabric which views homosexual people in a discriminatory way. Instead of focusing on lesbian and gay persons themselves, much recent research in homosexuality has centered on the characteristics of those who espouse negative beliefs about homosexuality. A general prejudice against homosexual people has come to be called homophobia. The word *homophobia* literally translates as "fear of the same," its etmyology being based on a Greek prefix and root. While some researchers properly designate this phenomenon homo-sexphobia, meaning "fear of the same sex," most writers have persisted in employing the former term in their nomenclature.

Homophobia can be understood from a personal, internal perspective or from an external, cultural point of view. George Weinberg (1972) popularized the use of the term *homophobia* to describe an irrational fear, intolerance, or dread on the part of heterosexual people of being in close proximity to people they believe to be homosexually oriented. Homophobic feelings are not always easily detected. Subtle innuendos or obviously blatant jokes about "fags," "dykes," or "queers" may indicate an underlying fear of or uncomfortability with the subject of homosexuality. A heterosexually married spouse may gradually come to discover some same-sex erotic attractions. Confused, distressed, and fearful, she or he may inadequately cope with these same-sex desires by general negativity to the subject of homosexuality. Similarly, homophobia may be manifested in the ridicule of an adolescent male toward an effeminate peer in order to prove his own masculinity.

From the external or cultural dynamic, homophobia can be defined as "any belief system which supports negative myths and stereotypes about homosexual people" (Morin and Garfinkle 1978, p. 30). More specifically, it is any structured belief which does not equate the value of same-sex life-styles and opposite-sex life-styles. A societal unwillingness to sanction any sexual behaviors which depart from an established norm may be a symptom of homophobia. For those individuals situated in a cultural matrix which legitimates sexuality only within a monogamous, permanent, heterosexual marriage, total freedom from homophobic feelings is extremely difficult.

In some cultures homosexual prejudice does not constitute a serious social problem. In 64 percent of seventy-six nonindustrialized cultures surveyed, "homosexual activities of one sort or another are considered normal and socially acceptable for certain members of the community" (Ford and Beach 1951, p. 130). The Greeks and Romans of antiquity condoned and even advocated same-sex behavior among males as an expression of the highest form of love. (The subordinate status of woman inevitably contributed to the attitude that same-sex relationships were superior to heterosexual ones.) Excepting the Hebrews and possibly Assyrians, the ancient cultures surrounding the Tigris and Euphrates rivers, the Nile, and the Mediterranean Sea approved of same-sex behavior.

Even European cultures such as the Scandinavians, Celts, and Cretans accepted homosexual practices. Some Oriental cultures tolerated homosexuality at various historical times. During the feudal period of Japan, male homosexual love was esteemed as more virile than heterosexual love. Male geishas adorned Japanese teahouses until the middle of the nineteenth century. Relative to history and anthropology, homosexual prejudice is not a universal phenomenon (Gramick, in press).

Homosexual prejudice is found among lesbian and gay persons themselves as well as among heterosexual individuals. It takes the form of self-hatred resulting from the internalization of other people's irrational fears. Gay men have internalized many of society's beliefs about homosexuality, although they do not hold these beliefs to the same extent as heterosexual men (Lumby 1976; May 1974).

This sociological examination of prejudice, religion, and homosexual people will consider (1) some characteristics of homophobic people which may offer some insights into the causes of homosexual prejudice, (2) gender differences among those who exhibit intolerance against lesbian or gay individuals, and (3) the relationship between religion and homosexual prejudice.

1. Characteristics and Root Causes of Homosexual Prejudice

Studies have revealed that individuals who manifest homosexual prejudice also exhibit other attributes. Generally such people tend to be:

   a. more authoritarian, intolerant of ambiguity, status conscious, and cognitively rigid (MacDonald 1974; Smith 1971);
   b. more dogmatic (Hood 1973);

    c. more sexually rigid and more guilty about their own sexual im-
    pulses (Berry and Marks 1969; Brown and Amoroso 1975; Dun-
    bar, Brown, and Amoroso 1973; Dunbar, Brown, and Vourinen
    1973; Smith 1971).

Individuals who are afraid of or intolerant of lesbian or gay people seem
to be afraid or intolerant in a great many other social situations as well.
The personality characteristics of homophobic people can easily be attributed to any other highly prejudiced group of people.

    Some sociologists have examined the personal correlates of homosex-
ual prejudice with a view to explaining the root causes of homophobia.
Churchill (1967) believed that personal homophobic attitudes are influenced by general cultural values regarding appropriate sexual behavior.
Social attempts to repress homosexuality, Churchill believed, were the
direct outcome of socialization in "sex-negative" cultures. He describes
contemporary American culture as exercising negative social judgment
upon all sexual behavior outside of the Judeo-Christian tradition of monogamous heterosexual marriage; homosexual prejudice is merely an
extension of attitudes of denial toward most other kinds of sexual behavior. According to Churchill, the sex-negative individual represses or suppresses his or her own sexuality and seeks to restrain the sexual practices
of others; the sex-positive individual accepts her or his own sexuality
and, consequently, accepts the sexuality, behavior, and values of others.

    Support for Churchill's contention can be found in studies which com-
pare attitudes of Brazilians, Canadians, and West Indians (Brown and
Amoroso 1975; Dunbar, Brown, and Amoroso 1973). Brazilians had the
most conservative attitudes toward sex-appropriate behavior of the three
cultures studied. Brazilians also showed the most homosexual prejudice.
West Indians, who demonstrated moderately conservative attitudes toward sex-appropriate behavior, were intermediate between the highly
sex-negative Brazilians and the less sex-negative Canadians. To further
substantiate this belief, it was found that individuals exhibited more
negative attitudes toward homosexuality if they grew up in the strongly
sex-negative subcultures of the midwestern and southern regions of the
United States than if they were reared in other parts of the country (Levitt
and Klassen 1974).

    Despite the above research linking conservative attitudes toward sex-
ual morality in general with homosexual prejudice, traditional attitudes
toward sexuality may not be the only nor, indeed, main source of homophobia. A more basic component of homophobia may be the need to
preserve a double standard between women and men. A direct association was found between negative attitudes toward homosexuality and
acceptance of sex-role stereotyping among men (Brown and Amoroso

1975; Dunbar, Brown, and Amoroso 1973; Dunbar, Brown, and Vourinen 1973).

Another study (MacDonald et al. 1973) tested these two differing explanations for homosexual prejudice. Which attitude is more responsible for generating homosexual intolerance: Conservative standards toward sexual behavior or support for a double standard between the sexes? It was found that permissive attitudes toward premarital sex correlated highly, but not as highly with homosexual intolerance as the acceptance of traditional sex roles. Some people condemned the homosexual person, whom they erroneously believed to be feminine when male, and masculine when female. Any threat to the traditional masculine-feminine dichotomy was abhorred. Inappropriate gender characteristics were rejected in order to reduce sex-role confusion and in order to preserve the dual role standard. While it was found that homosexual prejudice is more closely linked with a support for a double sexual standard than with nonpermissive attitudes toward premarital sexual intimacy, it must be pointed out that permissive attitudes toward premarital sex represent a limited index of "conservative morality." The hypothesis concerning conservative sexual morality must be tested over a much broader spectrum of definitions.

Some claim that the best predictor of homosexual prejudice is a belief in the traditional family power structure, i.e., a dominant father, submissive mother, and obedient children (Morin and Wallace 1976). The same researchers also found that the second best predictor of homophobia was advocacy of traditional attitudes toward women. Traditional religious beliefs were also predictive of both traditional beliefs about women and negative attitudes toward homosexuality. All of these studies lend support to Churchill's theory that socialization concerning appropriate roles for women and men is an impetus which influences hatred and fear of homosexual people.

From the cultural perspective, fears regarding gay men appear to be rooted in a general belief system; these fears affect individuals by the process of socialization. Acceptance of stereotypes which view homosexual people as sick and dangerous seems to be particularly associated with negative attitudes toward homosexuality. The more a person agrees with the stereotypes which consider homosexual individuals sick and dangerous, the more rejecting of lesbian or gay people he or she tends to be (Steffensmeier and Steffensmeier 1974).

From the personal perspective, homosexual prejudice can be a form of anxiety regarding one's own sexual feelings. Freud's theory (1911) relating paranoia to the projection of repressed, unacceptable passions has been extended to explain prejudice. Prejudice has been interpreted in terms of irrational fears and unconscious impulses projected outward by the prejudiced individual onto the object of his or her own prejudice (Adorno et al. 1950). Among the most acceptable emotions involved in all of this process are unconscious heterosexual and homosexual desires.

A widespread ignorance about the nature of human sexuality readily results in anxiety and fear in the person who experiences even minimal same-sex physical attractions. Unfamiliar with Kinsey's continuum of sexual orientation, many individuals erroneously regard human sexuality as bipolar: heterosexual or homosexual. They fail to understand that most people experience both the same- and opposite-sex attractions in varying degrees. To cope with their repressed or denied homosexual desires, individuals may develop an unhealthy fear of homosexuality which may induce vehement opposition to same-sex expression in others. The hostility which would naturally be directed toward self is diverted or projected onto another.

This projection occurs because the individual is uncomfortable with his or her own homosexuality. Afraid of latent homosexual feelings, the person seeks personal reassurance and self-conviction that she or he is really healthy or normal by trying to suppress all same-sex impulses in self or others. Fear of lesbian women or gay men is then the projection of the fear of one's own same-sex inclinations onto any homosexual manifestation in others which the individual unconsciously considers unacceptable (MacDonald 1976; Weinberg 1972).

Another variant of the projection theory assumes that homophobic individuals are fearful of sexual expressions of any kind. According to this view, uncomfortability with one's own sexual feelings is projected as hostility toward those who are more open and expressive about their sexuality. Such people display negative attitudes and actions toward others who openly express homosexuality.

Churchill (1967) posited that homosexual prejudice flowed from negative attitudes toward one's own sexuality as well as from identification with the age-old sexual beliefs and mores of the culture. His theory that a primarily antisexual factor rather than a specifically proheterosexual factor accounts for homosexual intolerance has been substantiated by researchers (Berry and Marks 1969; Brown and Amoroso 1975).

2. Gender Differences

Having considered some qualities of homophobic people and potential causes of homosexual prejudice which merit further investigation, this essay will now present some gender variances among those who are intolerant of lesbian or gay people. The question of whether men or women in our society are more homophobic has received much attention recently. While homosexual prejudice has been found in both men and women, males seem to be more threatened by homosexuality than are females (Brown and Amoroso 1975; Gallup 1977; Millham, San Miguel, and Kellogg 1976; Minnigerode 1976; Nutt and Sedlacek 1974; Steffensmeier and Steffensmeier 1974).

Unfortunately, fear of homosexuality among many American men prevents them from forming intimate same-sex friendships. Because such friendships risk a homosexual label, many males limit their options regarding close relationships to maintain a strong independent male role. By thus excluding other males from their intimate circle, they deprive themselves of enriching experiences and potentially growth-producing opportunities.

It is not surprising that men show more personal anxiety regarding gay men than regarding lesbian women. Similarly, women express greater preference for homosexual males than for lesbian women. The threat or uncomfortability seems to be much greater if one is dealing with a homosexual person of one's own gender. Having a lesbian or gay friend or relative results in less negativity toward homosexuality by both men and women (Millham, San Miguel, and Kellogg 1976).

The fact that gay men are much more vulnerable to rejection and disapprobation than their lesbian counterparts has been explained culturally. Feminist analysis has pointed out that traditionally defined male roles have been more highly valued in American society. Women who deviate from the societal expectations of traditional feminine roles may not be harshly condemned for aspiring to a "superior" role. On the other hand, men who depart from the more valued masculine roles are severely judged by society. Since gay men are incorrectly perceived as espousing female roles and lesbian women as mimicking masculine roles, societal opprobrium toward homosexual males is much greater. This would seem to explain the legal harassment and prosecution of gay men and the relative lack of legal repression of lesbian women. Lesbianism is not defined as a serious social problem as is male homosexuality because the latter is viewed as a greater violation of culturally acceptable sex roles (Steffensmeier and Steffensmeier 1974).

In one study on attitudes toward homosexuality and femininity in men (Storms 1978), subjects disliked the homosexual male more than the heterosexual male regardless of his gender attributes. They did not, however, consistently dislike the feminine man more than the masculine man. The feminine heterosexual man was liked less than the masculine heterosexual man, but the feminine homosexual man or "pansy" was liked more than the masculine homosexual man or "macho gay." These results cast doubt on the notion that homosexual people are disliked because of

their presumed inappropriate gender attributes. Storms explains this surprising result in the following way:

> This last finding, that masculine homosexual men are liked less than
> feminine homosexual men, may provide the key to understanding the
> true relationship between attitudes about sexual orientation and atti-
> tudes about sex-roles. It appears that attitudes about sexual orienta-
> tion are predominant; people primarily dislike homosexuals. Be-
> yond that, people probably adhere to the stereotype that homosexual
> men are feminine. Thus, to the extent that people dislike feminine
> men, it may be because of suspected homosexuality. When a femi-
> nine man turns out to be heterosexual and when a homosexual man
> turns out to be masculine, both are disliked even more for violating
> the stereotype.
>   It seems paradoxical that violating a disliked stereotype would
> make one disliked all the more. It suggests that the feminine homo-
> sexual male stereotype is a powerful, important belief that people
> resent having disconfirmed. (p. 261)

Other factors besides gender variations have also been examined to see
if they relate to homosexual prejudice. However, neither occupation,
socioeconomic background, age, nor geographic location has been found
to be so related. Several writers stress that the variable of religion ought
to be given more attention. This brings us to the third point of consideration: the relationship between religion and homosexual prejudice.

3. Religion and Homosexual Prejudice

An individual's personal religious belief about homosexual behavior
might well be the foundation on which the majority of people make value
judgments about homosexuality. Social sanctions can either restrict homosexuality entirely or tolerate its presence and manifestations under
carefully and rigidly controlled conditions. These social sanctions towards homosexuality arise from a variety of personal and cultural factors. Religion may be a major factor in shaping people's attitudes towards lesbian and gay people, even more so than towards any other
minority group in our society.

The publication of Adorno's *The Authoritarian Personality* (1950) and
Glock and Stark's *Christian Beliefs and Anti-Semitism* (1966) aroused
intense sociological interest in the relationship between religion and prejudice. A large body of empirical evidence documents that those individuals who are more "religious" according to various definitions tend to be
less tolerant of racial, ethnic, and religious minorities (Rokeach 1960;
Allport and Kramer 1946; Williams 1964; Stouffer 1955).

Very little research has been conducted in the field of religion and homosexual prejudice. Irwin and Thompson (1977) explored this relationship using data from a nationwide opinion survey in the United States. Their study found some significant differences in attitudes due to religious affiliation. Protestants and Roman Catholics were less willing to grant civil rights to lesbian and gay people than either Jews, those affiliated with another religion, or those who do not associate themselves with any religion. The strength of association between denomination and tolerance was fairly strong. One may logically ask why persons who identify with one religious establishment seem to be more hostile toward granting civil rights to lesbian and gay people than members of another structured religion.

In this same study, frequency of church attendance was also related to attitudes towards homosexual people. Although attendance at religious services is not an adequate measure of religious feelings, it certainly represents identification with a religious institution. The more frequent the church attendance, the more negative or conservative the attitudes. However, the negative attitudes among the churchgoers may be confined to the Protestants, who comprised the majority of the sample, and may not hold true for the other denominations.

Catholics and Protestants seem not only less willing to grant civil rights but also to be more rejecting of same-sex behavior than Jews or those who claim no religious affiliation at all. Regular (i.e., weekly) churchgoers are the least likely to accept homosexual behavior as legitimate (Nyberg and Alston (1976–77). The same body of data suggests that societal attitudes toward homosexual behavior will become more accepting only along with the acceptance of more liberal attitudes toward sexual behavior *per se*. A group of Methodist, Presbyterian, Roman Catholic, and Lutheran clergy demonstrated that the more orthodox one's religion, the more likely one is to be prejudiced against homosexual behavior (Wagennar and Bartos 1977).

Within Western civilization, religion has been popularly considered the traditional enemy of the lesbian or gay person and the alleged cause of homosexual intolerance. Such an assertion is certainly in keeping with the findings which document a relationship between prejudice and religion. This long-standing thesis has been challenged by Boswell (1980), who asserts that neither Christianity nor any other religion is the cause of social prejudice toward lesbian and gay people. The crucial word, of course, is *cause*. Boswell contends that religious beliefs became the scapegoat. Society needed a justification or rationalization for an already existing and deeply rooted prejudice and animosity.

Such a theory is indeed logical: if certain moral precepts which censure a particular minority are strictly enforced while other equally grave strictures limiting the sexual freedoms of the dominant majority are taken lightly, then seeing religion as the root cause of intolerance becomes suspect. Of necessity, other forces—social, economic, political, or personal—must be operative to explain adequately the hostile response in the one instance and not in the other. If applied fairly, religious strictures would find both behaviors loathsome. For example, if religious sanctions are the cause of antipathy to homosexual people, why aren't adulterers treated as lepers and outcasts in Christian societies, since both homosexuality and adultery are judged equally immoral by traditional Christian religious standards?

The Scriptures purportedly condemn hypocrisy as well as homosexual practices. But Western civilization did not brand hypocrisy as "unnatural" nor punish hypocrites by death or castration. Christian Scriptures also list homosexual acts and greed as sins deserving eternal punishment; however, no Western society has even enacted laws to burn greedy people at the stake! Prostitution, a sexual offense more stringently condemned than homosexual acts in the New Testament, was socially licensed rather than designated a capital offense in late medieval times.

The early Christian sect did not consider itself ultimately bound to Levitical law. From an outsider's perspective, the external hallmarks of the Jewish religion were found in their dietary regulations, ritual laws, and circumcision. If, within the relatively short period of 100 years of the official establishment of the Christian Church, Christianity had already abandoned these three practices, why should it cling tenaciously to a taboo against some particular action merely because it was part of Jewish tradition?

Almost no theologians condemned homosexual behavior utilizing "proof texts" from the New Testament passages, which are now routinely presented as biblical data on homosexuality, until after their mistranslation into English. Therefore these Scripture passages were not, in fact, responsible for antigay attitudes in medieval Christendom.

The above analysis is very careful to distinguish between authorship and execution. While this distinction is conceptually valid, the difference between the two may be operationally ambiguous and is apt to be lost on the average lay person. In American government, for example, the legislative branch authors the laws while the executive branch executes them. A repressive law will most likely be attributed to its source, a repressive government, with little distinction being made in the public eye as to which particular branch of the government is ultimately responsible for drafting the offensive legislation.

One cannot deny that some expressions of Christianity cannot be completely extricated from the political structure of western Europe from the fourth century on. It is precisely the particular type of social structure to which Christianity was intrinsically bound which may be responsible for antihomosexual prejudice. Does the simple explication of this distinction, however, make us one step removed from the real source of oppression?

If Christianity is the conduit rather than the cause of homosexual prejudice, and if religious beliefs are used merely to disguise or to give a semblance of rationality to already deeply rooted feelings of intolerance, then future researchers must ask, "What *are* the factors responsible for antigay prejudice?" Perhaps these factors will help to explain why prejudice resides in many religiously motivated people despite the fact that religion basically teaches love and respect for persons. Many crusaders for social justice, peace, and human rights have been motivated by and committed to religious beliefs of equality and love for all humankind. Religion has traditionally valued and promoted such qualities as trust, acceptance, openness, and feelings of love. How then can the paradox of a prejudiced religious person be explained? This apparent contradiction may be accounted for by appeals to three main contexts: theological, sociocultural, and personal-psychological.

Contexts for Analysis

In the theological context, some religions may hold tenets which can lead adherents to bigoted attitudes. Such is the case with a doctrine of revelation which professes an exclusive possession of the truth. A doctrine of election in which a group is thought self-righteously to be chosen, special, set apart, or divinely called would also tend to foster oppression of those not so divinely chosen.

Within this theological context, Glock and Stark (1966) published data to substantiate their contention that orthodox Christian beliefs prompt a rigid stand with regard to those beliefs. Consequently, hostilities toward non-Christians, particularly toward Jews, emerge. This landmark study produced much critical analysis. Their assertion that Christian beliefs cause anti-Semitism was challenged in religious and professional literature on methodological as well as theoretical grounds (Furfey 1966; Hadden, Vawter, and Mowshowitz 1966; Monas 1966; Dittes 1967; Greeley 1967; Levinson 1967; Strommen 1967; Williams 1967). The furor created by their book had the beneficial effect of inducing others to probe more deeply into analyzing the roots of prejudice.

A second possible explanation of why prejudice exists among religiously oriented people may lie in a sociocultural distinction concerning the reasons why individuals associate themselves with organized religions. In this sociocultural context reasons for church membership have been divided into communal and associational involvement. Communal affiliation refers to those for whom church membership represents a status, fulfills a need for social involvement or entertainment, provides a gossip source or a balm for lonely feelings. Associational membership, on the other hand, defines those individuals whose motivation and involvement springs from desires of sharing religious community.

In a study conducted to determine the extent of racial prejudice among Detroit churchgoers, 59 percent of Detroit Catholics with high communal involvement and low associational involvement favored segregated schools. By contrast, only 27 percent of the Detroit Catholic sample with low communal involvement and high associational involvement similarly favored segregated schools. Among Detroit Protestants a significant trend in the same direction was also reported (Lenski 1961). This seems to indicate that racial prejudice is more likely to exist among those Christians who associate with a church for social status or the reduction of personal feelings of loneliness than among those Christians who seek to identify themselves with others who share similar religious and spiritual convictions.

A third approach to resolve the coexistence of religion and intolerance involves an individual's personal, psychological context. Distinctions between extrinsic and intrinsic values have been offered to describe two types of personal religious orientation. The extrinsic religious personality views religion in purely utilitarian terms, as "useful for the self in granting safety, social standing, solace, and endorsement for one's chosen way of life" (Allport 1966, p. 455). This concept bears a striking resemblance to the communal type of church member described above. On the other hand, the intrinsic religious personality regards religious beliefs as primary motivation for all behaviors. In simple terms, an extrinsically oriented person *uses* his or her religion, while an intrinsically oriented person *lives* it.

Intrinsically motivated churchgoers seem to be less prejudiced than those people with an extrinsic religious orientation. Furthermore, those individuals who are indiscriminately proreligious are the most prejudiced of all types (Allport and Ross 1967). It seems that those who seek shelter in religion or use it as a crutch tend to be more intolerant than those who genuinely adhere to religious beliefs.

As can be seen, to categorically assert that religion promotes intolerance is much too simplistic. Personality and cultural variables must certainly be taken into account. Some contend that both religious orthodoxy and minority intolerance are expressions of a personal view which is limited in breadth of experience and outlook. Less cognizant of diversified social systems, such persons tend to manufacture rationalizations for minority intolerance which may find their legitimation not their source in a religious context (Roof 1974).

Future Study

The minimal research conducted concerning the relationship of religion and homosexual prejudice has failed to take into account the various distinctions of the theological, sociocultural, and personal-psychological contexts of religion. In any further study of religion and homosexual intolerance, two important questions need to be addressed:

1. What causes the patterns of homosexual oppression that many religious individuals have developed?
2. To what extent do differences in the various kinds of religious contexts predict approval of change in social policy?

To begin to answer the first question of the causes of homosexual prejudice among religious people, a constellation of sociocultural and historical factors need to be investigated. Elements embedded within the personality structure of the religiously oriented person must be isolated in order to ascertain the degree to which such factors contribute to a manifestation of homosexual oppression. To identify that constellation of historical and sociocultural factors such variables as education, age, political affiliation, ethnicity/race, socioeconomic background, and type of religious membership must be examined. Personal-psychological constructs such as authoritarianism, gender-role stereotypes, localistic world view, and conservatism should also be taken into account. Essentially, then, a reconstruction of how religiously inclined persons arrive at their present patterns of homosexual intolerance is desired.

The second question to be investigated in future research involves changes in social policy. Public bias against homosexual persons extends beyond mere social disapproval. A significant number of employers, for instance, would deny certain jobs or positions of authority and leadership to lesbian or gay persons. Whether or not the denial of these particular jobs or occupations is in any way related to the employer's degree of religiosity needs to be determined. Would a highly religious employer or supervisor, for instance, be less comfortable in accepting lesbian or gay workers in some positions and not in others, and if so, why? Can religious individuals make any kind of distinction between personal, moral disapproval of certain kinds of sexual behavior and the civil rights of those individuals who choose to live by a different value system?

Toward an Unprejudiced Future

In the above pages I have dealt with (1) some common traits of those who manifest intolerance toward homosexual individuals which may provide a key to understanding the root causes of this kind of prejudice, (2) variations between males and females who feel a negative bias against homosexual people, and (3) the relationship between religion and homosexual prejudice. I have discussed these themes by referring to a vast amount of sociological research. But no amount of academic studies, no matter how prolific, can erase the societal prejudice that abounds toward lesbian and gay people. When the academic problems have been solved, the human question remains. How can homosexual prejudice be reduced and ultimately eliminated so that all people, regardless of their sexual orientation, may be treated with dignity and equality?

In any culture one manner of replacing prejudice with toleration and finally with acceptance necessitates a lengthy and often tedious educational process. This educational method will assume many forms. For example, intelligent discussion between homosexual and heterosexual persons will be facilitated if respected and trusted members of society come out or reveal their homosexual orientation. Such a revelation almost invariably results in the shattering of myths and stereotypes of what gay and lesbian people are imagined to be (Gramick 1973).

Legal modifications constitute another form of education and consciousness raising. In order for states to decriminalize same-sex genital behavior or for municipalities, states, or federal levels to enact protective civil rights legislation, public hearings are usually scheduled in which the issue of homosexuality is aired. By addressing the topic frankly and openly with a sufficiently substantial number of people, irrational fears can be challenged and overcome.

Education, I believe, is the primary vehicle for transforming the prejudice which society assigns to any taboo behavior considered "unnatural." A popular objection to homosexual activity rests on a general antipathy to anything which is thought to be inherently unnatural. The classification of nonprocreative sexuality as "unnatural" was advocated by some philosophical schools during the rise of the Christian state after the fourth century. This philosophy subsequently fell into disuse but was later resurrected by the thirteenth-century Scholastics. While such an approach to sexuality and nature has been almost totally abandoned by contemporary thinkers, its emotional impact on the masses has not. Religious systems based on certain concepts of "nature" have at various times opposed growing flowers and plants indoors, shaving, and regular bathing as unnatural.

It seems plausible to claim that cultural mechanisms have conditioned people to respond to heterosexual stimuli and to impede or repress innate homosexual responses by imposing powerful social sanctions. Strong social forces operate to support heterosexual behavior and to inhibit homosexual activity. Natural same-sex feelings and attractions have been interpreted as a denunciation of or threat to the heterosexual social order. But the monumental and pioneering work of Alfred Kinsey and the present day popular investigations of the Masters and Johnson team are convincing the American public that homosexual behavior is well within the normal range of human sexual expression.

Sound sex education is a responsibility of the family, the school system, and established religions. Responsible forums must be set up to discuss and study all aspects of human sexuality, such as cohabitation, contraception, sterilization, as well as homosexuality. Education is a key factor in developing some sense of understanding of many controversial or sensitive sexual issues.

Because human sexuality is so intensely personal, any attitudinal change toward homosexuality must be initiated on a personal level. The first step in this process rests with the reader, who is invited to engage in a critical self-examination of his or her own attitudes toward sexuality. Assume the responsibility of educating yourself through workshops or seminars, through professional reading and study. Attitudinal change can occur only through exposure, contact, and confrontation with the truth. Above all, meet with and learn from lesbian and gay people themselves. They represent a prime source of hope in educating for an unprejudiced future.

REFERENCES

Adorno, T. W.; Frenkel-Brunswik, E.; Levinson, D. J.; and Sanford, R. N. 1950. *The authoritarian personality*. New York: Harper.

Allport, G. W. 1966. The religious context of prejudice. *Journal for the Scientific Study of Religion* 5: 447–57.

Allport, G. W., and Kramer, B. M. 1946. Some roots of prejudice. *Journal of Psychology* 22: 9–39.

Allport, G. W., and Ross, J. M. 1967. Personal religious orientation and prejudice. *Journal of Personality and Social Psychology* 5, no. 4: 432–43.

Berry, D. F., and Marks, P. A. 1969. Antihomosexual prejudice as a function of attitude toward own sexuality. *APA Proceedings* 4: 573–74.

Billingsley, A. Black families and white social science. 1970. *Journal of Social Issues* 26: 127–42.

Boswell, J. 1980. *Christianity, social tolerance and homosexuality*. Chicago: Univ. of Chicago Press.

Brown, M., and Amoroso, D. M. 1975. Attitudes toward homosexuality among West Indian male and female college students. *Journal of Social Psychology* 97: 163–68.

Churchill, W. 1967. *Homosexual behavior among males: a cross-cultural and cross-species investigation*. New York: Hawthorne.

Dittes, J. R. 1967. Review article on Charles V. Glock and Rodney Stark, Christian beliefs and anti-Semitism. *Review of Religious Research* 8: 183–87.

Dunbar, J.; Brown, M.; and Amoroso, D. M. 1973. Some correlates of attitudes toward homosexuality. *Journal of Social Psychology* 89: 271–79.

Dunbar, J.; Brown, M.; and Vourinen, S. 1973. Attitudes toward homosexuality among Brazilian and Canadian college students. *Journal of Social Psychology* 90: 173–83.

Ford, C. S., and Beach, F. 1951. *Patterns of sexual behavior*. New York: Harper & Row.

Freud, S. The case of Schreber (1911). In *The complete works of Sigmund Freud*. Vol. 2 (1911–13). Reprint. London: Hogarth Press, 1958.

Furfey, P. H. 1966. Sociology and anti-Semitism. *Commonweal* 84: 558–59.

Gallup, G. Gallup poll on gay rights: approval with reservations. *San Francisco Chronicle*, 18 July 1977, pp. 1, 18.

Glock, C. Y., and Stark, R. 1966. *Christian beliefs and anti-Semitism*. New York: Harper & Row.

Gramick, J. 1973. The myths of homosexuality. *Intellect* 102: 2352–55.

Gramick, J. Homophobia: a new challenge replaces a disproven view. *Social Work*. In press.

Greeley, A. M. 1967. Review of Charles Y. Glock and Rodney Stark, Christian beliefs and anti-Semitism. *American Sociological Review* 32: 1007–9.

Hadden, J. K.; Vawter, B.; and Mowshowitz, I. 1966. Churchly particularism and the Jews: a trifaith symposium on the Glock-Stark anti-Semitism survey. *Christian Century* 83: 987–92.

Herzog, E. 1970. Social stereotypes and social research. *Journal of Social Studies* 26: 109–25.

Hood, R. W. 1973. Dogmatism and opinions about mental illness. *Psychological Reports* 32: 1283–90.

Irwin, P., and Thompson, N. L. 1977. Acceptance of the rights of homosexuals: a social profile. *Journal of Homosexuality* 3, no. 2: 107–21.

Lenski, G. 1961. *The religious factor*. Garden City, N.Y.: Doubleday.

Levinson, D. J. 1967. Review of Charles Y. Glock and Rodney Stark, Christian beliefs and anti-Semitism. *American Sociological Review* 32: 1009–13.

Levitt, E. E., and Klassen, A. D. 1974. Public attitudes toward homosexuality. *Journal of Homosexuality* 1: 29–43.

Lumby, M. E. 1976. Homophobia: the quest for a valid scale. *Journal of Homosexuality* 2: 39–47.

MacDonald, A. P., Jr. 1973. A time for introspection. *Professional Psychology* 4: 35–42.

MacDonald, A. P. 1974. The importance of sex-role to gay liberation. *Homosexual Counseling Journal* 1: 169–80.

MacDonald, A. P. 1976. Homophobia: its roots and meanings. *Homosexual Counseling Journal* 3: 23–33.

MacDonald, A. P., Jr.; Huggins, J.; Young, S.; and Swanson, R. A. 1973. Attitudes toward homosexuality: preservation of sex morality or the double standard? *Journal of Consulting and Clinical Psychology* 40: 161.

May, E. P. 1974. Counselors', psychologists', and homosexuals' philosophies of human nature and attitudes toward homosexual behavior. *Homosexual Counseling Journal* 1: 3–25.

Millham, J.; San Miguel, C. L.; and Kellogg, R. 1976. A factor-analytic conceptualization of attitudes toward male and female homosexuals. *Journal of Homosexuality* 2: 3–10.

Minnigerode, F. A. 1976. Attitudes toward homosexuality: feminist attitudes and sexual conservatism. *Sex Roles: A Journal of Research* 2: 347–52.

Monas, S. 1966. Reasonable bigotry. *Commentary* 42: 96–99.

Morin, S. F., and Garfinkle, E. M. 1978. Male homophobia. *Journal of Social Issues* 34: 39–47.

Morin, S. F., and Wallace, S. Traditional values, sex-role stereotyping, and attitudes toward homosexuality. Paper presented at the meeting of the Western Psychological Association, Los Angeles, April 1976.

Nutt, R. L., and Sedlacek, N. E. 1974. Freshmen sexual attitudes and behaviors. *Journal of College Student Personnel* 15: 346–51.

Nyberg, K. L., and Alston, J. P. 1976–77. Analysis of public attitudes toward homosexual behavior. *Journal of Homosexuality* 2: 99–107.

Rokeach, M. 1960. *The open and closed mind*. New York: Basic Books.

Roof, W. C. 1974. Religious orthodoxy and minority prejudice: causal relationship or reflection of localistic world view? *American Journal of Sociology* 80: 643–64.

Smith, K. T. 1971. Homophobia: a tentative personality profile. *Psychological Reports* 29: 1091–94.

Steffensmeier, D., and Steffensmeier, R. 1974. Sex differences in reactions to homosexuals: research continuities and further developments. *The Journal of Sex Research* 10: 52–67.

Storms, M. D. 1978. Attitudes toward homosexuality and femininity in men. *Journal of Homosexuality* 3, no. 3: 257–63.

Stouffer, S. A. 1955. *Communism, conformity and civil liberties.* Garden City, N.Y.: Doubleday.

Strommen, M. P. 1967. Religious education and the problem of prejudice. *Religious Education* 1: 52–59.

Wagennar, T. C., and Bartos, P. E. 1977. Orthodoxy and attitudes of clergymen towards homosexuality and abortion. *Review of Religious Research* 18, no. 2: 114–25.

Weinberg, G. 1972. *Society and the healthy homosexual.* New York: St. Martin.

Williams, R. L. 1971. Abuses and misuses in testing black children. *The Counseling Psychologist* 2: 62–73.

Williams, R. M., Jr. 1964. *Strangers next door.* Englewood Cliffs, N.J.: Prentice-Hall.

Williams, R. M., Jr. 1967. Review of Charles Y. Glock and Rodney Stark, Christian beliefs and anti-Semitism. *American Sociological Review* 32: 1004–7.

JAMES R. ZULLO AND

JAMES D. WHITEHEAD

The Christian Body and Homosexual Maturing

Introduction

In our beginnings are our end. Nestled discreetly within our starting points are the seeds of our conclusions. We have all learned—psychologists, theologians, educators—that there is no stepping out of our social contexts and religious values; no presurgical scrub that cleanses us of our own convictions and commitments. Whether we begin in the clinic or confessional, our environs shape our vision. This is not a curse of subjectivity, but a description of the human condition. The challenge at the outset of a reflection such as this is not cool objectivity, but a clarity and honesty about where we begin.

This reflection begins in an image of who we are as a believing people. Before examining the maturing of homosexual Christians, we begin in an image of corporate identity—aware that within this image lies our conclusion.

As Catholics and Christians we are the body of Christ. "Now you together are Christ's body, but each of you is a different part of it" (1 Cor 12:27). The starting point is religious unity amid extraordinary diversity; we begin not with questions of "them" and "us," or illness and health, but with unity. We are, first of all—and finally—one. This starting point is also corporeal—a fitting image for a reflection on sexual maturing.

We are the body of Christ and our body is part gay. This is how we find ourselves. Denials, apologies, disclaimers follow. But this is who we find ourselves to be: we women and men who seek to follow Jesus Christ share a body that is part homosexual and part heterosexual.

From the beginning we Christians have cherished and been bewildered by this image of our identity. Paul repeatedly turned to this corporate symbol to describe our group's coordination and gracefulness (see 1 Cor and Eph 4). In his letter to the Corinthians he pointed to the experiences of weakness and shame, experiences not irrelevant to this reflection: "It is precisely the parts of the body that seem to be the weakest which are the indispensable ones; and it is the least honorable parts of the body that we clothe with the greatest care" (1 Cor 12:22–23).

Traditionally we have called ourself "the mystical body of Christ." At times the *mystical* quality of our shared life has been so emphasized that our fleshliness was almost forgotten (or, more precisely, denied). It may be useful then to recall the less mystical aspects of our body. The body of Christ—we are talking about ourselves now—is at once lovely of limb and painfully scarred. Its loveliness is rooted in its God-shaped gracefulness and coordination. Yet this lovely body is also a wounded, disfigured one. Scarred, and still being wounded, we are a body in need of healing. This is not news.

If it is not news, it is important to savor the ambiguity of who we are: a body both beautiful and wounded. And the ambiguity deepens; the wounds of this body are not merely ancient scars nor the effects of external assault. Some scars mark what we have done to ourself. They are results—shameful as it is to admit—of "self-abuse." The postshock value of this term bears some scrutiny. Just as individual self-abuse includes such destructive compulsions as overworking and overeating, corporate self-abuse includes the variety of destructive behaviors we become skilled at—such as preventing our women members from official and sacramental leadership in the body. This use of the term may thus remind us of two aspects of our common life: sexuality is but one of the means we employ to hurt ourself; and the abuses of Christian living are "ours"—shared by all of us in the body. This last point prevents us from breaking up the body between "us" and "them" and invites a full ownership and participation in the life of the Church.

We begin with this image of the body of Christ because this reflection is an exercise in self-intimacy:[1] listening to our own body, that it may tell us about ourself. This is an exercise in befriending neglected, repudiated parts of ourself. Its goal is both the healing of our wounds and the recovery of a lost gracefulness. In the following pages we will chart the maturing of the Christian body, paying special attention to the mid-life challenges and invitations encountered by the gay and lesbian members of ourself. We will conclude with a reflection on a contemporary Christian spirituality and the role of the maturing homosexual Christian in ministering to the body of Christ.

The Mid-Life Moratorium

In mid-life we are likely to experience within ourself a few nudges to explore the meaning and direction of our life. Perhaps we begin to feel a little like Saul Bellow's Herzog: "overcome by the need to explain, to have it out, to justify, to put in perspective, to clarify, to make amends . . . he sometimes imagined he was an industry that manufactured personal history." Fulfilling this need to reappraise, take stock, and listen to our own personal history is essential to creating a new consolidation of our adult identity. Psychologist Erik Erikson uses the term *moratorium* to describe a "time-out" period, a "breathing space" in the development of the person that involves a threefold integrative process: recapitulation, consolidation, and anticipation. In the moratorium of young adulthood, it is our short past which helps to shape the initial decisions of adult life. It is a time for "getting ready" to make our moves, for achieving a stable enough sense of ourself that we may confidently enter the adult world of love and work. However, the mid-life moratorium is a time to reassess where those initial decisions have led us. Our past is now fuller and perhaps we are aware that more time lies behind us than stretches before us. This moratorium experience in mid-life calls us to examine the quality of our identity (who we are) and the integrity of our commitments (what we are for). It is a pivotal time for reassessment, reconstitution, and redirection.

Through the work of the moratorium in mid-life I encounter my homosexuality anew. I find myself thinking more frequently about my life and reflecting on the diverse paths I have walked. Perhaps I sense the question "Who am I?" receding into the background as I become more concerned with the question "What have I become?" I am amazed at how much I have learned about myself over these last two or three decades and hopefully experience a sense of achievement in the gay or lesbian identity that I have forged. This period of a mid-life moratorium can be a grace-filled time to discover the person that I have become and to savor the unique talents and gifts that I now bring to my adult love and work.

The mid-life moratorium invites me to a reorientation to the truth about myself. It is a challenge to "grow down" into life, a time to discover and make friends with the person I have become. Charles Peguy writes in his *Victor Hugo*:

> Forty years is a merciless age. It won't allow self-deception any longer. It doesn't tell any more fairy tales. It doesn't hide anything. Everything is unveiled, everything is revealed. Everything is betrayed. Because this is the age when we become who we are.

The lure of mid-life, then, draws me home to myself.

Questions begin to multiply: Why am I so restless? What does sex mean to me? Who are my trusted friends? What does being homosexual mean to me now? Why do I seem to know more people who are sick or have died? Why does God seem so silent? If these questions rattle us, it helps to recall they are also a part of a normal inquiry in mid-life. Rather than signaling an impending spiritual or psychological breakdown, these questions guide the reexamination of my life journey. The goal of this journey is a mid-life reconciliation—learning to walk once again with myself and with God, and listening more reflectively and prayerfully to how I am being revealed to myself.

Having examined the notion of the mid-life moratorium in the context of Christian homosexuality, we turn now to an exploration of two related tasks: a reconciliation with the past, and a reappraisal of sexuality and sexual orientation.

Reconciliation with the Past

One of the most painful yet healing tasks of the moratorium in mid-life is a reconciliation with the past. We are aware of how the unfinished business of the past continues to unsettle our life in the present. Patterns of behavior reveal how we have continually hurt ourself—ignoring intimacy needs, denying anger, resisting change. Feelings buried for years emerge and are attached once again to powerful images and memories from the past. Whether it be unresolved issues with our parents or a long-standing anger at our Church, it is often in mid-life that we struggle to reconcile these conflicts. Henri Nouwen, in his insightful book, *Reaching Out,* emphasizes the need to talk about this problematic past: "there will be no hope for the future when the past remains unconfessed, unreceived or misunderstood."[2] What Nouwen suggests and what our own personal experience bears out is that achieving a reconciliation with the past will necessarily involve an honest sharing of our untold stories with trusted others.

As we conduct this reconciliation with the past, we find our troubles mixed in with graces and good fortune. For example, we give thanks when we recall how our life has been graced by those dearest and closest friends who have loved us into our own middle years. We are also grateful for those affirming and challenging persons who entered our life for only a short time, but who invited us in many ways to grow beyond ourself. And we acknowledge the numerous opportunities we have had, both personally and professionally, to shape and enrich our own Christian vocation. As mid-life women and men of faith, we believe that our life has not been just a series of capricious or random events. But, rather, having reflectively tracked our journey into mid-life, we stand in awe of how our life has been gifted.

In revisiting our past and beginning the healing that this return demands, we learn another lesson about maturing: the past can be changed. When we forgive and become reconciled with our personal histories, they lose their power over us. Emptied of much of its anger and guilt, our past can become a friend and a resource.

I cannot change the facts, perhaps painful, of how I came to know myself as lesbian or gay. This awareness may have come through touring the bars or over a period of one-night stands. It may have been in the course of marrying and having children that my homosexuality was revealed to me. Priestly or religious life may have been the road I traveled in search of my sexual identity. Perhaps I came to accept myself as homosexual only after having lived many years "in the closet." Whatever my experience, now at age forty or fifty, I look back at that constellation of life events, decisions, and relationships and develop some new interpretations. I know that residues of anger and vulnerability still remain and that many facts about my past cannot be changed, but I also know that I can change my relationship to those feelings and facts. I learn that recurring memories and dreams, with their accompanying intense pain, are signs that the past is seeking to be brought into reconciliation. Gingerly, I enter into dialogue with my past to learn its challenging but graceful revelations. Wanting to befriend my past anew, I pray in mid-life for the gift of reconciliation.

However, I am well aware that a reconciliation with the past can be oversimplified. I know from previous experience that my attempts to reconcile myself to the events and people in my past does not always produce clarity or a sense of peaceful resolution. In this regard, I am learning to acknowledge the discrepancies that have become a part of my identity as a homosexual. I have not become everything I wanted to become when I imagined my life as a young adult. I have not achieved all that I had hoped to achieve. The gap that exists between the person that I have become and the person I wanted to be is larger than I had hoped for. Perhaps I see the ways that I have tried to project an image of myself as a person of certitude and security, wholeness and innocence. But mid-life calls me to integrate the uncertain and insecure in me, to admit the brokenness I have experienced in life and to own my unique patterns of sinfulness. Mid-life invites me to a greater toleration of the ambiguity and ambivalence I feel within myself, and teaches me once again that "terminal clarity" cannot be achieved. I learn a new definition of maturity: "Unresolved conflicts and unhealed parts of our past return to disrupt our lives in the present. Maturity does not imply that absence of such conflicts and inconsistencies, but the ability to accept this mosaic which is myself. Acceptance does not effect the transformation of these immaturities into health and wholeness; rather it reconciles me to the paradox of human maturity."³

Sexuality and Sexual Orientation: A Reappraisal

Accompanying the invitation to be reconciled with the past is the challenge to reexamine our sexuality. Over the past decades I have become increasingly aware that human sexuality will not be neatly divided between heterosexual and homosexual categories. Neither my life nor those I know well fit this rigid dichotomy. I am aware of the ways that my emotional life reveals a larger capacity for emotional attraction and affective expression than I realized as a younger adult. I have grown to appreciate the wide variety of people, women and men, gay and heterosexual, who have deeply affirmed me by their manifestations of care and love. I realize that as a person I am not constituted in such a way as to be *exclusively* homosexual. Rather, over a period of time, I have more accurately come to know my sexual orientation as *predominantly* gay.

Within the realm of my predominant sexual orientation, I have experienced my affective life within a continuum which ranges from a whole constellation of homo-sexed responses on one end of the polarity to hetero-sexed responses on the other. I have observed that my sexual orientation has not created barriers or blockades to the possibility of intimacy with persons of the opposite sex. As a gay man, I realize that mutual self-disclosure, declarations of liking or loving, and demonstrations of affection can genuinely take place with women, and yet heterosexuality as a predominant sexual orientation is not my preferred mode of intimacy. Perhaps some of my confusion stems from the fact that many in our society tend to define sexual orientation in terms of genital behavior. For example, the fact that a lesbian may be quite capable of having sexual intercourse with a man and even enjoy it does not constitute her as a heterosexual woman. While it is true that consistent preferences for genital expression are key indicators of sexual orientation, what constitutes sexual orientation necessarily goes beyond the genital. More central to a definition of myself as gay or lesbian is the accumulated awareness I have of the movements of my affective life. Persistent patterns of homosexual attraction, enduring experiences of intimacy, and continuing manifestations of devoted love—these are the more trustworthy signs of my sexual orientation. Coming then to affirm myself as homosexual beings with this task of self-clarification; gradually it leads me to an experience of self-appreciation.

My voyage of self-exploration in mid-life has helped me to accept the fact that the roots of my homosexuality lie far below the level of simple choice. I realize now that I did not make up my mind to be gay or lesbian, though I know that I have been free to accept or not accept that fact. I am also aware that as a Christian I am no more responsible for my homosexual orientation than my heterosexual brothers and sisters are for theirs. But rather what we share in common is that we are both responsible for how we respond to our sexual orientation. That I am homosexual is irrevocable; how I am homosexual is distinct. I find that I do have important choices regarding my relationships and my commitments, and while these choices are those of a homosexual Christian, they shape the goodness and maturity of my adult life. As William Kraft has observed, many different levels of maturity are available to me as a homosexual Christian: "Some are unhealthy and need help, others are normal in that they cope, succeed, look and act like most, and still others go beyond normalcy in their functional and creative endeavors."[4]

Passages Toward Mature Identity

That I am constituted homosexual is something I have in common with my lesbian sisters and gay brothers. I realize that my life and the lives of those closest to me share similar patterns of maturing. Yet I am also impressed by the distinctive passages that have characterized my formation as a homosexual Christian. In mid-life I become aware that the seeds of my lesbian or gay identity are contained in earlier stages of the life cycle. I learn that the initial search most likely took me through four different phases of identity development: diffusion, foreclosure, moratorium, and consolidation. Whatever way I journey through these phases, in young-life the task is to shape an identity for my adulthood; in mid-life the task is to reshape that identity. In young-life it involves an identity quest; in mid-life, it leads to an identity inquest.

In the following section we discuss these passages toward mature identity from the perspective of both the earlier life stages and mid-life. Often it is only in mid-life that we become aware of these earlier stages of growth. Our dialogue between the perspectives of young adulthood and mid-life will remind us that the work of identity formation is not a one-and-for-all developmental task; rather it is ongoing and involves change and continual adaptation.

Identity Diffusion

An expectable crisis of early adolescence, identity diffusion is a state of psychological fluidity where I was open to everything and committed to nothing. It was basically an experience of inner chaos which may have contained some fuzzy images of myself as homosexual. But I did not spend much time or give much energy to struggling with the larger questions of my life. Propelled by untrained desires, it was an impulsive, maybe even reckless and thrill-seeking exploration of the world. As a young adolescent, I was a bundle of ambivalence—fiercely independent yet childishly helpless, euphorically optimistic yet categorically negative about everything; wanting the whole world to be my audience, yet extremely self-conscious about being in the spotlight. Much later I learned that these qualities were normal in early adolescence.

But carried into the late teens and early twenties, these signs of identity diffusion were more ominous. Perhaps my experience of diffusion was evident in my fear to grow up and face those initial intuitions about my homosexuality. I may now think about the ways that I tried to avoid the inevitable crises and confrontations involving decision making, relationships, and responsibilities of adult life. Alcohol, drugs, or compulsive sexual activity may have been strategies I used to maintain some sense of control over my life. But soon it became clear to me that this state of identity diffusion would not serve me well as an adult. I needed more stable and clearer reference points against which I could test my own emerging identity and feel some progress of moving into adulthood.

Identity Foreclosure

A counterfeit resolution to the task of identity development, foreclosure occurs when I commit myself to an ideology, life-style, or vocation before having sufficiently explored or struggled with other significant options or possibilities. In mid-life I learn that identity foreclosure was often expressed in premature or postponed decisions concerning my adult life. In this state, I was notably susceptible to forces outside myself. For example, I may have discovered that, as a result of wanting approval from my family or feeling pressure from my peers, I entered into marriage, more with the hope of extinguishing my homosexual feelings than with the confidence that I could sustain this commitment of heterosexual love. Perhaps I made a premature choice for celibacy. I may have entered priesthood or religious life more with a need to quell my homosexual impulses and fantasies than with a readiness to integrate my homosexual identity into my celibate commitment. Foreclosure for me may have resulted when I chose to live a public gay life-style before I was emotionally ready to do so. Whatever the initial motivation for foreclosure, mid-life invites me to examine the ways that I may be still living in a state of foreclosure. My hope is that I am also able to appreciate the ways that I have moved beyond foreclosure into more genuine resolutions.

From my mid-life perspective I know that the "voices of foreclosure" were numerous as I was growing up. On the one hand, I encountered the homosexual world itself ready to offer me a prepackaged life-style. Being homosexual meant conforming to someone else's criteria. It meant surrendering some of my own personal freedom in order to adopt a lesbian or gay role often defined, maintained, and promoted by the subculture itself. Maybe I felt the homosexual world pushed me too hard or too soon to come to grips with my homosexuality. Because of my need to avoid confusion and ambiguity about my gay identity, I may have turned away from opportunities to discover my potential for heterosexual friendship. In short, I forged an identity around a too-exclusive definition of myself as gay.

On the other hand, I discovered that the louder "voices of foreclosure" came from individuals and institutions outside the homosexual world. These voices of society, Church, and mental health professionals had been recorded on "tapes" that I carried around in my head for years. Society's tapes told me that as a gay or lesbian person I was dangerous, unfit, undesirable, a sexual failure. The tones of these societal tapes were filled with fear, disgust, anger, dread, discomfort, hatred, and aversion. I found that my Church had also created its own library of tapes regarding homosexual life and played out the theme of homosexuality as spiritual sickness. Lastly, I was made well aware of the collection of tapes on homosexuality that were held by the mental health profession. Titles included homosexuality as development "arrest," "failure," "fixation," as well as the more sophisticated and isolating themes of "homosexual panic," "homophobia," "character disorder," and "ego-dystonic homosexuality."

Whether these "voices of foreclosure" came from the gay world itself, or from society, the Church, or the mental health profession, the basic issue has been one of my own interior autonomy and authority. How free have I been to determine how I will be homosexual? Based on my increased self-knowledge, how many new tapes have I made for myself? A mid-life learning is that while the "voices of foreclosure" may never be silenced and while many of the tapes I carry around in my head may never be erased, I can learn ways to soften their influence and reduce their volume. Hopefully I am learning to increase the volume on the new tapes that I have made for myself.

Identity Moratorium

The path to mature identity began with an experience in early adolescence of identity diffusion and often was seriously influenced by one or more of the "voices of foreclosure." Eventually what had been diffused or foreclosed needed to move toward the third phase of identity development, that is, the identity moratorium. This is basically a healthy stage of young adulthood where I attempted to enter as fully as possible into the crisis experience of searching, exploring, and actively pursuing various alternatives and possibilities for my homosexual adult life. Long-term commitments were not expected or encouraged at this stage, but rather, as a young adult, I was invited and challenged to "try out" many different roles and ideologies. It was a time when I learned to let go of the agendas and expectations of others, and attempted to listen more carefully to my own hopes and ambitions. This moratorium on the journey to adulthood was a time and space when I stopped long enough to allow my soul to catch up with my body. It was a time which conjured up images of "simmering" or "lying fallow." Often it was a confusing time of "uneasy serenity."

It was in the moratorium that I struggled with the persistent and consistent fantasies I had concerning my sexual identity and sexual preference. I could see the patterns of attraction emerging—sensed a growing desire to be more emotionally intimate with persons of my own sex. In fantasy and perhaps in behavior I was aware of my homosexual orientation emerging and yet I felt its tentativeness. It was also in the moratorium that I learned about my needs for adult intimacy. I began to sense that sexuality was a larger category than genitality. I felt that the deeper longings I experienced were for relationships, affirmation, and acceptance.

During the moratorium I searched for those select few trusted friends or mentors who would stand with me as I struggled to resolve the issue of my homosexuality. Hopefully I can recall or recognize one or two significant mentors, gay or heterosexual, who helped me to find out who I was becoming and to what and whom I might commit myself. The mentor's role for me was both affirming and confronting.[5] I felt encouraged, guided, and directed to reality-test this merging image of myself as homosexual against another person whom I trusted and admired. The mentor was there to make conflict conscious when I hid behind denial. And the mentor served as a type of "adult guarantor" for me, someone who gave me an entrée into the adult world, someone who served as a model of a well-adjusted, committed Christian. One of the more disruptive roles the mentor played was to invite me to end the moratorium, to resolve the crisis on my own terms and to make some long-range commitments for my adult life. Whether this involved making a commitment to stay together with another person or a decision for a religious vocation, the issue centered on my need to create a stable life structure for myself. The primary clue I had that the young-adult moratorium was reaching a healthy conclusion occurred when I perceived that my desire and readiness to create zones of stability in my life were greater than my need to continue examining and experimenting with more options.

Identity Consolidation

As the work of this moratorium comes to a close, I find myself drawn into a period of consolidation. The reexaminations and explorations of the previous years have helped clarify who I am and what my life is for. I have faced my sexual identity more honestly. I have managed, with the help of close friends or a mentor, to name some of my deepest feelings and hopes. I have tamed some of the energy that had mostly confused me in earlier years.

I emerge from the moratorium (often in the late twenties) with greater comfort with and confidence in myself. Now less busy or conflicted on the inside, I find I am able to love and work with more attention and commitment. Now, more consolidated in my sense of identity and purpose, I enter the next stage of adult life. And I am beginning to sense the pattern of my maturing: I head into a future that will reveal more of me to myself, demanding new reassessments and consolidations.

Identity Consolidation at Mid-Life

Most often it is only in a mid-life moratorium (usually in our forties) that we can recognize the patterns of our past maturing. The reexamination of our young-adult life and its consolidation launched us into our thirties and forties. And by mid-life we found ourself again asking important questions about our work, our love commitments, and our prayer.

The challenges confronted in mid-life moratorium, examined in the first section of this essay, lead to another consolidation. This mid-life integration of my identity effects a deeper resolution of those personal questions resolved a decade or two earlier. By mid-life we have a much longer personal history: the information accumulated over this history gives us a richer, if more mellow, sense of our identity and purpose.

This consolidation in mid-life is often experienced as a sense of hardiness. Looking back over my life, I come to a sense of myself as durable. I have come through what others (including Church persons) have done to me; I have survived what I have done to myself. With this sense of personal resilience, newly available now, I am able to live with less illusion and less pretending. In Levinson's vocabulary a mid-life crisis and its consolidation often involve "de-illusionment,"[6] a letting go of the illusions so useful and necessary in the launching of our adult life.

This "de-illusionment" (*not* disillusionment) touches both our identity and our efforts of intimacy. I am more able now to let go of personal illusions about myself and cultural illusions about homosexuality and how gays and lesbians are to act. More comfortable with myself as Christian and homosexual, I find I love others better—with fewer expectations of who I or they "should be," with less romanticism and more generosity. And in this connection between identity and intimacy we revisit the purpose of a mature identity: knowing who it is that we give in the loving that makes our life worthwhile. The love commitments of my adult life and the fidelity that these commitments strive for stand upon an enduring and resilient sense of who I am.

The sense of hardiness and resilience which is part of a mid-life consolidation is not only a culmination. It is also a preparation. The strength and confidence which result from a crisis lived through prepares us for the next stage of our life. The "crisis competence" that Kimmel[7] sees resulting from the young adult homosexual's crisis of identity also applies to a mid-life crisis. More flexible and confident after this moratorium, the gay and lesbian Christian are prepared for the next decades of life and the new challenges that await them (and await everyone) in their retirement and aging.

My readiness for commitment and recommitment and my desire for greater stability in my life represent healthy resolutions of the mid-life moratorium. I emerge a little less certain of the answers but more confident about the course my life is taking. I acknowledge the losses and changes incurred in the transition to mid-life and try to accept them for what they are, namely, new sources of information about myself and my world. The moratorium at mid-life leads me to a reorientation to the truth about myself. I am better at owning the disowned, acknowledging the still unresolved aspects of my past, and tempering some of my perfectionistic tendencies. Being more truthful about my own limitations has helped me to become a more compassionate person. Having learned to be less punitive and uncompromising with myself frees me to walk with others as a more empathetic companion. I know now that when I am clear about who I am and able to affirm the truth about myself, there is a better chance that I will be able to give myself over to others in ways that are more honest, believable, and trustworthy.

Maturity and Spirituality

Having explored the challenges and invitations which pattern the maturing of the mid-life homosexual, we might examine this journey from the perspective of Christian spirituality. The religious maturing of both the homosexual and heterosexual Christian includes movements of vocation, authority, and mutuality.

Vocation

The growth which occurs from our twenties to our fifties (and beyond) can be charted as an emergence of the authority of our own life and vocation. The psychological strength of identity can become as an emergence of the authority of our own life and vocation. The psychological strength of identity can become for the Christian a virtue or religious strength. As a Christian virtue, identity is my developing energy and gracefulness in being myself. For Christians our identity is more than a psychological discovery of who we are; it is a deepening recognition of who we are called to be. Thus our adult identity embodies our vocation.

We are talking here of "vocation" in its broadest and deepest sense. Whether as a lay person, a vowed religious, or a priest, we Christians find ourselves called, invited along certain paths. Before a vocation is a calling to a specific career or life work, it is a revelation of who we are and what we are for. And it is a gradual revelation: only over many years do we come to a confident sense of our adult identity. A Christian vocation is a lifelong revelation of us to ourself. Our vocation is not visited on us by some external edict; it is instead growing within: it is who we are, as this is gradually revealed to us.

Our vocations as Christians are shaped by two powerful forces: the abiding values of our religious faith and the gifts we find in ourselves. These gifts can be difficult to discern in our youth: they are so easily obscured by our fears or concealed by the sheer complexity of our inner lives. The maturing of our identity and vocation demands a careful and patient listening to our gifts, our deepest hopes and ambitions for our life; such listening leads to a greater clarity about who I am and a confidence in who I am called to be.

The maturing of a vocation for homosexual Christians includes a recognition and embracing of their sexual identity. This is how I find myself to be; this is how I am called to follow Christ in my adult relationships of love and work. Though not completely who I am, my sexual inclinations and affections are an important part of my adult identity—and so, of my Christian vocation. These specific movements of attraction and warmth, shaped and tamed by the values of Jesus Christ, will energize my adult commitments of love and work. The conversion that often accompanies such a maturing of identity is well known: from a denial or rejection of their sexual identity, gay and lesbian Christians can come to recognize that this is how they are called by God; this must be a part of their gracefulness as adult Christians.

Authority

This gradually growing confidence in who I am, the enduring pattern of my aspirations (sexual and otherwise), brings with it a new authority to my life. Without a strong sense of who I am called to be, I live under the authority of others' expectations—whether these are the ambitions of parents or the implicit demands of "the gay scene." Envy, jealousy, second-guessing myself: these all indicate an absence of an inner authority.

As we mature in our identity and vocation, the external authority of culture, parents, and Church become balanced and complemented by an inner trustworthiness of ourself. A Christian adult life is always a balance of authorities: the authority of our community's hopes and ideals in tension and dialogue with the authority of our own maturing insights and aspirations. This growth in personal authority, in my own inner dependability can also be charted as the seasoning of instincts.[8]

Psychological and religious maturing entail the taming of desire. Christian faith, long before Freud pointed it out, has been concerned with the question: "What am I to do with my longings?" Longings for sexual union, longings for independence; aspirations to nurture others and also to be cared for: angers and rages, righteous and otherwise. Our responses to these longings and desires pattern our maturing.

Christians believe that we can neither repress our desires nor simply abandon ourselves to them. Holiness is not calculated by escape from desire and feeling, but by the seasoning of passion. Religious growth is not deliverance from instinct and aspiration, but involves the forming of human feelings according to certain hopes and values. Christian maturing—and so, Christian spirituality—entails the education of desire, and the seasoning of instincts. The metaphor of "seasoning" suggests a number of aspects about the maturing of our feelings. Our longings, ambitions, and angers are gradually influenced and shaped by the values of our environment. We live in a Christian community for that very purpose—to allow the hopes and ideals of Jesus Christ to permeate and shape our desires. We ambition the shaping of our loving and angry passions in the pattern of Jesus Christ.

And gradually, amazingly (and with many reversals) this is what happens: during the many seasons of our twenties through our fifties our instincts of love and anger are seasoned by Christian values and ideals. Our instincts, once so confusing, unruly, and unseasoned (think of adolescence!), become more reliable and trustworthy. Never infallible, our instincts become dependable. Seasoned by the Gospels and by the loving Christians in our life, these instincts mature and give energy and resilience to our commitments of love and work.

This positive development is, of course, often not realized. Another, bitter seasoning occurs: we learn, in the religious "formation" of our homes and schools, the wretchedness and unholiness of our instincts. We are taught that they are unnatural and shameful. And so our instincts are not seasoned and matured, but repressed, punished, and closeted. Some of the scars on the body of Christ are, as we have observed, self-inflicted. And yet our body retains amazing recuperative powers; it is resilient and capable of forgiveness and healing. Part of this healing arises in listening to our body's needs: What does this wounded but lovely body of believers most ambition?

Mutuality

One longing that lingers in every human heart, a longing that the values of Jesus Christ would season, is the ambition for mutality. Mutality is the ability (really, the virtue) to sustain the ambiguity and excitement of being up close to another person. Without it, commitment and fidelity have mostly guilt and fear to stand on. Mutuality is an adult virtue because it lures us beyond both childish dependence and a standoffish, adolescentlike independence. It is built on a tough sense of identity and vocation: confident in the person I am turning out to be, I know I will survive this embrace; in this friendship or work situation, I do not need to manipulate others lest I be swallowed up by them.

Mutuality is a Christian virtue because Jesus taught a radical partnership that imperils every distinction of slave and free, male and female, black and white. The religious ideal of mutuality is cruelly mocked in the Church's hierarchical distinctions of "Reverend, Very Reverend, Most Reverend . . ." (and nonreverend). A severely hierarchical view of our Christian body isolates the head from the lower, more shameful members—be these womanly, gay, or lay. And while we mock our own ideals, we continue to pursue them. For the gay Christian, this virtue of mutuality has its own challenges. As a young single person, how to risk myself for the first time in a relationship, or how to risk again? As a gay celibate religious or priest, how to develop friendships faithful both to my longings for intimacy and to my public vocation? As a gay person in a heterosexual marriage, how to grow in mutual love with my spouse while not denying other movements of my heart?

The virtue of mutuality, gradually developed from an increasing comfort with and confidence in our own identity and vocation, can rescue us from a major temptation of our culture—narcissism.[9] It may be useful to recall that this affliction is not about self-love but its opposite. Narcissists busy themselves trying to discover and uncover themselves. In the realm of personal relations, they are "users." Whether in one-night stands or in more sophisticated strategies, they use others as mirrors, searching again and again for a lasting glimpse of themself. Mirrors are important but futile tools: in you, and you, and you, I seek a reflection of myself, as Narcissus searched the mirroring pond for insight and identity. Lacking an enduring and truthworthy sense of myself and unable to allow myself to be known well, I am compelled to use others to find out how I am doing (in physical appearance, in sexual prowess, etc., etc.)—to find out who I am. The magic of narcissism is all done with mirrors, but it is an unhappy magic and one that cannot conjure up a mutual, enduring relationship.

The gay and lesbian Christian, as well as the heterosexual believer, feels the curse of narcissism in today's culture. If narcissism is an "indigenous disease," flourishing in our present climate, homosexuals may be especially vulnerable to its punitive effects because our culture and religious tradition often undermine their sense of worth and vocation. Our religious values and ideals, inherited from Christ but so easily and often twisted, call us away from isolating ourselves and cutting ourselves off from each other. And this call draws us toward confident identities and vocations where mutual love and commitment have a chance to thrive.

Conclusion

In this essay we have attempted to chart some patterns of mid-life maturing that the gay and lesbian Christian may experience. A goal of every kind of maturing is to bear fruit: to reach a point where our strength becomes not just a personal gain to be banked, but becomes fertile. Maturing as Christians through our thirties, forties, and fifties, we become able to, we need to, give something to the next generation of believers, gay and heterosexual. We become generative. This happens at the personal level, helping a younger member of our community, and at the level of the social system that is our Church. What does this mean concretely for the gay and lesbian Catholic?

Adult maturing, when it amazingly and gracefully occurs, carries us beyond the dependence of childhood and the confused antagonisms of adolescence. These earlier stages of religious growth survive in us when we find ourselves either waiting passively for someone to tell us how to act, or petulantly complaining about our hardships. Christian maturity is always a matter of balancing authorities: the authority of our religious heritage with the growing authority of our own life. Each authority is deeply ambiguous and full of pitfalls. The grace of revelation of our Christian faith is bounded by and compromised by all the perversions we as a people have wrought on it; thus its authority endures, though in a wounded fashion.

And the authority of our own lives knows the same compromise and fragility. We come gradually to trust and to love the peculiar journey of our vocation; yet this does not blind us to, or excuse us from our failures, and the purification that our lives are constantly subject to. Maturity is the balance of authorities that has an offspring. The fruit or offspring of this maturity can be the adult Christian's willingness to care for and minister to the Christian tradition itself. The "child" (whether age ten or thirty-seven) waits for her Christian heritage to change her understanding of homosexual holiness; the "adolescent" (whether age seventeen or fifty-two) rails against the narrowness of his Church. Homosexuals who are both adult and Christian are equipped—by the strength of their seasoned instincts and sense of vocation—to care for the wounds of their faith community. This can become part of their vocation.

How does such an extraordinary service occur? Happily, it is already happening in the lives of gay and lesbian Catholics who are teaching the Christian community the possibility and form of mature homosexual love. As Christian homosexuals venture out of the closet—where darkness and secrecy occluded any practical witness—they are making visible to the Church the patterns of their religious maturing. These patterns illustrate modes of sexual sharing, of career, of generative service to the community quite like those of heterosexual Christians. If no biological offspring issue from gay and lesbian intimacy and commitment, religious and cultural gains do spring off, reminding us—as does our tradition of celibacy—that Christian fecundity is not restricted to biological fruitfulness. And we are coming to see that the generosity possible in homosexual relationships is threatened by the failures common to adult commitments—selfishness, infidelity, and stagnation.

As the larger Christian community is instructed in the differing patterns of gay religious maturing, it will be exorcised of some of its homophobia. It will come closer, if belatedly and reluctantly, to its own ideal of Christ's radical mutuality: gay and lesbian Christians are more like heterosexual Christians than they are different. Called by the same God, and with instincts seasoned by the same hopes and values, we share the same body. The radical quality of this unity suggests that we will be pursuing it for a very long time.

The larger lesson is twofold: this ideal of mutuality within our religious body has survived and would season our instincts and vision if we will let it; secondly, this ideal is not to be awaited like helpless children or rebellious adolescents, but is to be assertively and maturely pursued. In the pursuing, we are about the healing of our lovely body, the body of Christ.

NOTES

1. This virtue, which combines an awareness of our strengths and weaknesses with a growing comfort with ourselves, is explored in some detail in chapter 21: "Self-Intimacy: The Foundation of Fidelity," in *Marrying Well* (New York: Doubleday, 1981) by Evelyn Eaton Whitehead and James D. Whitehead. These authors discuss this virtue in the development of gay and lesbian Christians in their essay "Three Passages of Maturity" in Part II of this book.

2. Henri Nouwen, *Reaching Out* (New York: Doubleday, 1975), p. 68. Maggie Scarf, in *Unfinished Business: Pressure Points in the Lives of Women* (New York: Doubleday, 1980), examines the complex ways we rework troubled parts of our past. See especially pages 211 and following.

3. Evelyn Eaton Whitehead and James D. Whitehead, *Christian Life Patterns* (New York: Doubleday, 1979), p. 201.

4. William Kraft, "Homosexuality and Religious Life," *Review for Religious* 40 (1981/3): #372. While this statement articulates a balanced view of homosexual maturity, Kraft's overall judgments concerning homosexual life represent a more traditional stance. For other views, we recommend: Edward Vacek, "A Christian Homosexuality," *Commonweal*, 5 December 1980, 681–84; and James B. Nelson, *Embodiment: An Approach to Sexuality and Christian Theology* (Minneapolis: Augsburg, 1978)—see especially chapter 8, "Gayness and Homosexuality: Issues for the Church."

5. The important role of mentoring is explored by Daniel Levinson in his *The Seasons of a Man's Life* (New York: Knopf, 1978), pp. 97 and following. In *Unfinished Business* (see note 2 above), Maggie Scarf examines mentoring and the lack of it in the lives of American women today—see especially pages 222 and following.

6. See Levinson, op.cit., p. 193.

7. See Douglas C. Kimmel's "Adult Development and Aging: A Gay Perspective," *Journal of Social Issues* 34 (1978/3): 117. On questions of lesbian maturing, see Sasha Lewis's *Sunday's Woman: A Report on Lesbian Life Today* (Boston: Beacon Press, 1979); Ginny Vida, ed., *Our Right to Love* (Englewood Cliffs, N.J.: Prentice-Hall, 1978); and Del Martin and Phyllis Lyon, *Lesbian/Woman* (New York: Bantam, 1972).

8. Christian maturity and the "seasoning of instincts" are treated in greater detail in chapter 12 of *Community of Faith* by Evelyn Eaton Whitehead and James D. Whitehead (New York: Seabury, 1982).

9. Christopher Lasch, in *The Culture of Narcissism* (New York: Norton, 1978), presents an excellent overview of recent psychoanalytic thinking on this personality disorder. Unfortunately, after this overview, the book degenerates into a diatribe against most humanistic efforts of self-development and group development.

GREGORY BAUM

The Homosexual Condition
and Political Responsibility

The reason why I wish to discuss the relation of the homosexual condition to the political order is the new emphasis on social justice in the recent teaching of the Catholic Church. The turning point, in my opinion, was the 1971 Synod of Bishops, which declared that the redemption wrought by Jesus Christ included the liberation of people from the oppressive conditions of their social lives. In ecclesiastical documents, social justice has come to be defined in terms of the liberation of oppressed people, of the outcasts, the marginals, the colonized, and the exploited. The Church's concern for social justice is here linked to the very core of the Christian message. Pope John Paul II accepted this teaching and extended it. In his first encyclical he argued that because Jesus has in some way identified himself with every human being, the struggle for human dignity, human rights, and social justice is a service offered to Jesus and his kingdom and hence belongs to the very nature of the Church's mission. To be a Christian means to develop a socially concerned heart and look for an appropriate political orientation.

In Latin America and others parts of the Third World this new emphasis on social justice has led many Catholics to identify themselves with revolutionary movements. They are convinced that in their countries, a gravely unjust and, in fact, inhuman social order is held in place by a military government protecting the wealth of a small minority, while the great majority of the population is kept in poverty, deprivation, and misery. Catholics in the developed countries have begun to criticize their own governments, which, for reasons of national self-interest, support and protect the right-wing military regimes in Third World countries.

The new emphasis on social justice and human rights in the Church will, in my opinion, eventually demand a reconsideration of the homosexual condition and make Catholic bishops recognize the equality of straights and gays in the church. For if God creates some people heterosexual and others homosexual, who are we to argue with God?

Critics of Society

Gay men and women find it easy to follow the Church's summons to social justice. First, they themselves know from experience what oppression is. They know what it means to be excluded, despised, slandered, vilified, discriminated against, and legally excluded from human rights. And because they themselves are an oppressed minority, they find it easy to be in solidarity with other oppressed minorities and demand with them and for them social justice and civil rights. Secondly, I contend, gay men and women as a largely invisible minority have an ambivalent position in society. They often belong to the cultural mainstream and are deemed perfectly integrated into society, while they themselves realize they are different, marginal, and threatened, and belong to the mainstream only because they disguise themselves. This ambivalent position of belonging and not-belonging allows gay men and women to become perceptive critics of the social order. They know society so well because they are insiders; and at the same time they stand apart. They are able to detect the hypocrisies of society, the social lies and cultural distortions, all of which are designed to protect the structures of subordination. For these two reasons, I wish to argue, homosexual men and women are called to be social critics and agents of social change. If they are Christians, they will find it easy to follow the summons to social justice uttered by the contemporary Church.

Since society is in need of criticism to continue its evolution toward public well-being, one may ask whether this is not one of the special contributions gay men and women make to the common good and the progress of culture. Gays not only demand human rights and free acceptance for themselves; they also ask themselves what special contribution they can make to the advancement of the whole community. When God created men and women as gays, what function did God expect them to exercise in society? Perhaps their existential inability to be like the majority hides a divine call to become prophets, critics of society, agents of social change, reformers, or radicals.

Some gay people do not agree with this at all. The think that it is more prudent to be conformist in culture and society. Since they deviate from the recognized norms on one point, they try their best to conform to all the other norms prescribed by society. They might even argue that if you want society to accept you and recognize your rights, then it is more strategic to present yourself as a defender of society, not as its critic. Because you want society to acknowledge your rights, you are willing to close your eyes to all sorts of things that are wrong in public life. We sometimes find gay men who in their desire for social prestige, high culture, and sartorial elegance transform themselves into aristocrats of sorts, not always escaping the ridiculous.

Such a social outlook comes close to an elitist conception of homosexuality. There is an ancient tradition according to which homosexual love among men is a sign of cultural superiority appropriate for members of the elite. Educated men were able to unite spirit and flesh in their sexual friendships. Since women and lower-class men were excluded from education, they had no right to homosexuality. Women and men not belonging to the elite were to be the laboring animals of society, charged with producing food and perpetuating the race.

Related to this elitist understanding of homosexuality is the male bonding observed in many social institutions. Men get together to share their virility in a common task, from which women are rigidly excluded. They create a male world for themselves defined by their own values, vowed to the subordination of women. While this sort of male bonding is not usually accompanied by homoerotic fantasies or practices and hence passes as being fully respectable, it resembles a certain elitist homosexuality. It is equally harmful to women, and hence it also damages and distorts the common good of society. The male bonding found in the army, the police force, the clergy, and certain sports clubs creates a one-sided image of maleness and protects the subordination of women in society. These all-male organizations also generate public contempt for homosexuality: the male bonding in their own ranks must appear as wholly nonsexual. Everyone must come to know that that there are no homosexuals in the army, the priesthood, the police force, or the football team.

These varying stances of conformism, elitism, and male bonding are not in keeping with Catholic social teaching nor the Christian call to social justice. In recent years, the Catholic Church has come to recognize and endorse the aim of the women's movement, namely, the social equality of men and women. The turning point here was John XXIII's encyclical *Pacem in Terris* (1963), which acknowledged as the significant "signs of the times" in the present world the movement of workers for participation and greater control, the movement of colonized peoples for autonomy, and the movement of women for equality in society. Through these "signs of the times" God addresses the Church and demands that it reinterpret its message and reorientate its course. In this light, any form of male homosexuality that fosters the domination of men over women is irreconcilable with Christian teaching. Gay men as critics of society must be supporters of the women's movement. In light of this "sign of the times," one might add, the existence of an exclusively male clergy be- ✕✕✕ comes problematic.

Does Marxism Have Answers?

Some activist gay people, in search of a new social philosophy, turn to Marxism. We read their views in radical gay publications. At first it seems strange why gays would turn to marxist social theory for help. After all, the countries that call themselves Marxist and socialist strongly discriminate against homosexuals. This is true of Russia and the Soviet bloc countries of Eastern Europe, and this is true of Cuba. When socialists were the agents of social change in the nineteenth and twentieth centuries, they favored civil rights and sexual freedom, and this included respect for gay people. On the whole, this is still true for the democratic socialist parties of the West: they tend to defend gay rights. Demographic research has shown, moreover, that in the Western countries that have socialist parties, the majority of gays support these parties by their vote. Communist parties, on the other hand, usually exclude gay activists. Communist countries have harsh laws against gays. Why then do some gay activists in the Western nations turn to Marxism?

Marxists argue rather convincingly that there is a relation between capitalism and oppression based on race and gender. Capitalism widens the gap between the rich and the poor, and between rich countries and poor countries; in its present form, thanks to an increasingly sophisticated technology and the search for an ever cheaper labor force overseas, capitalism creates a growing number of unemployed in the United States and thus generates regions of underdevelopment and destitution in which people are condemned to perpetual marginality. What capitalism needs in this situation is people of low status or prestige, whose presence on the lowest level of society does not produce public protest. If the unemployed and the marginalized are largely black, Mexican American, or members of other nonwhite groups, there will be no public outcry. If there is a disproportionate number of women among those doing the most menial tasks or those who are pushed to the margin, public opinion, largely created by middle-class white men, will not be outraged. The present form of capitalism seems more acceptable, therefore, if there are low-status people to occupy the lowest ranks of society. Racism and sexism fulfill a useful function in the stabilization of the present social order. While this argument does not directly apply to gay people, who are for the most part an invisible minority, it applies to them indirectly. For the lower rank assigned to women in society demands a clear definition of sexual roles and publicly acknowledged ideals of what it means to be a man and a woman. These public values seem to be challenged by homosexual life. In such a society gays are often deemed subversive. They question the roles assigned to men and women in society.

While it is correct to argue that in capitalist society racism and sexism exercise an important function, it does not follow from this that racism and sexism have their origin in capitalist society nor that once capitalism has been replaced by a socialist economic system racism and sexism will necessarily disappear. We know that racism and sexism antedate the capitalist system of production: they existed in previous societies. Racism and sexism are forms of oppression that are never simply derived from the economic order: they have their own evil origins. They are vicious distortions of the divinely created pluralism-in-equality among the races of the world—and among men and women. Because these two evils are not produced by the economic system, even though they can be used and made more oppressive by such a system, there is no guarantee whatever that a socialist economy will by itself overcome racism and sexism. If Marxists make that claim, they are wrong. The history of the existing socialist countries give ample evidence for the persistence of racist discrimination and the subordination of women.

It is worthwhile to look more closely at the existing socialist countries. We find that they are not only hostile to gay life, they also promote strict norms of sexual behavior for heterosexuals and underplay the role of pleasure in human life. Sociologists have spoken of "the puritanism" of the Eastern European countries. Since, in these countries, the transition to socialism was accompanied by entry into industrialization, the government had to educate people for the sustained, systematic, and efficient labor demanded by industrial production. The socialist countries searched for a functional equivalent of the "Protestant ethic." The rhythm of preindustrial labor was more relaxed. Since agriculture and manufacturing recognize seasons and pauses, adjustments to the needs and powers of the human body, and a speed of work largely determined by the workers themselves, the entry into industrial production makes ascetical demands of efficiency, punctuality, and regularity for which preindustrial culture did not prepare people. In the absence of the Protestant ethic, the socialist countries had to set their own moral tone, create their own secular ideal of human life, place high priority on dedicated and systematic work, and restrict people's desire for pleasure, leisure, and the free run of the sensual imagination. Communist "puritanism" is thus strictly necessary for the functioning of industrial society. Cuba had to import the same secular spirit to make its people work. In this context sexual nonconformity and the stress on sexual happiness are symbols of middle-class decadence. Gay life suggests subversion.

We note in this connection how foolish the Marxist rejection of religion has been. By rejecting in doctrinaire fashion Christianity in all its forms, countries which called themselves Marxist found themselves without spiritual resources and had to create their own secular symbols to inspire people to dedication, selflessness, and sustained work. And since secular symbols do not transform the soul very deeply unless they are blessed by some religion, these countries found that work—daily production in industry, agriculture, and administration—became a problem. In many parts of Latin America, the Catholic Church is determined not to allow the coming revolution to be wholly in the hands of secular forces. Catholics participate in the revolution so that they can take part in the building of the new culture, released from the bondage of foreign ownership and foreign political control. In revolutionary Nicaragua, the Church tries to unfold the meaning of the Christian symbols and the Christian message to enable people to leave behind the passivity to which they had been condemned, and become active in sustained and cooperative labor to build their country.

Let me add that the harsh condemnation of gay life and sexual nonconformity found in Cuba and possibly in revolutionary movements of Latin America also has to do with their sad history of oppression. For many North American visitors, Havana was a foreign bordello without limits, where they could indulge in pleasures forbidden to them in their own country. In the struggle to survive, Cubans sold themselves to lustful foreign masters. Easygoing sexual mores and especially homosexuality then symbolized subservience to the colonial lords. In the new Cuba, there is to be no such subservience. Gay life is now seen as an expression of nostalgia for the old days of private luxury and public shame.

A Pluralist Society

These remarks on the attitude toward homosexuals in socialist countries lead us to ask the fundamental question why present-day capitalist society, especially the United States of America, is the place where for the first time in Western history gay people have succeeded in creating a strong movement that aims at emancipation and equality. Previous cultures were occasionally tolerant toward some homosexual practices, but there never existed a culture in which gay people consciously affirmed themselves as different but equal, and sought an alternative life-style that was distinct from the majority and yet capable of integration into society as a whole. What are the sociological conditions that made such an evolution possible?

The first condition, I wish to argue, is Protestant pluralistic culture. Catholic countries have always produced monopoly cultures, defined by a single ideology, clearly defined social roles, and an organic imagination of solidarity. Critical movements and countercurrents in Catholic countries were obliged to reject the entire cultural project, become monopolistic themselves, and offer an alternative vision of society to replace the old. Thus secularism and socialism in Catholic countries presented themselves as total ideologies, opposed to Catholicism in principle. Protestant countries, on the other hand, produced pluralistic cultures. With the stress on personal conscience, even the established churches, like the Church of England, could not successfully oppose the rise and spread of the free churches. Critical movements and countercurrents in Protestant cultures advocated only partial rejection of the tradition. There was no need for them to present themselves as an alternative culture. They wanted to reform the existing society, make room for oppressed groups. and change the social structures; and hence even though they repudiated elements of the tradition, the critical movements continued to provide legitimation for the whole of society. Protestant cultures were pluralistic. Protestant individualism undermined the organic imagination of Catholic cultures. It weakened the sense of solidarity, it allowed society to integrate nonconformity, and it enabled critics of the social order to remain loyal citizens. While Protestant societies resisted the entry of Catholics, they eventually admitted them as a religious minority faithful to its own perception of religion. Catholicism itself, living in a pluralistic culture, eventually changed its character and abandoned its dream of religious and cultural monopoly. Because of the American revolution and the total separation of church and state, pluralism is most advanced in the United States of America. Only in such a pluralist culture could gays lay claim to an alternative life-style. Since religion itself is so pluralistic in the United States, the gay movement did not have to turn against Christianity; it was in fact accompanied by movements within the churches that sought to vindicate gay rights in society.

The second condition necessary for the emergence of the gay movement is urbanization. The concentration of the population in cities creates a social mobility that weakens kinship bonds, undermines the extended family, and initiates people into individualism and isolation unknown in villages and small towns. In the modern city, people become estranged from their own background and set out on a private journey of their own: depending in part on the economic class, these personal journeys may end badly in anomie, failure, or meaninglessness, or they may end well in personal fulfillment and sustained dedication. Without the modern city, the gay movement is unthinkable. Everyone knows this. Gay people from rural areas and small towns move into the big city to experience a greater degree of freedom.

The third condition for the gay counterculture is the late phase of capitalism. Early capitalism had a special affinity for the Protestant ethic. In early capitalism the principal problem was the production of goods. What counted above all was hard work and dedication. In a previous paragraph we have compared this with the needs of the existing socialist economies, which also depend on hard work and dedication. In this early phase of industrialization there are few rewards for the people who do the heavy labor. All efforts at the beginning go into the accumulation of capital to buy better machinery and more modern technological equipment to increase production. During this phase of the first accumulation of capital the system of production, whether organized along capitalist or socialist lines, is cruel and oppressive, demands endless sacrifices, and offers benefits only for the few people at the top. During this period, as we noted above, what counts is the "puritan" spirit of discipline and frugality.

But in the late phase of capitalism, the problem of production has been solved. There is enough capital to improve the existing machinery and perfect technology and automation. The problem has now shifted to the consumption of goods. Can we sell all the goods we produce? Who shall buy them? We may be in need of markets overseas so that we can get rid of our merchandise. And—who knows?—we may need armies protecting the overseas markets. More importantly, we have to become customers ourselves. We have to create a culture of consumption in which people are made to dream endlessly of how commodities can make their lives more comfortable, more pleasurable, and more exciting. We may still need a bit of the Protestant ethic on the job, but after work and on the weekend we have to become customers, spenders, swingers, playboys, and playgirls. Pleasure and sexuality emerge here as possible factors stimulating sales. In late capitalist society, the taboos on pleasure and sexual freedom are broken because indulgence exercises a significant economic function. Every newfangled taste inspires a new market. Gay men and woman who have wrestled for their freedom are at this time still protected from the Anita Bryants of this world by the market interests of the business community. Because gay people as a largely invisible minority cannot be pushed to the lowest level of the social scale, they are distributed over all classes; and because they are not normally married and have children to feed and educate, they have proportionately more money to spend on manufactured goods. Gays are socially useful as customers. Fundamentalists, in their effort to restore the rural and small-town America of yesterday, may denounce gay people as wicked and sick, yet the needs of the present economy are such that gay people are likely to remain tolerated.

These are the three conditions for the emergence of the gay culture: cultural pluralism, urbanization, and late capitalism. It makes me very sad to arrive at this analysis because the very society that creates the possibility of freedom for gay people is also the source of grave injustice and endless misery in the world. The three conditions I have described are highly ambiguous. Protestant pluralism has produced a new individualism, undermining the possibility of organic solidarity with a people, a class, or a group; urbanization initiates people into anomie and loneliness; and the late phase of capitalism creates not only a culture dedicated to consumption but also generates giant transnational corporations with powers greater than many national governments, accountable to none, which rule the world with profit as their only goal. We touch here a dilemma of gay people. The society which has permitted them to engage in a realistic struggle for equality is precisely the society of empire and domination, the source of so much injustice in the world. Will the society that has generated the conditions for gay acceptance in the long run annihilate these conditions and return to gay oppression?

Recently a Jewish rabbi made an interesting remark during a Jewish-Christian dialogue. He said that Jews can only be comfortable in an "untidy society." By this he meant a society that was pluralistic, not united by a common ideology, made up of people and groups with different aims and purposes, each of them allowed to follow their own interests and each respecting the freedom of others. Only in such an untidy society can Jews live without disturbance. Societies that are homogeneous and united by a common faith or ideology do not leave enough room for a minority such as the Jews. When a society is united by Christian faith, nationalist fervor, Marxist ideology, or another set of common values, the Jews will stick out as different and hence eventually attract hostile feelings. It seems to me that the same can be said for Mennonites. This extraordinary group of Christians, looking back on centuries of persecution, can only be comfortable in an untidy society. I believe that the same can be said also of gay people. Only in an untidy society can gays be recognized as people following an alternative life-style. Whenever great uniformity of spirit emerges in society, in periods of war, in national awakenings, in revolutionary struggles, or in religious revivals, certain minorities, especially gay people, are liable to suffer public discrimination.

This remark sheds some light on what is happening in the United States at this time. For while America is both pluralistic and consumer oriented and hence an untidy society, strong trends at this time try to create greater ideological uniformity. The return of the cold war rhetoric, the recovery of the old-time religion, the emphasis on national security, the perception of America as the first nation under God, called by God to exercise its hegemony in the world, and the accompanying impatience with noncomformity and dissent—these are all signs of warning for the minorities, among them gay people. If the United States should ever become united by a single nationalist ideology, the modest freedoms which gay people have won in this country may well disappear.

In a previous paragraph I have outlined three social factors that promote and protect pluralism: Protestant culture, urbanization, and the consumer society. We saw that pluralistic culture is also threatened. Are there factors in modern society that undermine pluralism and create homogeneity? It is often said that the so-called Second Industrial Revolution, produced by electronic technology and the new communication media, has created the conditions for great cultural uniformity. The mass media of communication, which affect every aspect of human life, have an enormous influence on human consciousness. Marx provided good arguments for the theory that labor, the work people do, affects their consciousness; in today's society it must be said that the influence of the mass media on people's mind is greater than the conditions of labor. The things that happen at the center—the language, style, taste, dreams, operative ideas—communicate themselves to the periphery and often devour the style of the small town, the village, the region, and even the slum. This movement toward uniformity does find itself opposed by a new emphasis on regionalism and cultural differences, but even when minorities are able to protect their own tradition, they often achieve this precisely because their methods and style imitate the cultural thrust coming from the center. Evangelical movements hostile to the cultural mainstream successfully promote their cause by adopting the most modern techniques of mass communication and thus, against their will, promote the soulless conditions of modern mass society. The Second Industrial Revolution has created conditions for making society uniform that could be used by governments to enlarge their own ideological perception. It is conceivable that the ideology of capitalist America as God's empire can be made into the common self-understanding of the American people. Minorities, including gay people, must stand against such a trend.

The Authoritarian Personality

Let me make a few more general remarks about politics and sexual liberation. It has often been observed that there is a certain parallelism between people's perception of society and their perception of the self. If their view of society is strongly hierarchical or authoritarian, if they perceive society as strictly divided according to levels of authority, where order is created above all by the obedience of the lower ranks to the orders given from the top, then they also have a hierarchical view of the self, vertically divided between the rational, emotional, and sexual components, where order is created by the obedience of the emotions and sexuality to the commands of reason. People who long for an authoritarian society and stress obedience as the first civic virtue also have an authoritarian perception of the self and stress the submission of sexual feelings to commanding reason. Some social scientists have spoken of "the authoritarian personality." This refers to people who easily adjust to an authoritarian society. They find it easy to submit to authority and, if they are superiors, to give orders, but they find it difficult to cooperate and share responsibility with others. The same people also exercise strict control over their feelings and sexual drives.

Once people struggle for social change and greater freedom, they discover a more cooperative view of society, one in which the various levels of society are in conversation with one another and cooperate in constituting the social project. Obedience is here situated in a context of collaboration. As people change their vision of society, they also arrive at a different self-perception. They envisage the self as constituted through an ongoing conversion of reason, feelings, and sexuality. Sometimes people who were trained in strict obedience do not know the language that brings reason, feelings, and sexuality into conversation. Once they abandon their strict obedience, they lose control altogether. They may be in need of some therapy to arrive at the inner conversation that produces a peaceful and yet passionate life.

It is not surprising that people who make sexual morality the big public issue, campaign against pornography, or oppose the emancipation of gays belong to the political Right. Their authoritarian perception of society demands strict obedience of the lower sectors of society; at the same time they are constantly worried that these lower classes will become unruly and undermine the order of the whole. Since they see sexuality as the lower sector of the personality that must be brought under control but that is difficult to suppress, sexual conformity becomes for them the symbol of social control and sexual nonconformity the symbol of social rebellion. To deviate from a highly contained sexuality is politically dangerous. To demand sexual freedom undermines the social order. Gay life is seen as positively subversive.

Democracy versus Capitalism

Gay people must be opposed to authoritarian governments on the Right and on the Left. They must favor liberalism, pluralism, democracy, and a cooperative society. I cannot deny that I am uncomfortable with this conclusion. For liberalism means laissez-faire, which allows the rich, the talented, and the shrewd to gain power and establish structures of subordination for the majority. Catholic social teaching has always opposed laissez-faire. Church teaching has always stressed the common good, the protection of the poor against exploitation by the rich, the creation of bonds of solidarity. Are gay people really called upon to be defenders of the present order? In this context I recall the analysis presented in a preceding paragraph, according to which racism and sexism exercise a significant function in the present capitalist system. Is this the society which gay people are asked to support in order to protect their freedom?

To shed some light on this dilemma, allow me to clarify the inner contradictions of American society. There are institutional trends in American society that promote cooperation and participation, and there are opposing institutional trends that encourage authoritarian rule. According to C. Wright Mills, the great American sociologist, the contradiction in American society is between democracy and capitalism. Democracy stands for pluralism and cooperation and is embodied in American political institutions and expressed in American political ideals; and capitalism is built on the authoritarian rule over workers exercised by the owners of industries. Democracy is foreign to the economic institutions. The people who work in factories, offices, and banks have no voice whatever in the running of these enterprises. Only the owners and appointed directors have the power to make decisions. Here organization is rigidly hierarchical. The capitalist class is profoundly shocked when employees demand the introduction of democratic procedures in the work place. They regard this as disloyal. But the logic of democracy demands that the people who actually do the work share in the profit and participate in the decisions regarding production and distribution. The great contradiction of American society is between democracy and capitalism. Those who support a cooperative society will favor the introduction of democratic procedures in the running of industrial and financial institutions.

Certain neoconservative writers today like to praise "democratic capitalism" as the system operative in the United States of America. This is propaganda. Capitalist institutions are nondemocratic. Anybody who has ever worked in a factory or a large office knows that employees have no voice and that decisions are made at the top. Workers are unable to participate in policymaking. At present, democracy is banned from the work place. Against the neoconservative writers, I wish to argue that the genius of American democracy must eventually penetrate the economic institutions, overcome the domination by the owning and managerial elite, and generate co-ownership for workers and codetermination in the planning of production and distribution.

The conclusion of these reflections is that gay people are called to be critics of society and agents of social change. This is true especially of Christian gays. Catholics will want to follow their Church in its new affirmation of human rights and social justice, especially in Latin America and other Third World countries. Gays want to be in solidarity with all oppressed groups in their struggle for emancipation. At the same time I have argued that to protect their own existence gays must support pluralism, the freedom for nonconformist life-styles, the untidy society. They must be both defenders and critics of American society. This may well lead to some dilemmas. Gay people realize that the social order that has allowed them to hope for emancipation is also the one that undermines solidarity, creates individualism, produces loneliness and meaninglessness, and offers to its members either a superficial commercial culture or a messianic nationalism. As critics of this society, gays committed to social justice will become conscious of the contradictions in American society, discern in it the trends toward cooperation and pluralism as well as the trends toward domination and uniformity, and ally themselves with the forces of democracy. It is the democratic tradition that guarantees the pluralism of religion, race, ethnicity, and life-style, and will eventually penetrate the economic system itself and make it cooperative and subservient to the common good.

Some committed Christians follow this lead and become radicals: they think it important to reject the present system and demand radical social change, and they have little patience with efforts directed toward slow improvement. Other committed Christians become reform minded: they are ready to involve themselves with others in the gradual transformation of the present society. In secular society radicals and the reform-minded usually find it impossible to remain in solidarity. It is my conviction that in the Church it should be possible for radicals and reformers to stay together. Both Daniel Berrigan and Robert Drinan think of themselves as following the Christian call; and while the former has become a great radical and the latter an important reformer, they have remained united in spirit and support one another. It is my opinion that neither the reformist nor the radical option alone exhausts the social meaning of the Christian Gospel: we need the two approaches in the Church. Christian gays want to be loyal to one another, whether they choose to follow the radical or the reformist way.

JOHN McNEILL

Homosexuality, Lesbianism, and the Future: The Creative Role of the Gay Community in Building a More Humane Society

Over the past one hundred years the greater part of all intellectual efforts to understand homosexuality have been given over to an etiological study—a search for causes. Most of this theological, psychological, and moral speculation concerning homosexuality, I believe, was prejudiced and vitiated at its very source, because it was based on a questionable presupposition. This presupposition was that heterosexuality is of the very essence, at the very center, of the mature human personality, with the result that maturity and heterosexuality are identical.

Many theologians see heterosexuality as a reflection of the divine image: "Male and Female he created them—in his own image" (Gn 1:27). They end up with an uncritical acceptance of Western culture's sexual stereotypes as God-given roles. They conveniently ignore the second older account of creation in Genesis, where emphasis is not on procreation but on companionship and equality: it was not good that a human should be alone, so God created another human person to be his (or her) companion (Gn 2:18).

The psychoanalytic community, or at least one influential segment of it, accepted Irving Bieber's statement: "We assume that heterosexuality is a biological norm and that unless interfered with all individuals are heterosexual."[1] This assumption effectively blinds the investigator to any evidence that a homosexual relationship can be a truly constructive and mature expression of human love. Consequently, the only avenue of

investigation open is etiological: What causes this deviation from the
norm? Where do they come from? Implied is this: Where did he or she go
wrong? Thus an attempt was made to search out presumed causes of
deviation, for example, in faulty parental relations or in some constitutional factor. The more paranoid and homophobic spoke of "recruitment" and used analogies of a contagious disease.[2]

Further, this presupposition left only one course open to society; to do
everything in its power to prevent this deviation, or, failing that, to seek a
cure for its victims or, failing that, to punish and drive underground any
homosexual expression. Just a brief comment on the etiological question:
We are now more aware of the extreme complexity of both the physical
and psychosexual developmental process. There are at least nine stages in
that process and each of these stages leaves room for considerable variety. It seems to me that the obvious conclusion from the past century of
research into the etiological question is that we are still not certain why
anyone is homosexual or heterosexual. In fact, to see humans in simplistic terms as purely male or female, homosexual or straight, is to falsify
reality. There is an infinite variety of ways of being sexual in this world.
In the end everyone is unique. Consequently, to prescribe unequivocal
roles for males and females in society is to destroy the richness and
variety of God's creation, the unique human person.

A Teleological Perspective

In contrast to the etiological search for causes in the past, I would like
to consider homosexuality and lesbianism in a developmental perspective, both individual and collective. This developmental perspective is
meaningful because what the fullness of human sexuality precisely as
human is, does not lie in the past but in the future. The full implications
of Christian values for human sexuality have yet to be realized. We see in
recent thinking the beginning of a totally different, more hopeful, orientation of reflection. The truly worthwhile question is not "from whence"
the homosexual comes, but rather "Where is he or she going? or better
yet, "For what purpose do they exist?" This is what I call the teleological
perspective.

The importance of this perspective lies in the fact that human sexuality
participates in the radical freedom of the human person. Consequently, it
is only by posing the question "Why?" "For what purpose?" that we can
begin to detect in what sense the homosexual can be not contrary to, but
part of human development and the divine plan. By posing this question
we can begin to see what intrinsic role homosexuality and lesbianism

have to play in the development of a more humane society. Only when we arrive at some understanding of that role can we who are gay freely and truly accept and affirm our gayness not just as harmless deviations from the norm, but as an essential element in building a more humane society.

Much of the recent positive moral theological thinking, including my own,[3] has been directed to freeing homosexuals from ethical condemnation. However, no matter how much we relativize the sexual norm, or personalize the ethical exigency concerning homosexuality, we still are not shedding any light on the obscure question of why homosexuality exists. As Pierre-Claude Nappey, a French philosopher, put it:

> Homosexuality must be seen as corresponding to a definite finality. My feelings is that not only is it possible for homosexuals to be of equal value with heterosexuals in individual cases, but that it has an overall significance and a special role to play in the general economy of human relations; a role that is probably irreplaceable.[4]

I believe one urgent task that faces the human community is the difficult and complex undertaking of determining that finality. For on its discovery depends both the ability of the homosexual community to accept itself with true self-love and pride, and the ability of heterosexual society to accept a homosexual minority, not just as objects of pity and tolerance at best, but as their equals, capable of collaborating in the mutual task of building a more humane society.

The Positive Contribution
of the Homosexual Community

What then, is the collective role of the homosexual minority in human society? Under what circumstances can that potential be realized? I would like to begin my exploration of that positive role with a quotation from the psychologist Jung:

> If we take the concept of homosexuality out of its narrow psycho-pathologic setting and give a wider connotation, we can see that it has positive aspects as well . . . . This homosexuality gives them a great capacity for friendship, which often creates ties of astonishing tenderness between (members of the same sex) and may even rescue friendship between the sexes from its present limbo of the impossible.[5]

If Jung's observation is correct, then, far from being a threat to the family, homosexuals and lesbians can be a help in leading the whole human family to a new and better understanding of interpersonal love between equals as the true human foundation for the family, rather than the patriarchal role-playing of tradition.

One often hears the opinion that homosexuality represents an immature form of sexual development at a narcissistic stage, which prevents the individual from appreciating the difference of the opposite sex. Other psychologists, however, see the narcissistic factor of the homosexual stage of development as essential to the development of all interpersonal love, whether homosexual or heterosexual. To love your neighbor as yourself presupposes that you are capable of loving yourself. Nappey sees the homosexual community as objectifying a necessary stage in human sexual development. The homophobe who suppresses his or her homosexual feelings frequently destroys, by the same act, his or her ability to reach out and love the other, any other.

If this is true, then, if the day should come when it is possible to suppress or eliminate all homosexual tendencies so that homosexuality could disappear from the face of the earth, we would face the danger of removing a creative catalyst for the progressive development of sexual relations toward a fuller, more humane reality. In Nappey's words: "If heterosexuals honestly hope to see the establishment of the best possible condition for the fulfillment of individuals and society as a whole, they will have to try and accept their own homosexuality through the acceptance of those whose homosexuality is explicit."[6] Again in Nappey's words: "Why shouldn't everyone be delighted that homosexuals (and lesbians) have been entrusted with the task and mission of attending the two original flames which, if they were allowed to go out, would no longer serve as catalysts of heterosexuality, thereby bringing about the downfall of the entire system."

Factually, however, Western culture has constructed heterosexual role models for both male and female based on a vigorous repression of any homosexual self-love. We can begin to understand the role gay liberation can play in the liberalization of society if we consider for a moment the frequently dehumanizing and depersonalizing role that prevailing sexual identity images play in our culture. Men are supposed to be strong, tough, assertive, objective, courageous, independent, insensitive, unemotional, aggressive, competitive, promiscuous, and persuasive. Women are supposed to be weak, passive, irrational, emotional, unassertive, subjective, dependent, devoted, self-effacing, impractical, artistic, and receptive. As every gay man or woman knows with bitter memories, God help the man or woman who displays a quality which society presupposes belongs exclusively to the opposite sex.

An even more serious consequence follows if we assume that these heterosexual identity roles constitute the total mature content of the human personality. For this results in the tendency to understand the human individual as essentially partial and incomplete. Some theologians carry this to the theological extreme of finding the image of God not in man or woman alone, but only in the heterosexual couple united in marriage. They seem to overlook the fact that this would leave out Jesus, who presumably never married. As Jung observed, true friendship and love between men and women who accept and identify with these cultural images is impossible. Precisely this understanding of the absence of any direct personal relationship of friendship between the sexes led the philosopher Hegel to despair of solving the problem of human isolation and alienation on the interpersonal level and to seek that solution on the political level in the unifying concept of citizen. Marx, in turn, used the concept of class identity to escape the same dilemma. The frustrations that result in trying to live out these partial images leave modern humanity open to all forms of exploitation, both economic and political.

Married love, from both a human and religious viewpoint, can only exist fully between persons who see themselves somehow as total and equal. As Rainer Maria Rilke put it over a century ago:

> We are only now beginning to look at the relation of an individual person to a second individual objectively without prejudice and our attempt to live such associations have no model before them. The humanity of women, borne its full time in suffering and humiliation, will come to light when she will have stripped off the convention of mere femininity . . . . Some day there will be women whose name will no longer signify merely an opposite of masculine but something in itself, something that makes one think, not of any complement or limit, but only of life and existence. This advance will . . . change the love experience, which is now full of error, will alter it from the ground up, reshape it into a relation that is meant to be of one human being to another . . . and this more human love . . . will resemble that which we are preparing with struggle and toil—the love that consists in this—that two solitudes protect, border and salute each other.[7]

Carter Heyward made the same observation from a lesbian perspective:

> There is little room in the enormous socially constructed box of heterosexual roles for real mutual love between the sexes and no

allowance at all for mutual love between women and between men
. . . . If our world and civilization have a future, it may be that in
some future decade sex roles will be transcended; persons will be
defined as persons and models of relationships will be chosen, not
imposed. It is with other lesbian Christians that we can witness to the
power of God's presence in mutuality—in a relationship in which
there is no higher and no lower, no destructive insecurities fastened in
the grip of sex role expectations. Lesbian relationships can make a
prophetic witness within and to society, a witness not on behalf of
homosexuality per se but, rather, on behalf of mutuality and friendship in all relations.[8]

Priest-psychologist Eugene Kennedy puts the same idea in the perspective of healthy adolescent development:

> When we can face with less fear the complex of feelings and impulses
> that are part of each person's sexuality, we will be able to accept and
> integrate our experience into a less prejudiced and more creative self
> identity. That is to say, when persons can be more friendly toward
> what really goes on inside them, they will feel less pressured to deny
> or distort the experience of themselves. The achievement of their
> masculine or feminine identity will be less the acceptance of a rigidly
> imposed social stereotype and more the attainment of a multi-dimen-
> sioned truth about themselves. Greater openness can only increase
> our chance of more successful gender identity.[9]

All these quotations underscore the truth that in the very act whereby
society allows the homosexual to be him or herself, it will liberate everyone to be in touch with the fullness of themselves.

I do not wish to appear naive in my awareness of what is frequently the
reality of the gay life-style. I am consciously dealing here with ideals and
possibilities. Many homosexuals are still filled with self-hatred and act
out that self-hatred in self-destructive ways. As Neil Alan Marks observed in a recent *Christopher Street* article: "Many homosexual men
[who have integrated themselves into the prevalent gaycult] have not yet
accepted themselves as valid and fully functional human beings."[10] Many
homosexual men have felt compelled to buy heterosexual society's dehumanized macho image and are engaged in a self-destructive persecution
of their feminine self and an active outward rejection of women. In
keeping with their macho image they actively strive to suppress all feelings and to reduce their sexual activity to an impersonal, unloving fantasy sex that downplays their sexual object's subjective and human reality. This systematic destruction of their feelings makes sense because
society and the Church have done everything in their power to force

homosexuals to experience their gay feelings as immoral and socially unacceptable and, therefore, invalid. Many lesbians, in turn, are acting out a self-destructive form of anger against men.

There are, however, many gay men and women who have accepted the many dimensions of themselves. I have frequently found these gay people are more human and vulnerable, less smug and self-satisfied, more honest in seeing their own fraility and fallibility, over against so many heterosexual people who seem to live totally unexamined lives. It takes a lot of intelligence and courage to be successfully gay in our society and, unfortunately, many fail to make this grade. Homophobes tend to read into these failures something intrinsically wrong with homosexuality itself. More often than not, however, these failures represent the failure of society to allow the gay person to be him or herself.

Homosexuality and Violence

There is still another function that the homosexual community could perform within society toward the liberation of all to a more humane existence. That function has to do with diminishing one of the psychic foundations for violence. Psychologists are fully aware of the deep all-pervasive relation between the male cultural identity image and the proneness to violence in American culture. As Dr. Weinberg observed in his book, *Society and the Healthy Homosexual*, it is homophobia which frequently underlies male aggressiveness and fear of passivity.[11] The prophetic few who have chosen nonviolent means to correct injustices in our society have frequently been the victims of a popular hatred and antipathy that borders on the hysterical. Anyone who has participated in a peace demonstration or an antinuke or civil rights march knows from firsthand experience the type of emotional hostility their acts can provide from male onlookers and police. There is no doubt that many sense in the passive resistance of pacifists or conscientious objectors a menace to the male image itself.

Hitler's Nazi party was well aware of the association of pacifism with male homosexuality. In 1928, the Nazi party published this statement concerning a proposed reform of the sodomy laws in the German criminal code:

Community before Individual:

It is not necessary that you and I live, but it is necessary that the German people live, and they can only live if they can fight, for life means fighting, and they can only fight if they maintain their masculinity. They can only maintain their masculinity if they exercise discipline, especially in matters of love . . . . Anyone who even thinks of homosexual love is our enemy. We reject anything that emasculates our people and makes them a plaything of our enemies; for we know that life is a fight and it is madness to think that men will embrace fraternally. Natural history teaches us the opposite. Might makes right. And the stronger will always win over the weak. Let's see that once again we become the stronger.[12]

In 1937, the SS newspaper, *Der Schwarze Korps*, estimated that there were two million homosexuals in Germany and called for their extermination. Himmler gave orders that all known homosexuals were to be sent to Level 3, that is, death camps. The second largest group to die in Hitler's gas chambers after the Jews were our gay brothers and sisters.

Because they have the possibiliy of escaping the negative influence of the prevailing male identity image, the homosexual community is potentially free from the psychological need to establish their male identity by means of violence. This ability, however, is linked to and conditioned by their ability to accept and celebrate their sexuality. As Carter Heyward put it: "Sexuality is, I believe, the one most vital source of all our other passions, of our capacity to love and do what is just in the world . . . the capacity to celebrate sexually is linked inextricably with the capacity to court peace instead of war, justice instead of oppression, life instead of hunger, torture, fear, crime and death."[13]

My point is not that every homosexual can realize such a freedom at present; any more than every heterosexual necessarily succumbs to the depersonalization of the heterosexual image. Occasionally homosexuals imitate in an exaggerated way the worst features of the heterosexual image. They confuse masculinity with sadism. However, while violence on the whole seems remarkably absent from the life-style of self-accepting homosexuals, it is particularly prevalent among those who have strong homosexual desires they hate and seek to repress. Consequently, by liberating the heterosexual male to the possibility of recognizing and accepting the homosexual tendencies in himself, a self-accepting homosexual community could make a positive and even decisive contribution to bringing violence within control in our society.

Homosexuality and Human Services

Another change is going on in our culture which also tends to place the person who is living out the traditional male image at a disadvantage.

Traditionally, the male was programmed to be the worker. Rendered relatively insensitive to the needs of persons, he had to find his role in the hard work of dealing with material things. As a result, service roles in the community such as care of the young and the aged, education, counseling, nursing, and social work in general have been seen as primarily feminine roles, not fit occupations for the true male.

Among the special gifts he attributes to the homosexual, Jung observed that "frequently the homosexual is surprisingly gifted as a teacher because of his almost feminine insight and tact."[14] Thielicke, in turn speaks of a "pedagogical eros," a heightened sense of empathy to be found in the homosexual.[15] Many observers note the attraction of homosexuals to artistic roles, such as actors, dancers, decorators, beauticians, etc. There is no doubt that the homosexual male is freer than his heterosexual male counterpart to develop aesthetic taste. What has escaped attention, however, is the frequency in which gay people fulfill service roles with remarkable success. Many people presume that gays lead selfish lives because they have no children, yet many gays creatively express their unselfish love for others in such positions as teachers, social workers, nurses, counselors, therapists, clergymen, in fact, in any form of occupation where they can be in direct service to their fellow humans.

How often, too, have elderly and sick parents been supported and cared for selflessly by a bachelor son or daughter whose homosexuality was carefully hidden from them; whereas, if they had been left to the care of their married heterosexual offspring, they would have been committed to the impersonal care of some institution. These and other reasons have led me to believe that every family is blessed that has a gay son or daughter. Once again there is the hopeful possibility that the homosexual community could serve the human community as a whole by helping its male members feel free to develop empathetic feelings and do works of service without feeling guilty about betraying standards of male identity.

The Homosexual Community and Values

Another positive aspect Jung attributes to the homosexual community is that they have a "feeling for history and a resultant tendency to be conservative in the best sense and cherish the values of the past."[16] Most values are incarnated in customs, mores, and taboos imposed from without as tradition, to which the heterosexual majority gives uncritical assent. When Bert Parks chanted "There she goes, your ideal" at the Miss America contest, heterosexual middle-class America would not dream of being critical. Most of these value structures, however, are breaking down, especially the traditional procreative sexual ethics, and many people feel lost and bewildered.

Forced by their condition, for the most part, to live outside traditional value structures, self-accepting gays have been thrown back on themselves and their own experience in order to establish the values which merit their acceptance. Almost in direct proportion to the extent that they are cut off from traditional patterns, they must seek out and re-create the real values which these patterns were meant to convey, and reincarnate these values in their life-style by a personal commitment.

I see the gay community struggling to find both the human and spiritual meaning of their sexuality and their love independent of traditional heterosexual patterns. Once again, there are excesses and many gays are involved in very dehumanized and depersonalized sexual life-styles. They seem to strive to live out the worst fears of their enemies in a self-punishing way. But many others, I believe the majority, are seriously engaged in the difficult search for the full human and spiritual meaning of their sexuality, and they have no guides or models before them. Once they make the breakthrough into the full meaning of sex outside a procreative context, however, they will have performed an essential service by guiding their heterosexual brothers and sisters to a new, happier, more fulfilled and human sexual life as well.

In all the comments so far on homosexuality and sex roles, the relation of the sexes to each other, violence, human services, and developing a new understanding of human sexual values, it should be evident that there is an intrinsic connection between gay liberation and women's liberation. One cannot take place without the other. Any real advance in one will necessarily involve a real advance in the other. G. Rattray Taylor, in his book *Sex in History*, finds a universal phenomenon in patriarchal cultures. These cultures always tend to combine a strongly subordinated view of women with a repression and fear of male homosexuality,[17] whereas cultures based on a matriarchal principle are inclined to combine an enhancement of the status of women with a relative tolerance of male homosexual practices.

The late Dr. Mark Freedman concluded from a series of tests administered to both male homosexuals and lesbians that "a clear picture of homosexuals today would show a great many men and women who live by their own values and whose emotional expressions are not limited by traditional sex roles. Many gay people respond to social pressures against homosexuality with an intense quest for identity, purpose, and meaning. Consequently, they rate superior to their heterosexual counterpart in such psychological qualities as autonomy, spontaneity, ability to be present and increased sensitivity to the value of the person."[18]

The Homosexual and Religious Leadership

Jung's final surprising observation concerning the positive aspects of homosexuality has to do with the special contribution the homosexual community can make to the spiritual development of humanity. "They [homosexuals] are endowed with a wealth of religious feelings which help them to bring the *ecclesia spiritualis* into reality, and a spiritual reciptivity which makes them responsive to revelation."[19]

Homosexuals have always played a hidden leadership role in humanity's religious life. The shaman, the medicine man, the monk and nun, and, frequently, the priest and minister have been gay. John Boswell, in his book *Christianity, Social Tolerance and Homosexuality*, documents the leadership role of the gay men in the monastic tradition.[20] The components of this particular gift have already been recognized. As we have seen, the homosexual community enjoys a special freedom which allows it to be passive and receptive; attitudes essential to prayer and meditation. Whenever a machismo image reigns in a culture, prayer and worship are usually seen as fit activities only for women. Homosexuals can be free from violence and dedicated to a quest for peace. They can have a special sensitivity to the value of the person, especially persons of the opposite sex. They can dedicate themselves to a life of service of their fellow humans. Further, we have seen that the homosexual community, if it were granted freedom to be itself and develop its potential, could contribute to the liberation of all humanity, to a fuller realization of personhood and interpersonal relations based on equality.

At this point it is interesting to note that each of the special qualities Jung attributes to the homosexual is usually considered a striking characteristic of the traditional historical portrait of Jesus Christ, the qualities that distinguished him from the ordinary man. Christ had an extraordinary ability to meet the individual as a unique person. Where others saw a class, an alien, a sexual inferior (e.g., the woman at the well), Christ manifested the ability to encounter the person as his human equal with understanding, compassion, and love. He also frequently expressed the desire to free his disciples from stereotypes and cultural prejudices. Christ refused to establish his identity and accomplish his mission by means of power and violence, and called on his disciples to be men and women of peace, resisting injustice by their own suffering. Above all, Christ presented himself as the loving servant of all humanity, pointing out that anyone who wishes to follow him must seek not to be served but to serve.

The point I am trying to make here is *not*, obviously, that Christ was a homosexual, any more than he was a heterosexual with the significance the cultural context gives that designation. Rather, he was an extraordinarily full human person and an extraordinarily free human being.

The New Testament makes the claim that there was a seed planted by Christ, the seed of the Spirit of love, whose eventual fruit will be the overcoming of all divisions that separate one human person from another and thus each of us from the totality of ourselves (see Gal 3:28). Paul mentions three such divisions: master and slave, that is, all divisions based on power and helplessness; Jew and Greek, that is, all divisions based on racial and cultural differences; and finally, male and female. Obviously, Paul is not referring to an elimination of the biological and, if any, psychological differences between men and women. Rather, he is referring to the learned cultural distinctions which render women culturally inferior to men, deny them the full status of persons, and, thus, militate against a true interpersonal love encounter between men and women. It is this same cultural distinction that lies at the base of cultural homophobia and leads to the active persecution of the homosexual.

Ideal human nature and ideal interpersonal relations lie in the future, not in the past. It is up to the creative freedom of all of us, with God's grace, and for the Christian with the model presented in Christ, to direct our development toward that ideal. That ideal is the fully mature human person who has totally integrated his or her sexuality into their personality so that they can use their sexual powers to express genuine unselfish love for another person.

The essential point I have tried to establish in stressing the positive aspects of homosexuality is that the tendency to identify oneself as a person with one's sexual identity image can, and frequently does, lead to a one-sided stress on certain qualities and the elimination of others. The heterosexual tends to define himself in contrast to the homosexual and vice versa. The result is a narrow, impoverished, and dehumanized image for both parties. The objective acceptance of the homosexual community will leave both communities free to develop all the qualities that belong to the fullness of the human personality. Thus the homosexual community if it is allowed to develop all its potentialities freely, has a very special role to play in bringing about the ideal of the total mature human being both for its own members and for its heterosexual brothers and sisters as well. It is my belief that gay liberation has occurred at this moment in history because the achievement of this maturity is essential to the survival of the human species. May we all, in Paul's words, ". . . reach mature humanness, and that full measure of development found in Christ Jesus" (Eph 4:13).

A CHALLENGE TO LOVE

NOTES

1. Irving Biber, *Homosexuality: A Psychoanalytic Study* (New York: Basic Books, 1962), p. 5.

2. Oriana Fallaci in an interview with Khomeini quotes this response to a question concerning the recent execution of homosexuals: "If your finger suffers from gangrene, what do you do? Do you let the whole hand and then the body become filled with gangrene? Or do you cut the finger off?"

3. I developed this new orientation in a series of articles: "The Christian Male Homosexual," *Homiletic and Pastoral Review* 70 (1970): 667–77, 747–58, 828–36. Also in my book *The Church and the Homosexual* (Kansas City: Sheed, Andrews and McMeel, 1976).

4. Pierre-Claude Nappey, "An Open Letter on Homosexuality," in *Sex: Thoughts for Contemporary Christians*, ed. Michael Taylor (Garden City, N.Y.: Doubleday, 1972), p. 211.

5. C. G. Jung, *The Collected Works*, trans R. F. C. Hull (New York: Pantheon, 1959), 9:86–87.

6. Nappey, art. cit., pp. 210–18.

7. Rainer Maria Rilke, *Letters to a Young Poet*, trans. M. D. Herter (New York: Norton, 1962), pp. 53–59.

8. Carter Heyward, "Coming Out: Journey Without Maps," *Christianity and Crisis* 11 June 1979.

9. Eugene Kennedy, *The New Sexuality: Myths, Fables and Hang-Ups* (New York: Doubleday, 1973), pp. 179–80.

10. Neil Alan Marks, "New York Gaycult, The Jewish Question . . . and Me," *Christopher Street* 5, no. 10 (November 1981), p. 10.

11. George Weinberg, *Society and the Healthy Homosexual* (New York: St. Martin, 1972), pp. 1–21.

12. Wolfgang Harthauser, "Der Massenmord an Homosexuellen im Dritten Reich," in *Der Grosse Tabu*, ed. W. S. Schlegel (Munich: Rutten and Leening, 1967).

13. Heyward, art. cit.

14. Jung, op. cit.

15. Helmut Thielicke, *The Ethics of Sex* (New York: Harper & Row, 1967), p. 284.

16. Jung, op. cit.

17. G. Rattray Taylor, *Sex in History* (New York: Ballantine), pp. 72–78.

18. Mark Freedman, "Far from Illness: Homosexuals May be Healthier Than Straights," *Psychology Today* 8, no. 10 (March 1975): 27–33.

19. Jung, op. cit.

20. John Boswell, *Christianity, Social Tolerance and Homosexuality* (Chicago: University of Chicago Press, 1980), especially pp. 218–41.

II

BIBLICAL-
THEOLOGICAL
PERSPECTIVES

MICHAEL D. GUINAN

Homosexuals: A Christian Pastoral Response Now

In a large, metropolitan area of the United States, a group of seminarians for the Roman Catholic priesthood were watching the evening
news on television. A report was given on homosexuals in San Francisco
being attacked and beaten. During this report, one of the seminarians
cheered on the muggers. "That's right! Punch 'em out. Teach 'the boys' a
lesson!" The following news story dealt with the killing of the baby seals.
The same person was deeply touched. "Oh, that's awful! The way they're
clubbing those cute, defenseless animals. They ought to stop them!"
Another member of the seminary tried to console him. "Look at it this
way," he said. "Maybe the baby seals are gay."

About the same time, an item in the daily newspaper reported a "gay
backlash" in Key West, Florida. One person is quoted as saying, "If I
were the chief of police, I would get me a hundred good men, give them
each a baseball bat and have them walk down Duval Street and dare one
of those freaks to stick his head over the edge of the sidewalk. This is the
way it was done in Key West in the days I remember and loved. Female
impersonators and queers were loaded into a deputy's automobile and
shipped to the county line." The speaker was the minister of a Christian
church in Key West.[1]

The homosexual question abounds in unsolved problems and areas of
confusion. The question has been only recently formulated and addressed
to various fields of inquiry, e.g., psychology, sociology, biology, theology, biblical studies, etc. Each of these fields has its own methodology
and resources, and we are far from clear-cut answers to many aspects of
the question. In this essay, I am concerned with a Christian, pastoral
response to homosexuals now. We do not have to, in fact cannot, wait for
all the evidence to come in, for all the questions to be answered. We have
to begin now to respond in a Christian way. In what follows, I do not

propose to offer any new solutions, nor to base my remarks on problematic evidence. Drawing on biblical inspiration, I wish to suggest four principles which I believe can guide us now. I do not believe any of these is particularly problematic. They do overlap a bit and are interdependent, but they can be distinguished clearly enough.

I

The beginning of prejudice is the violation and denial of the common humanity of the group in question. We are here; they are there. We are "good people," they are "queers, perverts, fags" (or: "niggers, jigs, kikes," etc., pick your group). The last thing that can be admitted is that we are all equally human beings, sharing the same basic needs, desires, hopes, and life. That is why I prefer to speak of "homosexuals"—we must keep clearly in focus that we are speaking of concrete human beings with whom we interact, knowingly or not, every day. "Homosexuality" is an abstraction; there is no such thing.

If the first step of prejudice and persecution is the denial of common humanity, the second step frequently is to quote the Bible in support of this. It is acceptable to segregate blacks because (we are told) Ham, the father of Africans, was cursed by God (Gn 9:22–25). It is acceptable to oppress Jews; after all, read what John's Gospel says about "the Jews," not to mention other remarks in the New Testament. We should not be surprised then to find the Bible being quoted in the current debate over the rights and dignity of persons who are homosexual.

In the Gospels, we meet religious, "Bible-quoting" people, people whose moral approach began with their own self-righteousness, which provided the norm against which other people were measured. The Gospels characterize these people as Pharisees. (In fairness we must note that this attitude was not true of all Pharisees, nor of Pharisaism at its best; but the problem was real.) These people "load heavy burdens to lay on other people's shoulders and do not lift a finger to help" (Mt 23:4). In one situation they want to stone a woman taken in adultery (Jn 8) and are told by Jesus, "Let the one who is without sin throw the first stone." In Matthew's Gospel, they are called "whitened sepulchers" who "look well on the outside but inside are full of dead men's bones and all kinds of filth. So it is with you: outside you look honest, but inside you are brimful of hypocrisy and crime" (Mt 23:27–28).

While the Pharisees seem to have pride of place in this attack, we should not overlook the fact that Jesus' own disciples are at times conspicuous for their hardheartedness and lack of understanding. They are very busy protecting Jesus and deciding what he should and should not hear, or whom he should or should not help. Two examples may suffice. A crowd is following Jesus, listening to his teaching; it gets late. His disciples tell him, "Dismiss the crowds; let them go to the villages and buy themselves food." Jesus has other plans (Mt 14:13–21). Again, a Canaanite woman cries out to Jesus to help her daughter. His disciples rise to the occasion. "Get rid of her; she keeps shouting after us!" (Mt 15:21–28). The approach and sensitivity of Jesus' disciples cannot always or easily be identified with Jesus' own attitudes.

This problem presented in the Gospels is hardly only of academic or historical interest. The two examples with which I began this essay are illustrative of the presence of the problem and its relevance to a discussion of a Christian response to homosexual persons. Two "thumbnail" indications that such an attitude is probably at work would be these: (1) "We're good and decent people and we are not going to put up with . . . ." The evil about to be committed in the name of goodness and decency is often worse than that which is being opposed. (2) "We should love the sinner, but hate the sin." While one could defend this in the abstract, in the concrete it is a cop-out. "Sin" is an abstraction which exists only when a someone does something. In practice, it is the sinner who is hated and violated.

Perhaps the basic underlying problem has to do with faith. For all their "religious" talk, such self-righteous people really do not have faith in God as much as faith in their own faith. The God of the Bible is a God of surprises, a God who calls us forward to new depths and new understanding. We need, as an integral part of our faith, a healthy sense of doubt, a doubt in our own faith. This point will return in our third section below.

My first guideline then is this: We must not be deceived or misled by the religious veneer on so much talk about homosexuals. When we encounter such attitudes, we should pause, be suspicious, have some reservations. Such an approach often masks something not only un-Christian, but even anti-Christian.

II

In the debate over homosexuality, a standard repertory of phrases and accusations quickly surfaces. Homosexuals are all sick; they are responsible for their condition and can change if they really want to (especially if they pray); they recruit from the young; they molest the young. Homosexual people find these statements ludicrous and the empirical evidence which exists thus far supports their opinion.

While there are specialists who maintain that homosexuals are by definition sick, a growing body of data suggests caution. As studies progress, especially of relatively happy and well-adjusted gays, the conclusion is emerging that "homosexuals meet with every reasonable standard of mental health in their relationships with themselves and with others."[2] When a group of tests were administered to relatively healthy gays and straights (and who is more than relatively healthy?), psychologists found great difficulty in determining who were the homosexuals and who were the heterosexuals, and in many instances there was no demonstrable pathology at all.[3]

The causes of homosexuality are quite obscure; in other words, they are just like the causes of heterosexuality. We are realizing more and more that there is a great deal about human sexuality in general that we simply do not understand. Is sexual preference biologically or genetically caused? Is it all learned behavior? If it is basically learned, it is learned very early and is deeply rooted in the personality structure. Here we meet a perverse double standard. If a homosexual, through therapy or prayer, begins to experience sexual preference for the opposite sex, we are told, "See, change is possible." But if a man is married, has children, and then "discovers" later in life that he really prefers same-sex relationships, we are told, "He was homosexual all along, but did not admit it to himself."

The idea of recruiting from among the young betrays the same kind of self-assured, simplistic evaluation of the causes of homosexuality. Gays are not recruited from the young, or from anywhere else. If they are, then so are heterosexuals recruited. The clichés involving children (e.g., Save Our Children) are geared to evoke such an emotional response that they can seldom be discussed in a reasonable way. What evidence exists strongly indicates that if a parent is really worried about sexual molestation of their children, they should demand only homosexual teachers, because the incidence of same-sex molestation is dramatically lower than that involving opposite sexes. Whether it is a question of "recruiting" or of molesting children, the charges are thoroughly specious in character.

In understanding homosexuality, the evaluation of empirical data is important, but we must also be aware that it can be misused. In an issue of *Christian Century* magazine,[4] psychologist James Harrison reviewed ten books on homosexuality within the Christian tradition. All but two or three came in for some strong criticism on this point. The author of one "evokes such a polarization between revealed biblical 'truth' and empirical scientific knowledge that the resulting epistemological dualism should make any Calvinist blanch. Furthermore . . . the author misrepresents what little scientific data he acknowledges." Another author "makes no effort to evaluate social science research, yet he uses its concepts incorrectly." Therefore his book is "an especially insidious one." Another author's "treatment of empirical evidence is a travesty."

I have no hesitation in saying that all of the clichés noted at the beginning of this section as characteristic of homosexuals are demonstrably false. That they persist in being cited in debate is the result of prejudice, bigotry, and demagogic sloganeering. My second biblical guideline comes from Exodus 20:16, "You shall not bear false witness against your neighbor."[5]

So far we have two guidelines: (1) not to be misled by religious persons who appeal to their self-righteousness to condemn, harm, or deny rights to other human beings, and (2) not to lie about our neighbor. Both of these are negative in tone. The following two guidelines are positive in orientation.

III

The point of departure for the third guideline—and in many ways it is the most important—lies in the Book of Job. We all remember the story. As a test of Job's faith and righteousness, he is despoiled of everything he holds dear. From the start, we, the audience, know that Job is innocent and that his protestations are sound. Three friends, Eliphaz, Bildad, and Zophar, come to comfort and console him. But slight consolation. They criticize him, presume he is guilty, and convict him of sin. If Job is suffering, it can be only because he has sinned. Job's experience contradicts this and he calls out to God to hear and justify him. His friends, though, are deaf to his pleas. They are so sure of what God does (their theology admits no doubts!) that they are unable to share or even to become aware of Job's experience, which does not fit their neat theory. This is especially ironic because one of the key characteristics of biblical wisdom teachers, to which Job's friends belonged, was remaining open to and learning from experience. In a nutshell, a conflict existed between a particular theological understanding and concrete, human experience which did not fit.

As Christians, we find ourselves in a similar position vis-à-vis homosexuals. We have a theory about homosexuality, and because of it we are unable to hear or understand the experience of homosexuals, which calls that theory, in some or all of its aspects, into question. I would like to first say something about the theory, and then something about gay experience.

The traditional theory is well known. Homosexual actions of any kind (e.g., a promiscuous one-night stand, or an expression of deep and committed love) are always seriously wrong morally because they are not open to procreation and thus violate the natural order of creation. The Christian tradition, the teaching of the Bible, and "empirical evidence" that gays are deranged, sick, etc.[6] are cited to support this theory.

The first element in the argument relies on tradition, i.e., the way Christian philosophers and theologians have dealt with the question in the past. Needless to say, these scholars were just as influenced by their own cultural and historical contexts as we are today. And today theologians have begun to question some of these past positions and reassess their continuing validity. Some examples: (a) the idea of natural law has played a big part in the negative evaluation of homosexuals; but what do we mean by "natural"?[7] This was often understood in the past to refer to whatever human beings had in common with animals. If this is one's definition, we can see how it might be difficult to take into account specifically human factors and variations. (b) Older philosophers and theologians shared a world view that was basically static; our world view today is marked by a strong sense of historicity and change, of being "on the way." Change and development are part and parcel of our view of reality. (c) It is also true that some elements in our older traditions have been passed over, neglected, or forgotten. For example, Saint Thomas Aquinas objects to homosexual practices because they are "against nature"; in another place he says that what is against nature, simply speaking, can become in some situations "connatural," and specifically mentions homosexuality. "For it can occur that in a particular individual there can be a breakdown of some natural principle of the species and thus what is contrary to the nature of the species can become by accident [a technical term] natural to the individual."[8]

The traditional argument also depends heavily on biblical texts. These too are coming in for closer scrutiny.[9] Is the biblical evidence really that unambiguous? These texts were written from two thousand to four thousand years ago in foreign languages, cultures, and times. We have to beware of reading our contemporary understanding of things, our questions and presuppositions, back into these texts; at the same time, we must beware of carrying forward into our times aspects of biblical data which are very much bound to their context in the ancient world.

Our modern understanding of homosexuality as a permanent, given psychological condition simply did not exist in the ancient world, if, in fact, it existed anywhere before the rise of modern psychology in the last century and a half. In our modern sense, then, there is no biblical text on homosexuality or homosexuals. It is stupid and unfair to expect biblical texts to provide detailed answers for all our modern problems, problems which either did not exist in the ancient world, or which were understood in quite a different way.

Just as we should not read all our problems and preoccupations back into the texts, we have to be careful not to carry ancient cultural characteristics over into our present time. A very few texts (Lv 18:22; 20:13; Rom 1:26–27) do mention acts which we today associate with homosexuality. Why are these acts condemned? The reasons are not entirely clear. Cultural factors may, at least in part, be operating. Certain actions may have been associated with particular idolatrous, pagan religious practices; the male role model in the ancient Near East called for a man to be a mighty warrior and to beget lots of children; the ancient culture had many elements of a shame culture, and one of the most shameful things for a man was to be treated like a woman, especially sexually.[10] One so treated was certainly not a mighty warrior. These are some suggestions which have been offered. Whether or not they all hold up, they do serve to highlight the problem of interpreting biblical evidence.

A further question must be faced. Once we have tried to recover the meaning of the biblical texts, how are these to be applied today in our moral theology? What relevance do they have today? This too is a complex question.[11] Discovering what the biblical teaching actually is and then applying it today is not nearly as neat and easy as at times we may be led to believe.

If it is only recently that this traditional theory with its theological and biblical underpinnings has come under attack, it is fair to ask, "Why?" What is the source of the attack? The answer is simple: the experience of gay people. In the past, many gay people, when faced with this rigid theory which did not fit their experience, simply said, "Your theory is wrong; so is your religion. Who needs it?" and left the churches. Now, more and more gays are saying, "Your theory does not fit our experience; religion and the Church are important to us, and we are not going to go away!" If we are to relate to homosexuals in a truly Christian way, we must try to share, in some way, the deep human experiences of gay men and women.

We should not understand this sharing only in an abstract, watered-down sense, i.e., we read books and articles about homosexuality, its causes, problems, etc. This is not unimportant, and it should not be overlooked, but it is too cerebral. Human beings are more than minds; they are thinking, feeling, sharing, loving, suffering, embodied individuals. We must somehow share this level as well.

The best way for heterosexuals to do this is to share with their gay relatives and friends. While I am quite convinced that all of us have gay relatives and friends, this avenue, unfortunately, is not always open, and for obvious reasons. It is important though to see gay men and women at their best. No one denies that the gay world has its unhealthy side (in this respect, it is just like the heterosexual world), but we should try to contact and see the healthy, normal side.

Since, given the present situation, it is not always possible to share and discuss the experiences of gays directly, some ways are open to us to share indirectly. Especially significant is the area of artistic representation, which engages us on a deep personal level. While gay men and women have long been involved in the arts (is this not part of the stereotype? we might mention that gays are also involved in professional atheletics; there have even been gay boxing champions!), it is only recently that explicitly homosexual experiences have been treated. Plays such as *Crimes Against Nature, Boys in the Band, Fortune and Men's Eyes, The Elocution of Benjamin Franklin,* and films like *Word Is Out, La Cage aux Folles, Sunday, Bloody Sunday, The Consequence* (based on the autobiographical novel of Swiss actor-playwright, Alexander Ziegler) dramatize the agony, humor, hopes, and struggles of gays. TV films like *That Certain Summer* and series like *All in the Family, Alice, White Shadow,* and others have dealt with the topic in various episodes. Novels like Patricia Nell Warren's *Front Runner, Fancy Dancer, The Beauty Queen*; Andrew Holleran's *Dancer from the Dance*; Rita Mae Brown's *Rubyfruit Jungle*; John Reid's autobiography, *The Best Little Boy in the World*; Joseph Pintauro's *Cold Hands,* while of varying artistic merit, can help us to a greater understanding and sharing of the situation of homosexuals in our modern society. This can help us to sympathize (in the literal sense of the term) with gays as fellow human beings.

From a religious point of view, a last and very important observation is worth making. Our theory says that homosexual relationships are unhealthy, destructive, and sinful. I have personally known gays and gay couples whose relationships (including sex) are a clear and positive force for growth in their lives, not only as persons, but as religious and Christian persons. They are aware of the religious horizon of their lives and try to live responsibly within it. They have grown in faith and charity. The presence of Christ in their lives and the effects of his presence are experienced precisely in and through their homosexual relationships. If we have a theory which denies this *a priori*, we are putting our heads in the sand, and if one's head is in the sand, what view is presented to the world?

Harvard biblical scholar Paul Hanson focuses the problem very concisely. "Job describes a pernicious kind of idolatry which is frightfully common among religious people today and yet seldom recognized as such. Humans conceptualize God, lay claims to the infallibility of their image, buttress their claims by arguing that their concept of God is proven by divine revelation objectively drawn from the Bible, and then appoint themselves as God's envoys to proclaim divine judgment on all who differ. Thus the religiously elite contribute to the breakdown of community and to the increase of intolerance and human misery, all as a means of safeguarding their own vindictive sense of moral and spiritual superiority. Job has little patience with such self-appointed spokespersons of 'god.' Living religiously is not a question of constructing and defending a definitive theological system but of responding faithfully, at the intersection of religious heritage and contemporary existence and experience, to an encounter with the living God."[12]

My third point should be clear. If we are to relate to homosexuals in a responsible, Christian pastoral way, we must begin to relate to the gay question with intelligence, understanding, sympathy, and compassion. We noted above that the first step to bigotry is the denial of our common humanity. Homosexuals are human beings just like all of us. We must keep Job and his friends in mind. The friends held their theory with great conviction and had no room for doubt. The best comment on this is the startling statement near the end of the book: "When the Lord had finished speaking to Job, he said to Eliphaz, the Temanite, 'I am angry with you and your friends because you have not spoken rightly concerning me, as my servant Job has done' " (42:7).

IV

My fourth point is brief. The society of Jesus' time, just as now, had its marginal people, those others looked down on, despised, and denied basic justice to: lepers, prostitutes, publicans (who became wealthy by collecting and extorting tolls for the occupying Romans), Samaritans. Wherever there was pain, suffering, oppression, the denial of justice, Jesus faced a choice. He could have said, "If I go to these people, work with them to put an end to their oppression, the injustice they suffer, I may be accused of agreeing with them in every detail; I may be identified too much with them. I'd better stand aside and criticize them, and people will see how religiously correct I am." Or he could have said, "I will be present there with mercy, healing, compassion, and strength." He was there with them and he was roundly criticized for it. "He eats with publicans and sinners!" (Mk 2:16; Lk 5:30–31; Mt 9:11, 11:19), He was there.[13] "You are a human being; you have dignity; you count. I treat you with respect and call you to grow to the fullest humanity you can, to a life of peace and love and justice. And I expect my followers to do the same." The Gospels could not be clearer. Religious arrogance, self-righteousness, and hardheartedness are much greater obstacles to the kingdom of God than human weakness and other forms of sin. When religion is used to deny life, to oppress the outcast, to despise the marginal, to do violence to others, we are not dealing with Christian behavior.

V

These then are my four guidelines—based on biblical examples and inspiration—for a Christian pastoral response to homosexuals. (1) We must avoid religious arrogance and self-righteousness, which would set us over against our gay neighbor and enable us to violate his/her common humanity. (2) We must not bear false witness against our neighbor, and the homosexual is our neighbor. (3) We must be open to the experience of our homosexual neighbor, even when this puts in question some aspect of our "certain" theories. We might, as did Job's friends, close ourselves off to a meeting with the living God calling us to new and fuller life. (4) In reaching out to share compassionately with gays, to work for justice for them, we are merely following the steps and example of Jesus, who did the same in his society. I do not see any of these principles as particularly problematic. We can begin to act on them right now. They do not, however, exhaust the meaning of Christian pastoral ministry to gays. To challenge, critique, educate, comfort, console in the light of the gospel is essential to and common to all Christian ministry. But if we do not, in some way, incorporate these guidelines, the other aspects of ministry will not—in fact, cannot—be heard.

NOTES

1. *San Francisco Sunday Examiner and Chronicle*, 15 April 1979, "Sunday Punch" section.
2. John McNeill, *The Church and the Homosexual* (New York: Pocket Books, 1976), p. 126.
3. Ibid.
4. "Building Bonds: The Church and Gays," *Christian Century*, 2 May 1979, pp. 500–504.
5. On these and other psychological issues, see J. Marmor, "Homosexuality and Sexual Orientation Disturbances," in B. J. Saddock, H. I. Kaplan, and A. M. Freedman, *The Sexual Experience* (Baltimore: Williams & Wilkins, 1976) pp. 374–91. The application of this commandment to the gay issue is well made by L. Scanzoni and V. R. Mollenkott, *Is the*

Homosexual My Neighbor? Another Christian View (New York: Harper & Row, 1978), e.g., p. 87.

6. I discussed this "empirical evidence" in point two above, so will not return to it here.

7. The complexities of this have been well discussed by J. Boswell, *Christianity, Social Tolerance and Homosexuality* (Chicago: University of Chicago Press,1980), pp. 11–15, 111, 145–56, 201–2, 303–32.

8. McNeill, *Church and the Homosexual*, p. 107. These passages are discussed at length by Boswell, *Christianity*, pp. 318–30, esp. 326–27.

9. A good summary and discussion of this can be found in Boswell, *Christianity*, pp. 91–117, 335–53. I believe that it is time for all of these texts to be reexamined vigorously by biblical scholars.

10. The more I study the motives of antihomosexuality, the more this point emerges as one of prime significance; it deserves study in its own right.

11. For discussion of some of the issues involved, see B. C. Birch and L. L. Rasmussen, *Bible and Ethics in the Christian Life* (Minneapolis: Augsburg, 1976).

12. *Divine Transcendence* (Philadelphia: Fortress, 1978), pp. 12, 18. Obviously, this applies to and overlaps with my first point above.

13. For God's consistent concern for the oppressed who cry out for justice, see my book, *Gospel Poverty: Witness to the Risen Christ* (New York: Paulist Press, 1981), passim.

LISA SOWLE CAHILL

Moral Methodology: A Case Study

C hristian ethics is made increasingly problematic in an era of ecumenical revision and expansion of traditional theological perspectives.
The conclusion now appears unavoidable that those accepted approaches
to moral issues which lack interrelated references to Scripture, tradition,
and both actual and ideal human experience are inadequate to the
breadth of the Christian religious experience and its theology. Our dilemma is complicated by the fact that contributions from these sources
are often unclear, in tension with one another, or both. This essay will
exemplify one way in which the multiple sources of Christian ethics
might work together to generate an adequate Christian response to a
concrete problem, homosexuality.

Narrow Approaches

In recent years, several theologians and denominational bodies have
attempted to develop a "Christian" perspective on this issue. Too frequently, however, the foundations of Christian moral insight are circumscribed narrowly, excluding or minimizing the authority of other sources.
An adequate approach would correlate several interdependent reference
points, and would attempt an appropriate and critical hermeneutic of
each in relation to all. For some, scriptural texts such as the story of
Sodom and Gomorrah (Gn 19:1–28) are taken to be definitive and clear
sources of moral rules which can be transposed from the biblical to the
contemporary setting, and which are normative for all Christians. Little,
if any, attention is given to historical-critical scholarship which might
explicate original contexts or subsequent interpretative appropriation by
the Jewish and Christian traditions. For example, it is not remarked that

* Reprinted, with permission, from *Chicago Studies,* where it first appeared in Summer
1980.

the destruction of Sodom and Gomorrah has been interpreted recently as *primarily* a condemnation of inhospitality rather than homosexuality.[1]

Others, such as Norman Pittenger, in *Making Sexuality Human,*[2] also appeal to a more general norm of ideal, "love," claiming that it has a biblical basis. Any genuinely self-offering love which respects the dignity of the beloved, whatever its sexual expression, is said to be a participation in the love of God. The various New Testament meanings of love remain undifferentiated. "Love" connotes sincere and honest interpersonal relationship, and is given little more specific content. The "loving" act is the good act.

In 1973, the trustees of the American Psychological Association voted to remove homosexuality from the list of psychiatric illnesses. Alan Bell, a psychologist, comments that "homosexuality . . . is a sexual variation well within the normal range of psychological functioning."[3] Implicit in such statements, and particularly in their assimilation by normative ethics, is the assumption that the morally commendable human act is the "healthy" human act. Further, what is healthy or sick can be determined by the empirical sciences. In the end, empirical, descriptive studies define the truly human, and conformity to that definition constitutes the moral "ought."

In the *Declaration on Certain Questions Concerning Sexual Ethics,* issued in 1975 by the Vatican's Sacred Congregation for the Doctrine of the Faith, we find an appeal to "natural law," a traditional basis of Roman Catholic ethics. "According to the objective moral order, homosexual relations are acts which lack an essential and indispensable finality," i.e., procreation (paragraph 5). The explicit presupposition of this analysis is that persons have a "nature" or certain essential characteristics, which they share universally, which are knowable by reason, which ought never to be violated in moral activity, and which conduce to specific and unchanging moral norms. In this instance, the law of nature demands that all sexual acts be open to the possibility of procreation, as well as expressive of the love of spouses. Scriptural texts are cited in a footnote, but they are a secondary rather than a primary consideration, adduced in support of a conclusion arrived at on other grounds.

Although the foundation of its argument is the law of nature, the *Declaration* bolsters its case with an appeal to Christian tradition, identified as "the constant teaching of the Magisterium" and "the moral sense of the Christian people" (paragraph 8). This insistence that present ethical judgments must maintain continuity with moral teaching of the Church presupposes that the Christian community in the past has articulated authentically and for all Christians the *concrete* significance of life in Christ.

Each of these evaluations appeals to one possible source of normative Christian ethical reflection, whether it be scriptural texts, broad scriptural themes, empirical evidence, essential human characteristics, or the experience of the faith community, authoritatively articulated. An adequate Christian ethics ought to attend to all of these sources, attempting to achieve their balance within a community of interpretation.

Integrated Approaches

These sources may be considered to exist in two broader categories and four more specific ones. The category "revelation" might be said to include within it *Scripture* and *tradition*. Within "human experience," are comprehended *descriptive* accounts of experience, such as those provided by the empirical sciences, and *normative* accounts, such as that proposed by natural law ethics. By "Scripture," is meant that body of texts (the "canon") which functions authoritatively in the Christian community as it defines and preserves its identity as faithful to Jesus Christ. To say this much is to already and inevitably enter the "hermeneutical circle" within which the Scriptures form the Church which interprets the Scriptures. Thus we arrive at the source with which, in another sense, we began, tradition. As the historical self-identity of the community which preserves and is preserved by Christ's presence within it, tradition is not really a distinct source, but a context for interpreting the others.

Descriptive accounts of human experience begin not with the explicit Word of God, or the presence of His Spirit within the Church, but with the existence of the creature in the historical process. A salient example in contemporary ethics is the findings of the empirical sciences, such as psychology, sociology, anthropology, and physiology. They enlighten our perception of what is in fact the case in actual experience. To such descriptions of what "is," can be juxtaposed and contrasted normative accounts of what "ought" to be. Descriptive accounts, even ones based on empirical investigation, are not always "value-free." Nonetheless, it seems a legitimate distinction can be made between accounts whose primary objective and function is to elucidate the historical reality of humankind, and those whose objective is to formulate an ideal by which to evaluate historical actuality. Some concept of "the normatively human," or the essentially, authentically or genuinely human, is necessary in order to transcend the particularities, intricacies, ambiguities, and distortions of concrete human existence.

Scripture and Homosexuality

The most obvious starting-point for Christian ethics, then, *as* Christian, is that body of literature which commemorates events of foundational significance for communal faith and practice. Importantly for ethics, the Scriptures provide images and symbols by which the moral orientation of the Christian is formed, as well as insight into what sorts of specific conduct are consistent with Christian character.

To use Scripture as a resource for any normative moral judgment would seem to entail appreciation of at least three of its dimensions. These are specific texts on the issue at hand, if any; specific texts on related issues; and general biblical themes or patterns. We might begin by recalling those familiar biblical texts which apparently yield clear prohibitions of homosexual acts, and even the homosexual condition. The compendia of laws in Leviticus and Deuteronomy outline the requirements of cultic and ritual purity essential to the integrity of the Chosen People. The Hebrews are enjoined to avoid the "abominable customs" of pagan nations (Lv 18:3, 24, 30). Twice it is repeated that "You shall not lie with a male as with a woman; it is an abomination" (Lv 18:22, 20:13). Although it is undeniable that, in these texts, homosexual acts are condemned as sinful, the attention of the author in each case seems to be directed elsewhere. First and foremost, the People of Yahweh are to resist idolatry and the temple cults of pagan religions, e.g., male prostitutes (Dt 23:18). These considerations may influence the way in which the central message of the text is interpreted, they inhibit any facile transposition of ostensible negative moral norms to other social and historical settings.

A similar situation emerges as the ethicist turns to the New Testament. Saint Paul is the only author to mention homosexuality explicitly, and includes it in lists of sins attributed to those who will be excluded from the Kingdom of God (1 Cor 6:9; Rom 1:26–27). Since Paul appropriated similar lists of sins from Jewish preaching of the time, they function as a rhetorical device in his letter, rather than as a moral discourse. It is nonetheless significant that they were preserved by Paul, and eventually by the Christian community in the canonical collection, but whether this incorporation is decisive for *ethics* in the light of the author's somewhat different concerns is problematic. Paul's Epistle to the Romans contains the only extended reference to homosexuality in the Bible. There it is portrayed as a consequence of abandoning God for idols. The sovereignty of the Creator and the futility of rebellion against the order he has made dominate the passage (1:20, 25). Violations of natural interrelationships among creatures and their Creator amount to forms of idolatry; perversions of appropriate relationships of maleness and femaleness are both the representation and the consequence of such disorder. Since idolatry is central, Paul does not embark on a discussion of sexuality in general, or even specify circumstances which would count as committing the sin mentioned. Paul's moral repugnance to homosexual acts was no doubt thoroughgoing, but a full response to this fact awaits the complementarity of other ethical insights, both biblical and nonbiblical.

Related Texts

The meaning of texts referring specifically to homosexual acts is enhanced when they are situated among texts on related issues, e.g., marriage, adultery, fornication, procreation. Many such texts coalesce with those negatively evaluating homosexual acts by indicating a positive heterosexual, marital, and procreative norm for sexual love. Perhaps the most paradigmatic are the Genesis narratives of the creation of humanity. In all three creation accounts (chaps. 1, 2, 5) humanity is constituted male and female, so that sexual differentiation is definitive of humanity from the beginning. Genesis 1:27 and 5:2 associate the duality of the sexes with the "image" and "likeness" of God in the creature; "So God created man in his own image, in the image of God he created him; male and female he created them" (Gn 1:27). In chapter 2, a union of two like but distinct beings is accomplished, when they "become one flesh" (v. 24). Neither man nor woman alone is complete humanity; only their duality, complementarity, and union give human nature its fullness. That the sexuality of the man and woman is part of their very creation suggests that the relation between the sexes is a profound part of human reality.

The union of Adam and Eve is succeeded by the mothers and fathers of the Judeo-Christian religious tradition, Abraham and Sarah, Isaac and Rebecca, Jacob and Rachel (along with Leah and two handmaidens), Moses and Zipporah. The convenantal commands of God forbid adultery (Ex 20:14, 17; Dt 5:18, 21), and enjoin filial respect for parents (Ex 20:12; Dt 5:16). In fact, the entire system of Hebrew law presupposes and institutionalizes the family and procreation.

The New Testament offers a similar picture. Jesus does not mention homosexuality, nor any sexual sins save that of adultery. It is possible, however, to distill an affirmative view of marriage and family from his teachings and deeds. Familial relationships are presupposed by many parables, e.g., wedding feasts (Mt 22:1–14; Lk 14:7–11), the bridegroom (Mk 2:19–20; Mt 5:14–17; 25:1–13; Lk 5:27–32); a wedding celebration is also the setting for a miracle story in Cana (Jn 2:1–11). More normatively, Jesus teaches his disciples to consider God as in the relationship of a parent to them (Mt 6:9–15; Lk 11:2–4), and compares God's forgiving love to that of a father for his prodigal son (Lk 15:11–32). Nonetheless, marital or familial status is not definitive of one's standing in the Kingdom of God (Mk 3:1–35; 12:25; Lk 18:29; cf. 1 Cor 7; Lk 14:26; Jn 4:1–42). The demands of discipleship take precedence over all human relations and loyalties.

Jesus' ethical teachings in general, e.g., on divorce (Mt 5:31–32; 19:9; Mk 10:11–12; Lk 16:18; 1 Cor 7:10–11), proclaim and enjoin those ideals of human conduct and relationship which are most consistent with God's intention in the creation, and with existence in the Kingdom. In challenging the Hebrew practice of divorce, Jesus appeals to the Genesis accounts of the equality and union of male and female (Mt 19:4–6; Mk 10:6–9). Herein the ideal is established. Exceptions to the permanence of this bond are not what God intended, but are allowances made only for "hardness of heart" (Mt 19:8; Mk 10:5). Also those who decide not to marry at all are considered to be exceptions to the norm, marriage. Jesus focuses on the ideal to which persons ought aspire in their conduct, rather than the casuistry of exceptions, even justifiable ones. Certainly it is a distortion of Jesus' own perspective to interpret his teachings as in themselves laws which exclude any exceptions they do not contain. The primary concern in the teaching of Jesus is not the definition of ethical criteria for inclusion in the Kingdom. Rather, he portrays God's relationship to us as merciful acceptance, and expects persons to respond with gratitude to God and reconciliation with even those among their fellows who are most antipathetic.

On the one sexual offense which Jesus mentions, his position is unambiguous. He presses behind adulterous actions to condemn with equal force even the lust which instigates them (Mt 5:27–28). Nevertheless, his attitude toward those who offend the norm is one of compassion and forgiveness, e.g., toward the woman about to be stoned for adultery (Jn 8:2–11), and the Samaritan woman at the well who has had five husbands (Jn 4:1–42).

The letters of Saint Paul provide a general perspective on sexuality, which, by contrast, appears quite negative (1 Cor 7:25–40). He advises Christians who are not already married to stay single, unless they require a spouse as a sexual outlet. Once married, husband and wife should love one another devotedly, but the one who remains a virgin has made the better choice. Since Paul, along with other early Christians, may have expected the end of the world and the return of the Lord in the relatively near future, he advises Christians to prepare, rather than to undertake any changes in their station in life. His central message, in the light of the eschaton, is simply that that which distracts one from single-hearted devotion to God is to be avoided. At the same time, he does compare the relation of Christ to his Church to marriage, and exhorts spouses to love one another faithfully (Eph 5:21–33).

Both Testaments also portray nonmarital love, including friendships between persons of the same sex. Yet these are colored by no clear sexual connotations. Between David and Jonathan (whose love is passionate, even sensual), Naomi and Ruth, Mary and her cousin Elizabeth, Jesus and Lazarus, Jesus and John, is the goodness of love between friends of the same sex, but no model of sexual relations between them. In the end, Scripture grounds via specific texts not only a negative appraisal of homosexuality, but a positive view of heterosexuality as normative for human love which has a sexual expression.

General Biblical Themes

Texts referring to sexuality need to be elucidated further by the larger biblical themes or patterns by which they are surrounded. Especially important for Christian ethics is the model of Jesus Christ which is presented in the Bible. Indeed, it is the self-disclosure of God in Christ that illumines the entire horizon of Christian existence. The Christian person is formed within a community rooted in a scriptural self-understanding and defined by certain common ideals, purposes, and symbols, e.g., Creation, Cross, Kingdom of God.

The qualities which ought to inform Christian character coalesce in Jesus. The focal events of his life for the Christian community are Cross and Resurrection. Christians know the reality of suffering to be the mark of sin, guilt, judgment, and to an equal degree, of obedience to the will of the Father. Reconciliation and exaltation are the converse of repentance and Cross. Jesus Christ, then, is a model not only of forgiveness, inclusive acceptance, reconciliation, and liberation, but also of suffering, guilt, judgment, sacrifice, fidelity, and service. His death on the cross, for example, reminds us of our universal sinfulness and the "brokenness" of creation. Since all of their descendants share in the sin of Adam and Eve, we are well advised to "Let him who is without sin among you be the first to throw a stone . . ." (Jn 8:7). The death of Jesus is for all persons, now redeemed, but first of all sinners, homosexuals no more and no less than anyone else.

Jesus associates with those whom the people of his time considered outcasts. Forgiveness is mediated to all in Jesus, even those whom "the righteous" condemn and shun. Fidelity to the Father in Jesus entails a responsibility to love others as Jesus loved, in conformity to the final paradigm of self-sacrifice, and in anticipation of the Kingdom which begins now. To the extent that homosexual love is characterized by fidelity and service, by sacrifice and liberation, by repentance and reconciliation, it follows Jesus' teaching and example. The larger community also must include homosexuals in their attitudes of love, forgiveness, and reconciliation, as well as judgment. Although these themes and their applications could be multiplied, it will suffice to take note of the fact that, while Scripture specifically affirms a heterosexual norm, and prohibits homosexual acts, it also affirms qualities of relationship which can be achieved by homosexuals. This positive view of the potential quality of homosexual love stands in tension with the negative implications of the specific texts on homosexuality and marriage. Is it adequate to the biblical witness to permit the larger biblical context to relativize all specific condemnations of homosexuality to the point of moral irrelevance? A final ambiguity on the issue of homosexuality in the Bible leads to the question whether Scripture is a sufficient as well as a necessary and primary source of Christian ethics. Does the community of interpretation for which Scripture is authoritative also assimilate appropriately other sources of insight within its perspective?

The Role of Experience

Paralyzed by complications and uncertainties in the hermeneutics of its primary source, particularly when that source is understood as a "text," contemporary Christian ethics often leans on the empirical sciences for assistance in the interpretation of human moral behavior, in particular, of sexual behavior.

Such evidence seems especially persuasive when it can be buttressed empirically, e.g., by sociology, psychology, anthropology, and studies of human sexual response, acts, and patterns of relationship (e.g., the pioneering work of Alfred Kinsey, and William Masters and Virginia Johnson). Such studies, too, seem to confirm heterosexuality, monogamy, and parenthood as prevalent crosscultural standards. However, they by no means are such without exception. Other forms of sexual relationship are reported with some frequency, and in many instances do not appear to be psychologically damaging or to render persons unable to function in society. Although sometimes homosexuality is associated with neurosis, same-sex preference as such is not in principle incompatible with psychological health, or with the capacity to enter into loving and faithful relationships. One particularly valuable contribution of psychology to ethics is the distinction between a homosexual *orientation,* or "constitutional" homosexuality, in which the person may be confirmed in a sexual orientation by little-understood factors largely if not wholly beyond his or her control; and homosexual *acts* of genital intimacy, performable either by a confirmed homosexual, or by someone having, in general, a heterosexual preference.

Although the empirical sciences are the most notable among those descriptive analyses of experience which have become influential upon formal ethical reflection, there are other varieties. It is worthwhile to note among these what might be termed the "personal story," which describes the experience of an agent involved in the sort of conduct under scrutiny.

Such a story is often offered as a morally persuasive "voice" for a class of persons, or for a generalizable dimension of experience. Verification then becomes consensual rather than empirical.

Descriptive assessments of morality in our own day are scarcely less problematic in their relation to Christian ethics than are biblical prohibitions addressed to foreign cultures and eras. Does normative morality depend on statistical frequency or on psychological and physical "health"? In most such studies, the underlying definition of human "health" is analogous to that pertaining to plant and animal life: the successful self-preservation and self-maintenance of an organism in its environment. Christian norms such as suffering, self-sacrifice, and self-denial for others at the very least challenge this definition.

Natural Law Tradition

A third alternative for the ethicist is to attempt to define or appropriate some concept of "the normatively human" or human nature, and thus to avoid the reduction of normative moral evaluation to descriptive or empirical analysis. The discovery of a methodology for deriving such a concept is an obvious barrier to this project, if it is not possible to derive it through empirical investigation. The Roman Catholic tradition of theological ethics nominates a candidate method, with attendant successes and shortcomings. This tradition has been committed to an objective moral order, under the providence of its Creator, which humans know and to which they conform by the powers of intellect and will. The essential human qualities, which reason discovers by abstracting from experience, and which choice ought to ratify, are not in any specific way epistemologically dependent on empirical verification, although it is expected that they will in general be confirmed by it. The "natural law" teaching that sex (in particular, sexual intercourse) is above all unitive and procreative is claimed to be consistent with biblical perspectives and with concrete experience.

The more egregious and notorious problems in this method arise at the level of the specific conclusions whose consistency with and, indeed, entailment by the heterosexual and procreative norm is asserted. The prospect of disagreement among those both within and without Christianity has not made the magisterium reluctant to articulate absolute prohibitions not only of adultery, prostitution, sexual promiscuity, but also all homosexual acts, premarital sex, and artificial contraception. To the Church's insistence that the presence of the Holy Spirit preserves its voice from falsehood, and obligates it to dispel the obfuscation of sin, error, and ignorance, it has been observed forcefully enough that even "authentic" teaching of the Church is articulated within the historical process and is subject to the contingencies and limitations that that process implies. A specific definition of "human nature" proposed with excessive certainty, abstraction, rationalism, rigidity, and authoritarianism exposes the intrinsic liabilities of the method by which it is derived more readily than would a more cautious or provisional proposal.

This brief investigation of the third source concludes with an insistence on the importance of deriving some working definition of the essentially human in the light of which the actually human may be considered. The commitment to this task is the indispensable contribution of natural law ethics. At the same time, it is necessary to consider whether carefully nuanced conclusions about exceptions to norms grounded in conceptions of the genuinely human are not only possible but advisable. As Aquinas had the good sense to remark, one doesn't really want to quarrel with the more general natural law principles, but as one gets down to specifics, there is increasing room for error (*Summa Theologica*, I–II, q. 94, a. 4. Considerable discussion has swirled around precisely what Thomas meant in so saying).

The Community

Obviously enough, scriptural images, scientific research, and insights into essential humanity are not discrete data with clear and distinct meanings apart from their ongoing relevance to the community within which they are discovered or received and understood. This community itself is the "tradition" of Christian faith and practice. In its function as an authoritative source for ethics, tradition is sometimes conceived as a series of propositions or even catalogues of sins transmitted from the past. Although tradition includes the articulation of specific moral directives for the life of the community, it is not limited to them. Specific criteria for what counts as "tradition" might include antiquity, widespread usage, consensus of the faithful, and authoritative definition. Tradition generally might be understood as the "story" of a people, for whom the Scriptures are formative, and whose historical self-understanding continues to form and inform present and future. (Stanley Hauerwas has eloquently developed the importance for ethics of "story," "vision," and "character.")

The question which expresses best the relevance of tradition for ethics is whether the purposes, decisions, actions, and relations of Christian persons are shaped by the story of the Christian people. Normative moral rules are subsequent and secondary; they delineate with varying degrees of specificity and reliability those sorts of conduct coherent with that story. The consistent positive contribution of the Christian tradition on sexuality is that "normative" human sexuality is heterosexual, marital, and has an intrinsic relation to procreation, love, and commitment. Hence the traditional condemnation of homosexual acts as not truly expressive of the meaning of human and Christian sexuality and even in contradiction to it. However, the sticky task of Christian ethics is determining when, why, and how to make exceptions to norms.

Summary

It becomes increasingly apparent that the sources of Christian ethics are several, and that their interrelationship in normative evaluations is exceedingly complex. The evaluation of homosexuality and homosexual acts is a case in point. It may be valid indeed to develop a negative rule about homosexuality within the Christian tradition, but not as a straightforward conclusion from Scripture or any other single source. The Christian ethicist is pressed to the nigh insuperable task of maintaining a "balance" among the dialectical reference points mentioned. (1) *Scripture:* (a) *Specific scriptural texts on the precise question.* Homosexual acts are unqualifiedly condemned, though in the context of discussions of other issues. (b) *Specific scriptural texts on related questions.* These yield a norm of heterosexual marital commitment. (c) *Overarching scriptural themes or patterns.* The lives of all Christians as individuals and in community are characterized by brokenness, self-sacrifice, forgiveness, and reconciliation, the paradigm of which is Jesus Christ. (2) *Descriptive accounts of human experience.* Empirical evidence points to the conclusion that homosexuals are a sexual minority, but can be psychologically and socially healthy, and can engage in loving relationships, whether or not these have a genital expression. (3) *Normative accounts of human experience (the normatively or essentially human).* The most authentically human expressions of genital sexuality respect the procreative and male-female unitive purpose of sexual acts. (4) *The tradition of the Christian community.* In the broad sense, tradition enjoins conformity to Jesus Christ. While homosexual persons are (in theory) not condemned, genital expression of relationships of love have been excluded for them.

Although my use of both biblical and nonbiblical sources is not beyond equivocation, I would suggest that these are the sorts of considerations to which normative ethics ought to attend. What, if anything, can be concluded from these sources? In the case of homosexuality, their complexity will be respected only by the proposal of a nuanced judgment, rather than a simple condemnation of homosexual acts as seriously sinful in all circumstances or blanket approval of all "loving" sexual acts. In my assessment, these sources together point unavoidably toward a heterosexual norm for human sexuality. This norm does not necessarily exclude exceptional applications, in cases where human and Christian values even more important than those protected by the norm are at stake, and where their realization cannot be accomplished without overriding the specific sexual norm. Descriptive or empirical accounts of human experience may be particularly helpful precisely at this point. They can serve to elucidate the situation in which the norm is to be applied, clarify the human options actually open to the persons involved, and question proposed applications of the norm which do not consider appropriately the "facts" of such a situation.

Orientation and Acts

The most important contribution of empirical research on the phenomenon of homosexuality is the distinction between orientation and acts. It is important to permit this distinction to influence applications of the heterosexual norm, even while continuing to uphold the norm itself. I would argue that heterosexuality *per se* is to be preferred to homosexuality. However, a normative judgment that the homosexual orientation is a less than fully human and Christian form of sexual preference does not necessarily entail a corollary prohibition of those genital acts through which confirmed homosexuals express and strengthen a committed relationship. It is essential to distinguish carefully between (1) normative evaluations of homosexuality, as a general sexual orientation, (2) evaluations of the concrete justifiability of homosexual acts in specific circumstances, and (3) the moral character and potential of homosexual persons. Far from branding all constitutional homosexuals as "sinners" in the specific sense, Christian ethics accepts the fact of homosexuality or heterosexuality as beyond the control of most individuals. Certainly homosexual persons (sexually active or celibate) are not inhibited by their sexuality from realizing in their character morally commendable qualities, or qualities consistent with their faith in Jesus Christ and life within his community. The cultivation of love, self-sacrifice, fidelity, and service are even more important for Christian moral agents than avoidance of the specific sorts of conduct which are *in general* not expressive of those virtues.

Given the heterosexual norm thus far delineated, a distinctively *Christian* perspective on homosexuality might perceive in it the suffering, tragedy, and irreconcilable conflict which are part of historical existence after the fact of sin, as part of the "brokenness" in which all creation shares. Although all human experience confirms the presence of evil and suffering within it, the faith community interprets this with the image of the Cross. With the corollary image, Resurrection, the Christian community expresses its distinctive confidence that evil, tragedy, and absurdity, are not the final word. The human situation, considered in the light of these central images together, is seen to be imbued not only by guilt, suffering, ambiguity, but also by mercy, forgiveness, reconciliation, redemption.

In view of these observations, two inadequate approaches to homosexuality can be discerned, as well as, hopefully, a more positive one. In one sort of evaluation, normative theological ethics relies too onesidedly on empirical studies which verify that the homosexual is psychologically and socially healthy. The ethicist then proceeds to the conclusion that the homosexual orientation is humanly and morally normative, and that homosexual acts are in no way morally questionable. The positive contribution of this approach is its affirmation of the homosexual person in his or her concrete reality. However, from a Christian viewpoint, this can also be understood as an attempt to deny the disconcerting reality of suffering and ambiguity concretized in the situation of the homosexual. This is to explain away the tragic dimension of our existence in history precisely when and *because* it thrusts itself painfully upon our experience. Such a solution also betrays frequently a confusion between affirming homosexual persons as persons, affirming the justifiability of homosexual acts in exceptional instances, and affirming homosexuality as an orientation. To see the orientation as nonnormative, and as in a real sense "suffering," is not to offer a negative moral judgment on homosexual persons, on their potential for praiseworthy relationships, nor necessarily on homosexual acts.

In another sort of evaluation, the association of the phenomenon of homosexuality with the brokenness of the creation, or with the "Sin" in which all persons and institutions share, is simplistically or uncritically identified with personal "sin," the sin of the homosexual person. If the orientation is evidence of the effects of Sin, then, it is inferred, genital acts expressing that orientation must be "sins." Some go even further, in insisting that the homosexual person, regardless of the level of his or her sexual activity, must be a "sinner." This evaluation falls short because of its imputation of guilt to individuals for a condition for which their responsibility is far from clear, or at a lesser level, for acts which, given that condition, are the concretely possible expressions of important human and Christian virtues or values.

A Judgment

A Christian perspective on homosexuality, then, would recognize suffering as such, but would interpret it by Cross and Resurrection. Both sacrifice and liberation are *positive* concepts, calling for embodiment in Christian life and action. Christian ethics focuses on character, formed by the biblical and communal vision, and enhanced by Christ-like qualities. Acts are not irrelevant to the development of character. The relation of specific sorts of acts to character is determined by consideration of the four sources mentioned, in combination or balance (tradition always forming the context for the interpretation of others, and Scripture always forming the tradition). In this case, those sources evidently conduce to the judgment that those sexual relations and acts which best embody the Christian vision are heterosexual and procreative acts within a permanent commitment. Even in this sort of specific assessment, the proper focus of Christian ethics, is character and moral values or characteristics (for example, honesty, fidelity, love, service, self-denial), rather than on physical values and material acts (for example, acts of genital sexuality). The latter are good or evil precisely because of their relation to the former, as generally accomplishing their realization and enhancement, or as generally excluding and inhibiting them. If because of conflictual situations, the material acts usually conducive to and expressive of moral values do *not* actualize them or in fact inhibit them, then these acts are not to be commended in the situation. The less-than-ideal ("broken") situation can and must be "redeemed" through fidelity to the higher religious and moral values, even if unavoidably embodied in less-than-ideal material decisions and acts. In the concrete situation this is the best alternative and therefore a positive and morally commendable one, which should be appreciated in the light of the Christian values, qualities, and ideals which it positively achieves. This amounts to a suggestion that while heterosexual marriage is the normative context for sexual acts for the Christian, it is possible to judge sexual acts in other contexts as *nonnormative but objectively justifiable in the exceptional situation,* including that of the confirmed homosexual.

Conclusion

There lately has been considerable discussion in Roman Catholic ethics of the viability of absolute moral norms and the concept of "intrinsic evil." This includes the distinction between moral and premoral evil.[4] I accept the distinction between moral and premoral or "ontic" evil, and see it as relevant to this problem. Another way to state my conclusion would be to say that genital homosexual acts are "evil" in that they are to be avoided generally. However, they are "premoral" evils in that their sheer presence does not *necessarily* make the total act or relation of which they are a part "morally" evil or sinful. The total act is not sinful if there is sufficient reason in *this* case for causing "premoral" or "ontic" evil. Killing in self-defense is analogous. Still, I consider the justifiability of any conclusions drawn within Christian ethics to be dependent on their consistency with Scripture, tradition, and the empirical sciences, as well as with natural moral reason.

This essay represents a tentative attempt to explore the problem of homosexuality from a perspective which considers several dimensions of theological ethics as it takes place within a faith community. I have highlighted four reference points (Scripture, tradition, descriptive and normative accounts of experience), and suggested the necessary relevance of all to any issue which the Christian ethicist might address. Although a "balance" of sources is recommended, the question of priority in cases of conflict is unavoidable. On the issue of immediate concern, I have tried to account for discrepancies among the sources by articulating a norm which contemplates exceptions, i.e., a nuanced position rather than an unequivocal yes or no. To assume that these sources can somehow be combined in a coherent position, however, is already to make a commitment in faith to the proposition that "revelation" and "human experience" are complementary realities rather than radically conflictual ones.

NOTES

1. D. Sherwin Bailey, *Homosexuality and the Western Christian Tradition* (New York: Longmans, 1965), pp. 1–28.

2. Philadelphia: Pilgrim Press, 1970.

3. "Homosexuality: An Overview," in *Male and Female: Christian Approaches to Sexuality,* ed. Ruth T. Barnhouse and Urban T. Holmes III (New York: Seabury, 1976), p. 141.

4. See Charles Curran and Richard McCormick, eds. *Readings in Moral Theology No. 1: Moral Norms and the Catholic Tradition* (New York: Paulist Press, 1979); and Richard McCormick, *Ambiguity in Moral Choice* (Milwaukee: Marquette University, Theology Department, 1973).

MARGARET A. FARLEY

An Ethic for
Same-Sex Relations

Nearly every traditional moral rule governing sexual behavior in
Western culture is today being challenged. Longstanding prohibitions have become so problematic that nations and states debate legal
changes, and major religious traditions struggle with new formulations of
ethical teachings. In the midst of all of this, there may be no question
more intensely probed, more politically volatile, more personally troubling or liberating, than that of the moral status of same-sex relations.
Like other questions of contemporary sexual ethics, it has emerged in a
context shaped by new understandings of human sexuality, changing
patterns of relationship between women and men, and increased control—through technology—of human fertility and reproduction.

Homosexuals today find themselves living in a society still greatly
influenced by the Christian churches. Moreover, persons with homosexual or lesbian orientation have often been nurtured by the Christian
community, and they seek to continue to give and receive life within it. In
acknowledgment of these facts, official groups within many of the Christian churches, as well as individual Christian theologians, have struggled
to review and reconstruct Christian views of homosexuality. Major attention in such studies has centered on the fundamental question of
whether or not homosexuality offers one of the possible ways for Christians to live out the sexual dimension of their lives; whether or not same-sex relations and sexual activity have a place within the Christian community. My concern in this essay is to move beyond this question to
another: What norms should govern same-sex relations and activity? It is
to move, then, from the question of whether homosexuality can be morally justified to what must characterize it when it is justified. In order to
make this move, however, I need to consider, at least briefly, the funda-

mental question of the general moral status of homosexual relations and activity.

When Christians look for light on an ethical question, they turn to basic sources: scripture, tradition (in the sense of the history of Christian belief discernible in the teachings and practice of the church and in the history of Christian theology), and other disciplines of knowledge (in this case, for example, philosophy and the biological and behavioral sciences), and contemporary experience. These are the sources, then, to which the Christian community must turn for an understanding of human sexuality in general and homosexuality in particular. But what have we thus far found by studying these sources?

Not an Absolute Prohibition

Scriptural Sources[1]

Although there is some pessimism in the Old Testament about the body as a hindrance to the life of the spirit and some fear of sex as a source of defilement, overall there is a clear affirmation of sex as a positive element in human life. Sexuality and sexual activity are natural, created by God, necessary for the well-being of human persons, and even a religious imperative. Central to the Old Testament tradition of sexual morality is the command to marry. Marriage is a religious duty, affirmed by all the codes of Jewish law. Two elements in the concept of marriage account for many other major laws regarding sexuality. The first of these is the command to procreate, which is at the heart of the command to marry. The second is the patriarchal model upon which the Old Testament ideas of marriage and society were institutionally based. These two elements provide a rationale for prohibitions against adultery and regulations regarding divorce, prostitution, polygamous marriage, concubinage, and to some extent, homosexuality. Thus, for example, adultery was considered a violation of a husband's property rights; polygamy and concubinage were accepted for a long time as a remedy for barrenness in a wife; homosexuality was looked upon as demeaning to males in part because it made them passive like females or at least did not allow them dominance over a female.

A third factor was influential in shaping Old Testament sexual rules: a concern to distinguish the practices of the Old Testament people from the idolotry of neighboring nations. The Leviticus prohibition against males lying "with a male as with a woman" is associated with this concern, as is the proscription of "improper emission of seed," whether through masturbation or homosexual activity. It is only later developments which tend to escalate specific prohibitions into paradigms of moral evil, obscuring the original intention of the laws. This seems to be true even in the case of the story of Sodom and Gomorrah, where the basic sin of the cities is described in other Old Testament texts as lack of hospitality, injustice, pride—but not as sexual sin in particular.

It is, of course, all too easy to explain away certain meanings of texts, or to relativize otherwise unambiguous passages by subordinating them to a larger context. Nonetheless, the simple recognition of the influence of factors such as patriarchalism, a concern for procreation, and a salutary fear of idolatry, alerts us to the problems we must encounter in any efforts to find in the Old Testament definitive answers to our questions regarding homosexuality.

The New Testament, too, sets problems for our search. It provides no systematic code of sexual ethics. The teachings of Jesus and his followers provide a central focus for the moral life of Christians in the command to love God and neighbor. Some fundamental virtues and principles fill out our understanding of this love. Beyond this, there are grounds in the New Testament for a sexual ethic which values marriage and procreation on the one hand and celibacy on the other, and which affirms a sacred symbolic meaning for sexual intercourse yet both subordinates it as a value to other human values and finds in it a possibility for evil. More specific guidelines for sexual morality appear in the New Testament only as responses to specific questions arising in specific situations. These responses have been used to support varying positions regarding such questions as divorce and remarriage, the status and role of women, and homosexual acts. Particular texts on homosexuality all offer problems for interpretation—whether because of our uncertainty about the meaning of terms, or ambiguity in the use of rhetorical devices, or disparity between the meaning of homosexuality during the time of Saint Paul and our own time (disparity between understandings of homosexuality as chosen debauchery or innate stable sexual orientation).

Whether one enters the battle of proof-texts, or stands before the biblical revelation as a whole, a modest conclusion that might be drawn is that neither the Old Testament or the New Testament offers us solid ground for an absolute prohibiton or a comprehensive blessing regarding same-sex relations and activity. Rather, determining the meaning and import of the scriptures themselves in relation to this particular ethical issue (as others) has been and is a part of the unfolding history of Christian doctrine regarding human sexual activity.

Tradition

Like other religious and cultural traditions, the teachings within the Christian tradition regarding human sexuality are complex, subject to outside influences, and expressive of change and development through succeeding generations. Within this tradition, however, two dominant motifs have been particularly relevant to the moral evaluation of homosexuality: procreation as the purpose of sexual intercourse, and male-female complementarity as the essential ground for sexual activity.

Christianity emerged in the late hellenistic age when even Judaism with its strong positive valuation of marriage and procreation was influenced by the dualistic anthropologies of Stoic philosophy and the Gnostic religions. Early writers in the church were persuaded by theories which idealized human virtue in terms of reason controlling emotion, mind controlling body. Thus, while they affirmed the basic goodness of sex (because it is a part of creation), they were deeply suspicious of the power of sex to overwhelm the mind and to introduce disorder contrary to reason into the attitudes and actions of the person. The disorder which characterizes sexual desire as a consequence of sin could only be corrected, they thought, by bringing it once again under the rule of reason. This was possible only if it could be given a rational purpose, an overriding value as its goal. Procreation served as this purpose and goal. Moreover, as medieval theologians argued, procreation could be discovered by reason as the natural goal of the physical organs of human reproduction. With a procreative norm, then, sex could be affirmed as good, and it could also be disciplined by restriction to a circumscribed sphere—the sphere of marriage. Only in marriage could there be adequate provision for the support and education of children.

Protestant Reformation theologians relativized the procreative ethic and prepared the way for a growing emphasis on male-female complementarity in sexual activity and gender roles. They shared the traditional pessimistic view of fallen nature in which human sexual desire is no longer ordered as it should be within the complex structure of the human personality. In their view, so great is the power of sexual desire that it cannot be ordered—even by giving it the rational purpose of procreation; it can only be restrained. Marriage is the remedy of restraint. Through marriage, sex can be channelled into the meaningful whole of human life (which includes the good of offspring); in marriage, sinful elements in sexual passion can be forgiven. New emphasis on the givenness of sexual desire and the almost universal need to institutionalize it in marriage deflected attention from procreation and turned it to an interpretation of sexuality as relational. What was "natural" was now not so much the proper functioning of reproductive organs but the need of man for woman, and vice versa, and the proper structuring of that need in complementary roles.

So long as the Christian tradition continued to justify sex primarily as a means for the procreation of children, or sex in marriage primarily as a corrective to disordered sexual desire, there was little room for any positive valuation of homosexuality. Heterosexual marriage had to be not only the general norm for Christian life, but along with celibacy the only acceptable choice for Christians regarding human sexuality. The twentieth century, however, has seen dramatic developments in both Roman Catholic and Protestant sexual ethics. The tradition has been deeply affected by historical studies which reveal the early roots of Christian sexual norms, biblical research which questions direct recourse to explicit biblical sexual norms, and new philosophical and theological anthropologies. The procreative norm (as the sole or even primary justification of sexual activity) is gone. Even in Roman Catholic ethics a wedge was introduced between procreation and sexual intercourse by the acceptance of the rhythm method of contraception, and new understandings of the totality of the human person have tended to support a radically new concern for sexuality as an expression and cause of love.[2] The view of sexuality as fundamentally disordered is also gone. Though Christian theologians still underline the special potential which sexuality has for evil, the almost total suspicion of its destructive power has been seriously modified. Rigid views of male-female complementarity have been softened; equality and mutuality, shared capabilities and responsibilities, now appear as central elements in Christian theologies of marriage and family. Finally, traditional notions of Christian friendship,[3] not dictated by gender lines, have received new attention, and there is a growing sense of the need to understand more clearly the dimensions and the criteria of friendship.

Although the Christian tradition has offered absolute prohibitions of homosexual activities (and sometimes relationships) in the past, it has not done so on the basis of arbitrary commands. Negative rules have depended upon rational justifications. However, past justifications, as we have just seen, no longer appear with the same clarity. They have sometimes been widely abandoned or changed. Those who stand within Christianity as a living tradition must either find new justifications for former prohibitions, or modify the prohibitions. Without offering the last word for the tradition, another modest conclusion may be drawn: Just as it is certainly not possible to draw from the tradition, at this point, a comprehensive blessing on same-sex relations and activity, so it is also not possible to draw an absolute prohibition. The wisdom of the tradition requires more labor if its best insights are to be brought to bear on contemporary questions of homosexuality.

Secular Disciplines

One reason why the separation of sources for Christian ethics into "tradition" and "other disciplines of knowledge" is not wholly satisfactory is that Christian theology has traditionally incorporated secular disciplines into its reflection on Christian faith. The ongoing presence of natural law theory within Christian theological ethics is striking evidence of this. Protestant ethics has, it is true, often understood natural law as "revealed natural law," whose conclusions about human nature are drawn from a biblical doctrine of creation. Roman Catholic ethics, on the other hand, has considered natural law to be discernible by human reason itself—aided and healed by revelation and grace, but human reason nonetheless. In this sense of natural law, secular disciplines can be important, constituting the ways of reason as it tries to interpret human reality.

Various human sciences have contributed to contemporary understandings of homosexuality. Chromosomes and hormones, behavioral patterns and psychological problems and adjustments, statistical deviations and cultural differences have all been studied. As a result of such studies, there exists today a variety of theories regarding the etiology of homosexuality and its status as a human phenomenon. Many Christian ethicists have drawn from this array some provisional, and minimal, conclusions: (1) The empirical sciences have not determined homosexuality to be of itself, in a culture-free way, harmful to human persons (nor have they finally ruled out this possibility). (2) Same-sex orientation may be natural for some persons if by "natural" is meant a given characteristic, impossible to change without doing violence to one's nature as a whole. (3) Same-sex preference in sexual relations may be an option for many persons since human persons have generally a greater or lesser capacity to respond emotionally and sexually to persons of both the opposite or the same sex. Persons exist on a continuum of possibilities in this regard—those on one extreme able to respond only to the same sex, and those on the other able to respond only to the opposite sex. (4) Same-sex orientation need not entail the denial of one's given gender or failure to accept the givenness of human embodiment. Members of the contemporary gay community tend to reject an artificial adoption of heterosexual stereotypes as the model for their relations, and to affirm their own maleness or femaleness in same-sex relations.

Perhaps even more important to a moral evaluation of homosexuality than the reports of the empirical sciences regarding homosexuality in particular have been the new interpretations of sexuality in general. The emergence of psychoanalytic theory brought with it new perceptions of the meaning and role of sexuality in the life of each person. What the Christian tradition had thought to be an indomitable need and desire, distorted by sin, has come to be interpreted as a natural drive, importantly constitutive of the dynamism at the base of the human personality. What for centuries was understood as an effort to order sexuality according to rational purposes has come to be understood as repression. However, psychoanalytic theory raised as many questions as it answered. Freud argued for liberation from sexual taboos, and from the hypocrisy and sickness which they entailed; but he also maintained the need for sexual restraint. Without the use of free choice to restrain sexuality, for Freud as for Augustine, the human spirit would be bound to lesser objects and occupations. Analysts, philosophers, sociologists, and criminologists have found connections between sex and violence, sex and exploitation, sex and insecurity.

Shifts have come in both contemporary psychology and philosophy regarding the meaning of human sexuality. Classical libido theory considered sexual desire a search for pleasure to be found in the relief of libidinal tension. Contemporary object-relations theory argues that the ultimate aim of libido is relationship with an object, not simple gratification of an impulse.[4] Contemporary philosophical theories have focused on sexuality as relational; as such, it can function for human conflict or union. It can destroy individuals and groups, but it can also serve both the individual and the common good. Sexual desire had been suspect because of what was thought to be its power to distract and cloud the mind; now it is maintained that sex not only need not be distracting but may enable a harmonization and concentration of powers so that the deepest and most creative springs of action are tapped close to the center of personal life. There is nothing in such theory that restricts sexual desire or activity to heterosexual relationships.

The last word is not in from reason's efforts to understand sexuality or homosexuality. At this point, however, it is difficult to see how on the basis of sheer human rationality alone, and all of its disciplines, an absolute prohibition of same-sex relations or activity could be maintained. On the other hand, the ambiguity of sex remains, so that it is equally difficult to argue that all sexual expression is for the benefit of human persons. We are pressed once more to the task of discerning what must characterize same-sex relations if they are to conduce to human flourishing.

Contemporary Experience

The final source for Christian ethical insight is as apt to be misleading in its designation as the others. Scripture, tradition, and secular disciplines all must reflect on experiences, past and present. What differentiates the source I am calling "contemporary experience" is the unsystematic way we have access to it. In this context, I am referring primarily to the testimony of women and men whose sexual preference is for others of the same sex. Here, too, we have as yet no univocal voice putting to rest all of our questions regarding the status of same-sex relations. We do, however, have some clear and profound testimonies to the life-enhancing possibilities of same-sex relations and the integrating possibilities of sexual activity within these relations. We have the witness that homosexuality can be a way of embodying responsible human love and sustaining Christian friendship. Without grounds in scripture, tradition, or any other source of human knowledge for an absolute prohibition of same-sex relations, this witness alone is enough to demand of the Christian community that it reflect anew on the norms for homosexual love.

Homosexuality and Justice

I began this essay by saying that my concern was to move beyond the question of whether or not same-sex relations and sexual activity can ever be justified. By arguing that no absolute prohibition and no absolute blessing can be established from the sources of Christian ethics, I have meant, of course, to imply that *some* same-sex relations and activity can be justified. I have not tried to settle questions of whether homosexual relations are as humanly fulfilling as heterosexual, or whether they can be justified only as exceptions to what is otherwise normative. I have focused on what I have called a "modest conclusion" because there is greater possibility of agreement with it, and because I am convinced that it is sufficient to move us on to what is the most important task for Christian ethics in regard to homosexuality. That is the task of articulating an ethic *for* same-sex activity and relations. This task, in my view, is finally the same as the task of articulating an adequate contemporary ethic for heterosexual relations and activity.

One way to begin to identify ethical norms for sexual activity is to refine a justice ethic for the sexual sphere of human life. This may prove to be only preliminary to a more adequate sexual ethic, but it has the advantage of moving sexuality away from a taboo morality, without assuming a contentless ethic of love. Moral criteria for homosexual relations must serve in particular as a corrective to remaining tendencies in the culture to associate sex with defilement in relation to taboos. (The culture's marginalization and oppression of homosexuals has at times manifested the worst of these tendencies.) On the other hand, it will not do to end all ethical discernment by saying simply that sexual relations and activities are good when they express love; for love is the problem in ethics, not the solution. The question ultimately is, "What is a right love, a good love?" The articulation of norms of justice will begin to answer that question, for these will be the norms of a just love.

Justice, of course, can have many meanings. The classic meaning of rendering to each her or his due can be, I think, most helpfully translated into the fundamental formal principle that persons and groups of persons ought to be affirmed according to their concrete reality, actual and potential. The formulation of material principles of justice depends, then, on our interpretation of the reality of persons. Contemporary efforts to develop a sexual ethic must take into account new interpretations not only of human sexuality but of the human person. Thus, for example, new emphasis on the element of freedom in the complex structure of the person must give rise to norms for sexual behavior which place great emphasis on the need for the free consent of both sexual partners. Similarly, new understandings of the nature and role of women must challenge traditional understandings of an order of justice in which men and women were affirmed (each given his or her due) in relations marked by hierarchy and subordination. Identification of such fairly obvious norms for sexual relations suggests a way of organizing a sexual ethic.

Contemporary concern for the nature of the person leads to a focus on at least two essential features of human personhood: autonomy and relationality. These two features ground an obligation to respect persons as ends in themselves and forbid the use of persons as mere means.[5] Moreover, together they provide the central content of the obligation to respect persons. Norms for a general sexual ethic, then, must not only satisfy the demands of these two features of personhood; they must serve to specify the meaning of the features.

The obligation to respect the autonomy of persons sets a minimum but absolute requirement for the free consent of sexual partners. This means, of course, that rape, violence, or any harmful use of power against unwilling victims is never justified; and seduction or manipulation of persons who have limited capacity for choice because of immaturity, special dependency, or loss of ordinary personal power, is ruled out. It also means that other general ethical principles such as the principles of truthtelling, promise-keeping, and respect for privacy are fundamental to an adequate sexual justice ethic. Whatever other rationales can be given for these principles, their violation hinders the freedom of choice of the other person. Deception and betrayal are ultimately coercive, ultimately not a just affirmation of persons as autonomous ends in themselves.

Relationality is equiprimordial with autonomy as an essential feature of human personhood. Individuals do not just survive or thrive in relation to others; they cannot exist without some form of fundamental relatedness to personal others. In relation, awareness of autonomy is born, and freedom either grows or is diminished. Insofar as sexuality qualifies the whole personality of persons, it also qualifies the relation of persons to one another. Sexual activity and sexual pleasure are instruments and modes of relation; they can enhance relation or hinder it, contribute to it and express it. Sexual activity and sexual pleasure are optional goods for human persons (in the sense that they are not absolute, peremptory goods which could never be subordinated to other goods or for the sake of other goods be let go), but they can be very great goods, mediating relationality and the general well-being of persons.

In so far as one person is sexually active in relation to another, sex must not violate relationality but serve it. Another way of saying this is that it is not enough to respect the free choice of sexual partners. Respect for persons together in sexual activity requires mutuality of participation. This, of course, can be expressed in many ways, but it entails activity and receptivity on the part of both persons—mutuality of desire, of action, and of response.[6]

Underlying a norm of mutuality is a view of sexual desire which does not see it as a search only for the pleasure to be found in the relief of libidinal tension, although it may include this. Human sexuality, rather, is fundamentally relational; sexual desire ultimately seeks what contemporary philosophers have called a "double reciprocal incarnation," or mutuality of desire and embodied union.[7] No one can deny that sex may, in fact, serve many functions and be motivated by many kinds of desire, but central to its meaning, necessary for its fulfillment, and normative for its morality when it is within an interpersonal relation is some form of and some degree of mutuality.

This leads to yet another norm, however. Freedom and mutuality are not sufficient to respect persons in sexual relations. A condition for real freedom and a necessary qualification of mutuality is equality. The equal-ity which is at stake here is equality of power. Inequities in social and economic status, age and maturity, professional identity, etc., render sexual relations inappropriate and unethical primarily because they entail power inequities—hence, unequal vulnerability, dependency, and limita-tion of options. Jean-Paul Sartre describes, for example, a supposedly free and mutual exchange between two persons, but an exchange marked by unacknowledged domination and subordination: "It is just that one of them pretends . . . not to notice that the Other is forced by the constraint of needs to sell himself as a material object."[8]

Strong arguments can be made for a third norm regarding relationality in a Christian sexual ethic. At the heart of the Christian community's understanding of the place of sexuality in human and Christian life has been the notion that some form of commitment, some form of covenant, must characterize relations that include a sexual dimension. In the past, this commitment, of course, was identified with heterosexual marriage. It was tied to the need for a procreative order and a discipline for unruly sex. Even when it was valued in itself as a realization of the life of the church in relation to Jesus Christ it carried what today are unwanted connotations of inequality in relation between men and women. It is possible, nonetheless, that when all the meanings of commitment for sexual relations are sifted, we are left with powerful reasons to retain it as an ethical norm.

As we have already noted, contemporary understandings of sexuality point to different possibilities for sex than were seen in the past—possibilities of growth in the human person, the gathering of creative power with sexuality as a dimension not an obstacle, the mediation of human relationship. On the other hand, no one argues that sex necessarily leads to creative power in the individual or depth of union between persons. Sexual desire left to itself does not even seem able to sustain its own ardor. In the past, persons feared that sexual desire would be too great; in the present the rise in impotency and sexual boredom makes persons more likely to fear that sexual desire will be too little. There is growing general evidence that sex is neither the indomitable drive that early Christians thought it was nor the primordial impulse of early psychoanalytic theory. When it was culturally repressed, it seemed an inexhaustible power, underlying other motivations, always struggling to express itself in one way or another. Now that it is less repressed, more and more free and in the open, it is easier to see other complex motivations behind it, and to recognize its inability in and of itself to satisfy the affective yearning of persons. More and more readily comes the conclusion that sexual desire without interpersonal love leads to disappointment and a growing meaninglessness. The other side of this conclusion is that sexuality is an expression of something beyond itself. Its power is a power for union and its desire a desire for intimacy.

One of the central insights from contemporary ethical reflection on sexuality is that norms of justice cannot have as their whole goal to set limits to the power and expression of human sexuality. Sexuality is of such importance in human life that it needs to be nurtured, sustained, as well as disciplined, channelled, and controlled. There seem to be two ways which persons have found to keep alive the power of sexual desire within them. One is through novelty of persons with whom they are in sexual relation. Moving from one person to another prevents boredom, sustains sexual interest and the possibility of pleasure. A second way is through relationship extended sufficiently through time to allow the incorporation of sexuality into a shared life and an enduring love. The second way seems possible only through commitment.

Sobering evidence of the inability of persons to blend their lives together, and weariness with the high rhetoric that has traditionally surrounded human covenants, yield a contemporary reluctance to evaluate the two ways of living sexual union. At the very least it may be said, however, that while brief encounters open a lover to relation, they cannot mediate the kind of union—of knowing and being known, loving and being loved—for which human relationality offers the potential. Moreover, the pursuit of multiple relations precisely for the sake of sustaining sexual desire risks violating the norms of autonomy and mutuality, risks measuring others as apt means to our own ends, risks inner disconnection from any kind of life-process of our own or in relation with others. Discrete moments of union are not valueless (though they may be so, and may even be disvalues), but they serve to isolate us from others and from ourselves.

On the other hand, there is reason to believe that sexuality can be the object of commitment, that sexual desire can be incorporated into a covenanted love, without distortion and loss. Given all the caution learned from contemporary experience, we may still hope that our freedom is sufficiently powerful to gather up our love and give it a future; that thereby our sexual desire can be nurtured into a tenderness that has not forgotten passion. We may still believe that to try to use our freedom in this way is to be faithful to the love that arises in us or even the yearning that rises from us. Rhetoric should be limited regarding commitment, however, for commitment is itself only a means, not an end. As Robin Morgan notes regarding the possibility of process only within an enduring relation, "Commitment gives you the leverage to bring about change—and the time in which to do it."[9]

A Christian sexual ethic, then, may well identify commitment as a norm for sexual relations and activity. Given a concern for the wholeness of the human person, and for a way of living that is conducive to the integration of all of life's important aspects, and for the fulfillment of sexual desire in the highest forms of friendship, the norm must be a committed love. This, of course, raises special problems in an ethic for homosexual love—problems to which I will return.

While the traditional procreative norm of sexual relations and activity no longer holds absolute sway in Christian sexual ethics, there remains a special concern for responsible reproduction of the human species. Traditional arguments that if there is sex it must be procreative have changed to arguments that if sex is procreative it must be within a context that assures responsible care of offspring. These concerns appear at first glance to have little to do with a sexual ethic for same-sex relations. Yet they suggest an important last norm for homosexuals as for heterosexuals in regard to relationality. Interpersonal love, in so far as it is just, must be fruitful. That is to say, it violates relationality if it closes in upon itself and refuses to open to a wider community of persons. The new life within it may move beyond it in countless forms (nourishing other relationships, providing goods and services for others, informing the work lives of the partners in relation, etc.), but all of them can be understood as the fruit of a love for which the persons in relation are responsible.

The articulation of this norm, however, moves us to another perspective in the development of a sexual ethic for same-sex relations. There are obligations in justice which others in the Christian community and the wider society have toward those persons who choose same-sex relations. Just as homosexual men and lesbian women must affirm one another and themselves in terms of autonomy and relationality, so they have claims to respect from the wider society and the Christian churches. Given no grounds for an absolute prohibition of same-sex relations, and none for an absolute blessing, homosexuals have the same rights as others to equal protection under the law, to self-determination, to a share in the goods and services available to all. Their needs for incorporation into the wider community, for psychic security, for basic well-being, make the same claims for social cooperation among us as do those of us all. The Christian community, in particular, is faced with serious questions in this regard. If, for example, a norm of commitment is appropriate for sexual relations among Christians; and if such a norm belongs to a homosexual ethic as much as to a heterosexual ethic, then the problems of institutional support must (like the questions of a sexual ethic) be addressed anew.

What I have tried to offer here is a beginning response to the question of what norms should govern same-sex relations and activities. My answer has been: the norms of justice—those norms which govern all human relationships and those which are particular to the intimacy of sexual relations. Most generally, the norms are respect for persons through respect for autonomy and relationality; respect for relationality through requirements of mutuality, equality, commitment, and fruitfulness. More specifically one might say things like: sex between two persons of the same sex (just as two persons of the opposite sex) should not be used in a way that exploits, objectifies, or dominates; homosexual (like heterosexual) rape, violence, or any harmful use of power against unwilling victims (or those incapacitated by reason of age, etc.) is never justified; freedom, integrity, privacy are values to be affirmed in every homosexual (as heterosexual) relationship; all in all, individuals are not to be harmed, and the common good is to be promoted. The Christian community will want and need to add those norms of faithfulness, of forgiveness, of patience and hope, which are essential for any relationships between persons within the Church.

It is not an easy task to introduce considerations of justice into every sexual relation and the evaluation of every sexual activity. Critical questions remain unanswered, and serious disagreements are all too frequent, regarding the reality of persons and the meaning of sexuality. What is harmful and what helpful to individual persons and societies is not always clear. Which sexual activities contribute to and which prevent the integration of sexuality into the whole of human life is not in every case evident. What can be normative and what exceptional is sometimes a matter of all too delicate judgment. But if sexuality is to be creative and not destructive in personal and social relationships, then there is no substitute for discerning ever more carefully the norms whereby it will be just.

NOTES

1. For a more detailed study of these sources, see my article, "Sexual Ethics," *Encyclopedia of Bioethics*, 4 (New York: Free Press, 1978), pp. 1575–89. See also similar treatments in A. Kosnik, et al., *Human Sexuality* (New York: Paulist Press, 1966), pp. 7–78; Lisa Cahill, "Moral Methodology: A Case Study," *Chicago Studies* 19 (Summer, 1980): 171–. 87, reprinted in this book. The Cahill essay comes to a somewhat different conclusion than I do.

2. The history of this shift, and continued concern for a procreative ethic, is much more complicated than this brief reference to it suggests. For slightly more detail, see my article, "Sexual Ethics," p. 1582.

3. See, for example, Aelred of Rievaulx, *Spiritual Friendship*, trans. M. E. Laker (Kalamazoo, Mich.: Cistercian Publications, 1977).

4. See, for example, W. R. D. Fairbairn, *Psychoanalytic Studies of the Personality* (London: Routledge and Kegan Paul, 1952), pp. 137–42.

5. See my article, "Obligating-features of Personhood," to be published by Medicine in the Public Interest, 1983.

6. The best analysis of sex in these terms that I have found is that by Sara Ruddick, "Better Sex," in R. Baker and F. Elliston (eds.), *Philosophy and Sex* (Buffalo: Prometheus Publishers, 1975), pp. 83–104.

7. See T. Nagel, "Sexual Perversion," *The Journal of Philosophy* 66 (1969): 5–17; R. Solomon, "Sexual Paradigms," *The Journal of Philosophy* 71 (1974): 336–45; J. Moulton, "Sexual Behavior: Another Position," *The Journal of Philosophy* 73 (1976): 537–46.

8. Jean-Paul Sartre, *Critique of Dialectical Reason*, trans. A. Sheridan-Smith (London: NLB, 1976), p. 110.

9. Robin Morgan, "A Marriage Map," *Ms.* 11 (July–August, 1982): 204.

EDWARD A. MALLOY

Point/Counterpoint

Several years ago I found myself dissatisfied with the current state of discussion within the Christian community on the issue of homosexuality. On the one hand, the defenders of the traditional prohibition against genital expression of a homosexual orientation seemed singularly uncreative in their appropriation of the classic arguments. Furthermore, they were not sufficiently attentive to the changed climate within which all discourse about sexual morality was taking place. On the other hand, the revisionists seemed to be curiously selective in their portrayal of the forms of homosexual affiliation and of the hoped for state of committed relationship. In addition, they cultivated a point of view which ranged from the compassionate understanding of the plight of this sexual minority to the deliberate advocacy of sexual anarchy. As a result, it was almost impossible to specify what the various revisionists held in common.

After some soul-searching (and repeated warnings from colleagues and friends to avoid such a contentious area of debate) I undertook some concentrated research, which resulted in the book *Homosexuality and the Christian Way of Life.*[1] Overall, I arrived at the conclusion that "the homosexual way of life, as evolved in the social structures and practices of the homosexual sub-culture, is irreconcilable with the Christian way of life. It fails to adequately embody the normative Christian values of chastity, love, and faithfulness to promise. Because it is centered in the pursuit of unrestricted sexual freedom, it can describe no limits to the function of sexuality in a life. As much as individual homosexuals may be chaste, loving, and faithful, they achieve this integration despite, and not because of, the values of the homosexual world" (p. 328).

The defense of this judgment forced me to review a whole series of claims and counterclaims in the biological, social scientific, and theological literature. Thus, having had one sustained chance to make my own case, I would like to concentrate in this chapter on a number of points which deserve further analysis. This contribution will take the form of a juxtaposition of various alternatives and an appraisal of their relative degrees of persuasiveness.

Homosexuality as a Descriptive Category

The deconstructionist current in contemporary philosophy promotes a skepticism towards so-called descriptive categories (with their seeming aura of neutrality) by picturing them as relatively arbitrary creations of the prevailing power structure.[2] *Homosexuality,* for example, is seen to appear at a given point in Western cultural history (the nineteenth century) when representatives of the dominant social group became concerned about the long-range viability of the prevailing (and desirable) institutions of heterosexual marriage and the family. In the eyes of the deconstructionists the coining of such a term isolates one aspect of the broader human phenomenon and concentrates the attention of the average person in ways heretofore unprecedented. Social scientists, physicians, legal scholars, and ethicists then begin to develop various explanations for the origins of the condition as well as evaluations of its acceptability. What had once been but one particular manifestation of the range of sexual expression was now seen to constitute an essential component of social self-definition.

Such a claim is not easily refuted. The pluriform ways of being a homosexual have led some sociologists to prefer the term *homosexualities.*[3] There are, in fact, no easy generalizations that can be made about causality, contentedness, or level of sexual consciousness. Homosexuals are first of all persons and they participate in the human saga according to genetic, environmental, political, economic, and axiological variables that defy glib explanation. And for a fairly high percentage of those with a same-sex orientation, there is minimal interaction with and recognition of other individuals of a similar propensity.

Nevertheless, the category "homosexuality" has sufficient usefulness in accounting for differences in sexual orientation and behavior along gender-specific lines that both the defenders and detractors of the homosexual alternative employ it regularly with the expectation of experiential recognition. At the same time that some spokespersons have been minimizing the importance of the homosexuality/heterosexuality distinction, others have been mobilizing the disparate elements of the homosexual subculture into a political and economic force with the assertion that the acceptance of a suppressed or unacknowledged sexual identity is destructive of personal well-being.

The rhetoric of gay and lesbian activism is charged with a positive, upbeat correlation between a homosexual world view and sociocultural liberation. Presumably, homosexual persons are gifted with an insight (perhaps accrued through membership in an oppressed class) that penetrates the obfuscations of status, role, and privilege and foresees a whole new range of social possibilities. Such claims to uniqueness, or at least difference, are based on the presumed adequacy of the heterosexual/homosexual distinction.

The danger of any set of descriptive categories will always be the development of a false consciousness. It is not necessary to make the question of the form of erotic sexual attraction in adulthood the definitive clue to an individual's personality or worth in order to defend the usefulness of the typology. If Kinsey is right and the pure types—heterosexual and homosexual—are rare, the parameters of the discussion have still been established. What may at one time have been a polymorphous, undifferentiated sexual continuum has now assumed a describable shape. The alternatives are contrapuntal—homosexuality/heterosexuality—and the ethical discussion must give this proper consideration.

Living by the Law of One's Nature

Seldom has the life story of an individual had such a profound impact on the evolution of collective understanding as was the case with the sexual ethic that derives from Saint Augustine of Hippo. Schooled in the Manichaean disparagement of the physical and retrospectively guilt ridden by his own sexual escapades, Augustine achieved a remarkable balance, all things considered. Yet the preeminence he assigned to the procreative end of marriage and his distrust of other forms of sexual expression led to a view of the natural (God-given) order of things that presupposed the inherent connection between genital activity and marital cooperation in the perpetuation of the species.

At a later stage in Christian reflection, Saint Thomas Aquinas developed a theory of natural law that, when applied to the sexual dimension of human experience, subdivided the various forms of sexual expression into those according to natural law (marital intercourse, fornication, adultery—in the latter two cases sinful only because the context is wrong) and those against natural law (masturbation, contraception, homosexuality). The operative paradigm was heterosexual, genital intercourse with penetration and ejaculation and openness to procreation (and less importantly, the male above the female). The sexual endowment was seen as a faculty with a predesigned purpose that alone validated its exercise.

Since the time of Saint Thomas, our store of knowledge about the male and female contribution to fertilization and about the gestation process has been enhanced considerably. As a result, human ingenuity has extended to the control of the reproductive cycle by both natural and artificial means. With the growing acceptance of family planning by married couples (and even more so with the deliberate increase in childless marriages) the natural ground for the claimed superiority of heterosexual forms of genital expression has been eroded. If sexual relatedness is primarily about mutuality, loving union, or shared intimacy, then it may be possible for homosexual couples to participate as integrally and consistently in genital intercourse as heterosexual couples.[4]

One objection to the classic version of natural law, therefore, is that human nature is not a static entity and thus even something as basic as sexuality is capable of being reinterpreted and subject to new types of rational control. Since this has already taken place in the realm of procreation among heterosexuals, the boundary line between responsible heterosexual and homosexual expression is more fluid and context-dependent.

The most effective rejoinder in Christian terms to this line of thought is to reassert the necessity of the procreative dimension in full genital expression in a given relationship. The controversy over contraceptive practice since Vatican II has, even in its more conservative versions, never demanded nor expected that all acts of sexual intercourse be fertile. This is a biological impossibility. Instead, the theme of responsible parenting has given proper weight to the unitive and sacramental dimensions of the lovemaking between the spouses. What this tradition continues to resist, however, is the elimination of the procreative dimension as somehow a nonconstitutive component of the marital bond as celebrated in the bodily intimacy of intercourse.

The argument of Christian spokespersons that the widespread acceptance of contraceptive practice among married people has eviscerated the main natural-law objection to homosexual activity among gay and lesbian couples only holds if *contraceptive* is equivalent to *permanently infertile*. While there are some married couples for whom this is true, such a perspective does not yet seem to have gained currency among the majority of Christians. And even if it did, the theological grounds for its defense are poorly developed. In the meantime, one sense in which homosexual genital activity can be said to be unnatural is that it is unable to embody the procreative dimension of the committed sexual relationship.[5]

A second objection to the natural-law prohibition against homosexual genital expression focuses more on causality than on function. Whether one accepts a nature (genetic, hereditary) or nurture (environment, social influence) etiological explanation (or some multicausal account, as I do), the argument takes the form: "Because some percentage of human beings are permanently homosexual through no choice of their own, it is unnatural to expect them either to act in a heterosexual fashion or to refrain from all sexual activity." It is presupposed that the personal consciousness of a homosexual identity of a confirmed sort in an adult is sufficient justification for allowing this orientation to be a guide to one's behavior.

What is at stake in the response to this formulation of the question is what the Christian community expects of its members in the premarital situation. What has been traditionally called the virtue of chastity (or proportionate pleasure) has been interpreted to require refraining from genital intercourse before marriage. Other forms of sexual expression were more or less appropriate depending on the circumstances and their proximity to the orgasmic experience. In this regard there was an equivalency or parallelism in the premarital situation of the heterosexual and homosexual person. The major difference being that the homosexual could *never* actualize his or her erotic drive since marriage was precluded as a possibility.

At face value, all of this seems so unfair. In an age when statistical surveys suggest that a high percentage of heterosexual men and women have participated in petting and oral and genital intercourse before marriage, why should homosexuals be held to a higher ethic. And what is even more puzzling is that a significant minority of Christian ethicists give some degree of validation to this experimentation. Furthermore, celibacy is understood to be a gift not given to all and therefore not able to be demanded for a whole category of human beings.

Despite their seemingly anomalous situation, homosexuals are called to a chaste existence by the Christian ethic. This does not entail a renunciation of the quest for friendship, love, or intimacy. Just as single or widowed or divorced heterosexual individuals need to be appreciated as unique persons with particular talents and disabilities, so gay or lesbian individuals must strive for a supportive network of relationships. To be deprived of the opportunity for genital intercourse with a loved other is not tantamount to being stripped of one's humanity. What would be unnatural would be for a homosexual to allow some degree of restraint in sexual gesturing to be an excuse for avoiding those steps in interpersonal relations which promote a fitting degree of human happiness.

Such a view may appear to consign homosexuals to a tragic disengagement from natural propensities. On the contrary, it groups them with that array of the unmarried who work and vote, pay taxes and take vacations, make friends and plan for the future. Whatever their vocational situation, they all fear loneliness and social isolation. It may be the particular challenge of the homosexuals among them to discover ways of refraining from genital completeness without sacrificing the legitimate desire for personal support and acceptance. If Christian homosexuals have a lesson to teach the wider community, it will derive from their prolonged (and sometimes heroic) effort to achieve a healthy integration of their sexual drive and consciousness with the value framework of the Gospel.

The Instability of Committed Relationships

The covenant between Yahweh and Israel, Christ and the Church, is symbolized in the Scriptures through the relationship between a loving husband and wife in marriage. Among all human forms of bonding, the marital relationship comes closest, it is suggested, to incorporating the elements of faithfulness to commitment and abiding self-donation that are among the highest human achievements. Up until the twentieth century, divorce and/or remarriage was a relatively rare occurrence. The presumption was, especially in Western society, that marriage was forever, whether or not it led to personal fulfillment and spousal endearment.

During the same period of time, the accusation was consistently made that homosexual relationships tended toward a promiscuous pattern in which multiple partners and fleeting commitments were typical. The one-night stand and the casual, anonymous encounter were seen as irreconcilable with the minimum expectations for stability and perdurance of commitment in the Christian scheme of reality.

But as societal patterns have shifted, there seems to be sufficient evidence that serial monogamy is becoming more common among heterosexuals (with bursts of promiscuity in between) and that there is a greater incidence of long-term relationships among homosexuals (especially past young adulthood).

One response to this emerging evidence is simply to lament the creeping decadence of our society. Another is to celebrate the growing sense of self-determination being exercised by those who find themselves to be in a bad marriage. And a third is to predict that the lifting of legal and economic strictures will lead to a rough approximation in the incidence of relational stability in both the heterosexual and homosexual contexts.

What is most important in the reaction to this changing state of affairs is that the Christian community continue to defend the human capability for promise making and promise keeping, especially in regard to those privileged relationships called friendship and marriage. The paradigmatic form of such commitment is the baptismal promise where a person pledges to a life of discipleship. What is alien about promiscuity is that it usually combines self-deception with a verbal lie. In effect, it treats one's sexual partners as objects to be manipulated rather than as persons to be nourished. Insofar as divorce violates a prior, freely given promise of the self, it is contradictory to a Christian perception of the good. Whatever mitigating circumstances might lessen the blame, it is always a tragic failure with a concentric or rippling effect on the quality of other relationships in society. The same can be said for homosexual interactions. The less personal, more self-serving, and capricious that homosexual liaisons become, the further they diverge from acceptable Christian standards. But, correspondingly, the homosexual couple who have forged a life together across a considerable period of time in the absence of normal societal approbation and who strive to be faithful to the commitment they share are worthy of respect and understanding.

In a time in history when so many factors work against the human fidelity to promise that is called forth by the example of our God, the greatest need is for a reaffirmation of its possibility. Wherever it appears, we find some token of a better world in the making. It is not that homosexuals lack the required will or clarity of purpose more than heterosexuals. No, the fear that I share is that there is some aspect of the homosexual situation (the absence of children, the fragility of complementarity, the heightened level of anxiety, etc.) which exacerbates the struggle and creates a social climate in which failure in commitment assumes the status of a self-fulfilling prophecy.

Homosexual—Male and Female

Feminist literature continues to argue a compelling case for the patriarchal origins of much of what prevails as sexual attitudes in Church and society.[6] The subordinate status of women throughout history is reflected in prejudicial laws, insensitive language, and demeaning stereotypes. Perhaps the most telling example of the inferior position of homosexual women in this story is that the civil codes of the past did not even include them in its condemnations of homosexual practice. Furthermore, social scientists have only recently directed their attention toward lesbian life and patterns of affiliation.

Despite this neglect, a spate of writing is presently attempting to fill in the portrayal. One claim that is common in feminist homosexual reflections is that this group is doubly burdened—as *women* and as *lesbians*—and therefore that gay men can, only with real effort, appreciate the plight that their sister homosexuals actually face. A corollary of this assertion of fact is that some hard decisions must be made about whether to concentrate the struggle for liberation first on the women's question or on the sexual-orientation question. The indications up to now are that lesbian political activists have decided that being a woman is more significant than being sapphic.

In some ways, this seems to be a matter of political strategizing rather than ethics. Yet it has broad implications for the future of the discussion. First of all, it posits gender-specific intentionality as a source of division rather than cooperation. It is not the residue of mystery about the heterogeneous sexual identity of male and female that attracts. Rather, it is the same-sex participation in structures of oppression that unites against a common foe. The cavalier imposition of male-derived theories like Freudian "penis envy" and the imagined yearning to be a male has been replaced culturally by an experientially justified hostility toward males that, at its worst, would promote a world of revenge and sexual isolation.

One scenario, therefore, would lead in the direction of so accentuating the importance of the male/female division that purposive interaction between gays and lesbians would be postponed for the foreseeable future. This, of course, would force the Church to decide whether priority should be given to reflection about the feminist problem (and related issues of injustice toward lesbians) at the same time that Christian gays argue the higher urgency of the treatment of sexual minorities. Especially since the leadership structure of Catholicism (and most mainstream Christian denominations) is male, the resolution of this imbroglio will not come easily.

A second feature of the male-female distinction among homosexuals that is important to consider is the growing evidence that lesbian relationships tend to include fewer partners and to survive for longer periods of time than do gay relationships. Is it just that women are inherently more stable or less preoccupied by the physical attributes of the other person or capable of intimate bonding with less game playing? Is it a matter of biology or psychology or something else? Up to this time, none of the commentators has given an adequate explanation of this phenomenon.

One ethical hypothesis that some have proposed is that, since the strictures against homosexuality are based upon the combination of nonprocreativity and characteristic promiscuity, they simply do not apply to the majority of female homosexuals. Lesbians (like their heterosexual counterparts) can still become pregnant and give birth (either through artificial insemination or a temporary heterosexual marriage). And they are more likely to remain content with the existing relationship, especially when the partners have attained sufficient maturity before beginning it.

In response to this hypothesis, it can be argued that procreativity is not satisfied simply by fertility. It hinges upon an integral combination of loving exchange, social support, and complementary completeness. In the situation of the lesbian couple there is a separation in time and in capability of realization between the enfleshed self-giving and the concrete manifestation that is a child. Procreativity cannot be willed into existence no matter how amenable the individuals involved are to its pursuit in their relationship.

As far as the promiscuity question is concerned, it would be almost impossible in the absence of multicultural and multigenerational research to determine whether the seeming stability of lesbian bonds would break down in a social environment which had more freedom of self-determination. From a Christian point of view, it appears to be the case that a higher percentage of female homosexuals come closer to approximating the Christian sexual ethic than do male homosexuals. However, if certain advocates of lesbian liberation have their way, such inhibitions about the type and frequency of sexual relationships will soon be cast aside.

Homophilia/Homophobia

Fear of the discovery of the hidden secrets of their hearts is probably present in all who share the human condition. The power of imagination and fantasy to provide an opportunity to explore the unknown and the forbidden confronts each person with paths not taken and alternate scenarios for a life. The dividing line between the saint and the sinner, the chaste individual and the lecher, is seldom a function of the absence of erotic stimulation. There seems to be large element of truth in the claim that the intense hostility toward homosexuals displayed by some heterosexuals (even to the point of physical beatings) is revelatory of some unacknowledged tension in the latter's sexual self-understanding. A homophobe is ultimately lashing out at a hated dimension in his or her own personality.

That there are homophobic individuals (as well as heterophobic ones) is a defensible proposition. What is not so obvious is that holders of such attitudes are finally responsible for the persistent cultured aversion for homosexual behavior. It may be that some critics of the gay scene are motivated by a combination of other factors: (1) a concern for the health and social viability of the family as an institution, (2) a judgment that immersion in the homosexual subculture will lead to patterns of destructiveness for those who are attracted to it, (3) an innate sympathy for conservative political and social programs, or (4) a loyal adherence to the teaching authority of the Church.

Secondly, homophobia is not to be confused with uncomfortableness in discussing the issue of homosexuality. For a variety of reasons, there are still many persons who have had no direct contact with publicly known gays or lesbians. Consequently, they hesitate to be caught in the clutches of those with more background, especially if it is in the public forum.

Third, in the Roman Catholic context, the requirement of a celibate clergy has confined theological reflection, until quite recently, to a group of males who do not enjoy the confirmatory sexual reaction that often accrues to marriage. One kind of subtle compensation can be a displaced suppression of whatever lingering homoerotic drives that may exist. To the extent that this occurs, clerical homophobia can influence the overall openness to the question in the Church community. On the other hand, a general liberality of spirit by representatives of the presbyteral office may blind them to the negative side of the gay experience. Homophilic compassion may be as little based on reality as its opposite.

Finally, it must be admitted that political demagogues have often utilized the general antagonisms toward homosexuals to their own advantage. False accusations directed at ideological opponents and occasional outbursts after incidents involving sexual crimes committed against youth are a familiar part of American political history. A climate of homophobia is probably as much determined by such displays of irresponsible power seeking as it is by the repressed sexual peccadilloes of the average citizen.

Conclusion

In this essay I have concentrated on five aspects of the debate about the morality of homosexual behavior. In each case, there has been some conceptual confusion in the discussion up to now. I am convinced that continued discussion of this important and sensitive issue will contribute to the twofold mission of the Church: (1) to be a proclaimer of the radical demand of the Gospel, including its teaching on sexual morality, and (2) to be a home for all people, especially the troubled and the outcast. The Church needs to be able to witness effectively to the compassion and love of Jesus without succumbing to a premature acceptance of activity that will turn out to be a countersign to the genuinely human.

NOTES

1. Edward A. Malloy, *Homosexuality and the Christian Way of Life* (Lanham, Md.: University Press of America, 1981).

2. See Michael Foucalt, *A History of Sexuality*, vol. I: *An Introduction* (New York: Bantam, 1978).

3. See Alan Bell and Martin Weinberg, *Homosexualities: A Study of Diversity Among Men and Women* (New York: Simon & Schuster, 1978).

4. Both John McNeill and Gregory Baum move in this direction in their respective ✓ analyses of the homosexual situation. See: John McNeill, *The Church and the Homosexual* (Kansas City: Sheed, Andrews and McMeel, 1976); and Gregory Baum, "Catholic Homosexuals," *Commonweal* 100 (1974): 479–82.

5. It is true that, if society allowed for it, homosexual couples could adopt children and to that extent manifest their mutual love in a manner similar to an infertile heterosexual couple. Nevertheless, the family dynamics in such an environment could be projected as too risky for the state to entrust the developmental well-being of the child to the couple. It would not be a matter of ill-will or false motives on the part of the adopting homosexual pair, but rather of an inability to replicate the dyadic diversity of the heterosexual partners.

6. In her transition from a prophetic Christian stance to a lesbian feminist one, Mary Daly represents one form of reaction to the recognition of the influence of religion on social institutions which affect the life and well-being of women. See: *The Church and the Second Sex* (New York: Harper & Row, 1968) and *Beyond God the Father: Toward a Philosophy of Women's Liberation* (Boston: Beacon Press, 1973).

DANIEL MAGUIRE

The Morality of
Homosexual Marriage

For a significant minority of persons in the human community, erotic desire is focused, primarily or exclusively, on persons of the same sex. Psychiatrists are divided on whether to label this *de facto* variation pathological or not. Similarly, moralists are divided as to whether this orientation is an inclination to moral perversion, or a simple variation in the human quest for intimacy. If it is pathology, medical science should look for a cure; if it is an ingrained tilt toward unconscionable behavior, ethicists must counsel its containment.

The psychiatric or ethical position that sees homosexuality as clinical or moral pathology is blessed with striking simplicity. Clearly, pathologies are not to be encouraged under the specious claim of freedom or self-fulfillment. We find in the human sexual lexicon such manifestly pathological conditions as zoophilia, pedophilia, necrophilia, fetishism, sadistic or masochistic sex, exhibitionism, voyeurism, and rape. If homosexuality fits somewhere in that listing, we need not labor long in discussing its moral or psychological status. We do not speak of a well-adjusted necrophiliac, nor do we consider necrophiliacs as having a moral and civil right to access to corpses. There is no cry for rapist or fetishist liberation. Some things are abnormal and harmful at least to the agent who acts out on them. Is this the case for homosexuality?

Those who say yes face two critical difficulties: (1) they must show that those who act in any way on their homosexual orientation victimize themselves or others and (2) they must show that celibacy is good for all nonheterosexual persons.

First, regarding the harm, it is empty nominalism to name something harmful in the absence of identifiable harm. It is illogical to speak of a moral or psychological cure for a harmful condition if we cannot show what harm the cure is to address. Illness is known by its symptoms. In the absence of symptoms, we assume persons are well. If psychiatry would label homosexuality a pathology or illness, it must show how it adversely affects persons who express their intimacy-needs homosexually. The delineations of these adverse effects must also show that these are due to the orientation itself and not to the sociocultural effects of seeing the condition as an illness. If a society falsely imputes negative meaning to a sexual orientation, this will adversely affect persons who act out on that orientation, though the fault would be with the social stigmatizing and not with the orientation itself.

Clearly, then, psychiatry and ethics must pass the "show-me" test when they speak of homosexuality as a malady in need of a remedy. The test is not met simply by stating that homosexuality is a "disorder" because it is a minority phenomenon or because anatomy and reproductive needs suggest male-female coitus as the unexceptionable norm. Minority status does not of itself mean objectionable deviance. Indeed, the presence of minority status is the spice of variety and thus of life. But is not anatomy destiny? The penis and the vagina do enjoy a congenial fit, and the species' need for reproduction relies on that. But sex rarely, in any lifetime, has to do with reproduction, and not even heterosexual persons are limited to coitus for sexual fulfillment. Also, the species' need for reproductive sex is being met and often overmet.

In ethics, the term *biologism* refers to the fallacious effort to wring a moral mandate out of raw biological facts. The male-female coital fit and its relationship to reproduction are basic biological facts. The biologistic error would leap from those facts to the moral imperative that all sexual exchange must be male-female coital in kind. The leap could only become likely if you reduce human sexuality to the biological simplicities of the stud farm. Given the infinity of meanings beyond baby-making involved in human eroticism and sexuality, such a leap is misdirected and, literally, unreal.

No. If homosexuality is an illness requiring a cure, if it is an orientation to sin, it is because it is harmful to persons. If that harm cannot be pinpointed, the charge of sin or illness must be reconsidered.

George Bernard Shaw reminded us that it is the way of barbarians to think of the customs of their tribe as the laws of nature. Is the homosexually oriented quest for intimacy contrary to the laws of nature or simply to the current customs of our tribe? That question is regularly sent to go a-begging. The discussion, however, depends on facing it squarely.

The second question confronting those who see homosexuality as pathology regards celibacy as the only moral option for nonheterosexuals. Moralists of this position say that the condition of being homosexually oriented is not evil in itself since it seems irreversible in many or most instances. (Some deviant Christian fundamentalists see homosexuality as a contumacious and wicked option that can be cast out by prayer and fasting. In the absence of any supportive data, we commend such a position to its own embarrassment.) The evil would be in acting out one's homosexual proclivities. The morally good homosexual, in this view, is the celibate homosexual. This position has inherent contradictions. Implicitly it is reducible to the position of the deviant Christian fundamentalists since it says: You may be homosexual but, with prayer and fasting, you will never have to express it. It insists that there is nothing wrong with being a homosexual as long as you do not act on it. That is too tidy. There is a lot wrong with being a homosexual if all the values that attach to sexual expression are denied you. Sex is more than orgasms; it is an important avenue to many personal values. If the sexual avenue is categorically closed off to gay persons, that is no slight impairment. It makes the condition itself an abridgment of personality.

This "be-but-don't-do" position rests on three errors: (1) a materialistic and narrow view of sex; (2) a stunted epistemology; and (3) a departure from biblical good sense. First, then, it views sex narrowly and materialistically, missing its linkage to such deeply felt human needs as intimacy, trust, and friendship. It would be gratuitous to say that a celibate cannot meet those human needs—that sex is necessary for human fulfillment—but it is equally gratuitous to say that a whole class of persons involving as much as 4 or 5 percent of the human population can be barred morally from the only kind of access to sexuality that attracts them.

1. Erotic desire is deeply interwoven into the human desire and need for closeness and for trusting relationships. The desire for a significant other with whom we are uniquely conjoined is not a heterosexual but a basic human desire. The programmatic exclusion of gay persons from the multiple benefits of erotic attraction, which often opens the way to such a union, is arbitrary, harmful, cruel, and therefore sinful.

Again, I am not saying that marriage or sexual activity are necessary for human fulfillment or psychological normalcy. Voluntary and involuntary celibacy is more common than is generally noted in a time of sexual overemphasis. Celibacy, voluntary or not, does not exclude human fulfillment. Sexually unfulfilled persons may be very fulfilled humanly. However, I stress that the sweeping exclusion of all gay persons from this important access route to meeting intimacy needs could only be based on a narrow and, I must insist, macho-masculine conception of what sex is and how it functions in human personal development.[1]

2. This position also lumps together without distinction all manifestations of homosexuality. Basically, the position is anthropologically naive.

Few areas of human life are as variegated as sexual activity. This holds also for homosexuality. Some manifestations of homosexuality are harmful to human personal and social good. A moral argument opposed to homosexual activity in those instances can be made. However, to claim to know, by some encyclopedic intuition, that only celibacy befits homosexuals in any culture, clime, or time is—to say the least—immodest. More accurately, it is epistemologically absurd. It involves a kind of *essentialist* approach to knowing. Thus, even before all the data is in on what homosexuality is, how it develops, what it means in persons and societies, how it interrelates with other aspects of human relating, etc.— before all of that is known, a formula-panacea has been found that exhausts the moral meaning of homosexuality by prescribing celibacy.

Such essential thinking in ethics has a poor track record. Once we thought we had intuited the nature of money so clearly that we could say that all interest taking was sinful regardless of circumstances. Once we thought that we had so intuited the nature of sex that we could know that all contraceptive sexual exchange was wrong. We also believed that we had so thoroughly plumbed the meaning of speech that even to prevent serious harm such as murder we could not speak untruth. All of these essentialist visions have been humbled. The road to truth is longer and more tortuous than we thought. But now, regarding homosexuality, we are again told that the nature of homosexuality can be so perfectly intuited (especially by heterosexuals) that we can, with majestic calm, make a transcultural judgment that any expression of it anywhere is wrong and dehumanizing. Such arrogance is not the hallmark of truth.

Any position about the complexities of human behavior and development that ignores the witness of experience is suspect. The position that asserts that homosexuality is all right as long as you do not act on it is innocent of and apparently unconcerned with the experience of homosexually oriented persons. The more one looks into that experience and hears sensitive witness from gay persons, the less comfortable one can be with the glib "be-but-don't-do" approach to this human mystery. This approach gratuitously and stubbornly assumes that homosexuality fits with such things as pedophilia and obsessive voyeurism. It assumes with signal cruelty that homoeroticism has no more humanizing possibilities than incest or zoophilia. In this view, homoeroticism is, like all of these demonstrably noxious realities, sick. Since the conclusion of this error is a prescription of universal celibacy for all gays, the burden is clearly upon those who would so prescribe. Instead we receive poor exegesis of religious texts, biologisms, and warmed-over biases in place of argument. Neither ethics nor persons are well served by such careless intuitionism and empirically bereft moralizing.

Jean-Paul Sartre has told us that the greatest evil of which persons are capable is to treat as abstract that which is concrete. That is precisely what the "be-but-don't-do" school does to homosexuality. It takes the infinitely diverse experiences of homosexual persons and classifies them without distinction as evil. Such a globular approach does not commend itself to intelligence.

3. The final error of the "be-but-don't-do" position relates particularly to Christians who should be nourished by the earthy wisdom of the Bible. Facile urgings of celibacy for persons who do not happen to be heterosexual fly in the face of biblical good sense. Saint Paul, in his celebrated First Letter to the Corinthians, talks about the possibility of celibacy. Even though he is writing in a state of high eschatological expectation, and with the expressed conviction that it is better not to have sex (1 Cor 7:1), he allows that sexual needs are such that it would be better to marry (7:12). He concedes that persons may lack self-control (7:15), and so even married persons would be better advised not to be sexually abstinent for long. He would prefer all to be celibate but notes that each one has his/her own gift from God (7:17), implying very clearly that not all have the gift of celibacy. Again, he would prefer the unmarried and widowed to stay celibate but, once more, allows for the possible lack of "self-control" and concludes that "it is better to marry than to burn" (7:19).

The "be-but-don't-do" position would certainly allow, with Paul, that it is better for heterosexuals to marry than to burn. But, apparently their message for our homosexual brothers and sisters is: "Burn, burn!" We should not be terribly surprised that gay persons do not see this as "the good news." They can point out that Paul in this passage is reflecting the good sense of Jesus, who also said of voluntary celibacy: "Let him accept it who can" (Mt 19:12). The Church itself, in the Second Vatican Council, has taken up this sensible idea, describing voluntary celibacy as "a precious gift," not as something indiscriminately given to whole classes of peoples.[2] The council points out that chastity will be very difficult, that it will face "very severe dangers" even for seminarians and religious with all the safeguards built into their life-style.[3] Those who would embark on a life of celibacy "should be very carefully trained for this state."[4] The council calls voluntary celibacy a "counsel," not a mandate, "a precious gift of divine grace which the Father gives to *some* persons," but not to all.[5] This gift of "total continence" is seen as worthy of special honor and as something "unique."[6] Celibate chastity "deserves to be esteemed as a surpassing gift of grace . . . which liberates the human heart in a unique way."[7] Persons entering religious orders should be warned in advance that celibacy, even in the sacred confines of religious life, is not easy.

Involved in the celibate project are "the deeper inclinations of human nature." Candidates for a celibate religious life should have "a truly adequate testing period" to see if "they have the needed degree of psychological and emotional maturity." They should be warned of "the dangers confronting chastity."[8]

To all of which, our gay brothers and sisters might reply: "If total continence is so difficult for nuns and priests, why is it so easy for us? If it is a counsel for them, why is it a precept for us? These are good questions. If celibacy is so difficult that only some heterosexuals can undertake it—and then with the most extraordinary systems of support—how can we say that all gays have this "unique" talent for self-containment? If celibacy is seen as it is in a religious context as a special charism, are all gays charismatically blessed with celibate graces? Is this not a radical theological restatement of the position that "gay is good?" It is a traditional axiom of Catholic moral theology that no one is held to the impossible (*nemo ad impossible tenetur*). Are gays, nevertheless, held to what is impossible for nongays? For nongays, in this view, celibacy is a gifted feat that symbolizes the special, generous presence of the power of God. For gays, it is just a way of life, and the least that they can do. There are problems here that even minimal insight and honesty could see and should admit. The pastoral position resulting from this contorted ethical position is equally strained. The only advice it leaves for gays is this: Pray and repress your erotic tendencies. God does not demand the impossible, and so God will give you the strength to do what moral theology, written by heterosexuals, has decided God wants you to do. If you fall from grace, appeal to God for forgiveness and your pastoral counselor will receive you with kindness and compassion.

Such pastoral advice embodies the theological error of "tempting God." It also harkens back to the medieval "ordeal," which contrived tests and put God on notice to come up with the response dictated by the test. If the fire burned you, you were evil. In this ordeal which we impose on gay persons, ethicists have boxed themselves into an arbitrary theological position which requires total celibacy from all gays and then leaves it up to God to pull off this implausible feat through prayer, sacraments, and pastoral counseling. Poor theology always puts God on the spot.

When we do theological ethics, we are painting a picture of our God. To say that something is good or bad is to say that it is in agreement or disagreement with the perceived will of God. In the position under discussion, we have God asking one thing from gays and considerably less from heterosexuals. If gay persons accept this particular ideological position on the ethics of homosexuality as the mind of God, *and* if they find it in contradiction to their own experience of reality, they have been pushed into the position of having to accept themselves *or* God. It is a position calculated to do precisely what pastoral theology should not do—alienate persons from the experience of God. Even at some risk to their professional situation, pastoral counselors are required not to offer either formal or material cooperations with a position that is so insensitive and religiously devastating.

Marriage as an Option for Homosexuals

Marriage is the highest form of interpersonal commitment and friendship achievable between sexually attracted persons. Nothing in that definition requires that the sexually attracted persons who are conjoined in committed, conjugal friendship must be heterosexual. Neither is the capacity for having children required. Reproductive fertility is not of the essence of genuine marriage. Even in the Roman Catholic tradition, sterile persons are permitted to marry, and, as a recent celebrated case in the Diocese of Joliet, Illinois, illustrated, even male impotence is no barrier to marriage. This means that the basic sense of the current Catholic position on the relationship of marriage and childbearing is this: If there are to be children, they should be born within the confines of marriage. Yet, even fertile heterosexual persons do not have an obligation to have children. As Pope Pius XII taught, there can be a variety of reasons—social, economic, and genetic—for excluding children from a marriage entirely. Marriage clearly has more goods than the "good of children," the *bonum prolis*. And those other goods, in themselves, are enough to constitute marriage as a fully "human reality and saving mystery."[9]

The Second Vatican Council produced a major statement on the dignity and value of married life. The council Fathers were, of course, speaking of marriage between heterosexual persons. In fact, however, aside from the "good of offspring," which they stress is not essential for a genuine marriage, the goods and values they attach to marriage are not exclusively heterosexual in kind. The needs that marriage fulfills are human needs. The values that marriage enhances are integral to humanity as such and not to humanity as heterosexual. In fact, the *indispensable* goods of marriage are those that do not relate intrinsically to heterosexuality. The *dispensable* good—offspring—is the only good that does relate to heterosexuality.

Let us look to the council's statement on marriage and see what "good news" we might find there for gay persons who seek a humanizing and holy expression of their God-given orientation.

The image that the council gives of marriage is, on the whole, very positive and sensitive to personal needs. Marriage is seen as "an unbreakable compact between persons" of the sort that must "grow and ripen."[10] "Marriage persists as a whole manner and communion of life, and maintains its value and indissolubility, even when offspring are lacking."[11] Married persons should "nourish and develop their wedlock by pure conjugal love and undivided affection."[12] The council continues in a decidedly personalist tone:

> This love is an eminently human one since it is directed from one person to another through an affection of the will. It involves the good of the whole person. Therefore it can enrich the expressions of body and mind with a unique dignity, ennobling these expressions as special ingredients and signs of the friendship distinctive of marriage. This love the Lord has judged worthy of special gifts, healing, perfecting, and exalting gifts of grace and of charity.
>
> Such love, merging the human with the divine, leads the spouses to a free and mutual gift of themselves, a gift proving itself by gentle affection by deed. Such love pervades the whole of their lives. Indeed, by its generous activity it grows better and grows greater. Therefore it far excels mere erotic inclination which, selfishly pursued, soon enough fades wretchedly away.[13]

To make married love prosper, the couple are urged to "painstakingly cultivate and pray for constancy of love, largeheartedness, and the spirit of sacrifice."[14] The married couple are to become no longer two, but one flesh by rendering "mutual help and service to each other through an intimate union of their persons and their actions. Through this union they experience the meaning of their oneness and attain to it with growing perfection day by day." The goal of marriage is "unbreakable oneness."[15] Such "multi-faceted love" mirrors the love of God for the Church. It will be marked by "perpetual fidelity through mutual self-bestowal." It should lead to the "mutual sanctification" of the two parties and "hence contribute jointly to the glory of God."[16]

The council does not look on this love as angelic and asexual. In fact, it stresses that this mutually satisfying and sanctifying love "is uniquely expressed and perfected through the marital act."[17] Sexual expression is extolled: "The acts themselves which are proper to conjugal love and which are exercised in accord with genuine human dignity must be honored with great reverence."[18] Again, reflecting the biblical sense of the natural goodness of sexual liturgy and its importance to conjugal love, the council warns that "where the intimacy of married life is broken off, it is not rare for its faithfulness to be imperiled and its quality of fruitfulness ruined."[19] Abstinence from sex, therefore, is viewed cautiously.

All of these texts of the council show a keen sense of the kinds of needs that are met in marital love. Married love will not survive on the thrills of early eroticism. What persons seek in marriage is total acceptance of all aspects of the self, the corrigible and the incorrigible, the lovely and the unlovely, the strong and the weak. Married love is not a selfish investment but an adventure in self-sacrificing, creative love. It is a school of holiness where persons may grow closer to God as they grow closer to one another and where their conjugal love may fuel their passion for justice and love for all people.

By what reasoning should values such as these be reserved for the heterosexual majority and denied to our gay brothers and sisters? By what twisted logic could we assume that gay persons would not experience the advantage of a love that produced such an "unbreakable oneness?" Why would gay persons in love be forbidden to aspire to and pray for "constancy of love, largeheartedness, and the spirit of sacrifice" to sustain their love? If erotic love between heterosexuals "is uniquely expressed and perfected" through sexual language, why would homoerotic love be judged moral only if sexually mute?

Two Objections to Homosexual Marriage

Two immediate objections might be these: (1) gay persons do not display the psychological stability and strength necessary for lifelong commitment in marriage, and (2) the data indicate that gay persons prefer promiscuity to closed one-to-one relationships, showing that marriage is a heterosexual ideal being imperiously imposed on homosexuals.

How stable are gays psychologically? In a recent important study, Professors Alan Bell and Martin Weinberg bring extensive research to bear on the common stereotypes our society maintains regarding homosexual persons. At the heart of the stereotyping is the belief that homosexuals are "pretty much alike." Accordingly, it is significant that Bell and Weinberg entitle their study *Homosexualities: A Study of Diversity Among Men and Women*. According to the stereotype, the homogeneous homosexuals are marked by "irresponsible sexual conduct, a contribution to social decay, and, of course, psychological pain and maladjustment."[20] The study presents strong evidence that "relatively few homosexual men and women conform to the hideous stereotype most people have of them." The authors describe as their "least ambiguous finding" that "homosexuality is not necessarily related to pathology."[21]

Regarding the psychological adjustment of homosexual men, Bell and Weinberg discovered that only one or two of the homosexual subgroups compared adversely to heterosexual men as to psychological adjustment. "The remaining subgroups tended to appear as well adjusted as the heterosexuals or, occasionally, even more so."[22] One quasi-marital subgroup, which the study styles "close-coupled" fared more than well in comparison to heterosexuals. "They felt no more tense, and were even happier than the heterosexual men."[23] Lesbians differed even less than male homosexuals in measures of psychological adjustment. In fact, close-coupled lesbians came out better in some regards than comparably situated heterosexual women.[24]

These findings are remarkable when we consider the stresses gay persons are subjected to in an antihomosexual society. All adolescents are vulnerable in their self-image. They are normally moving out from the nurturing closeness of family life, where their value has been consistently and reliably affirmed. In coping with this the adolescent vacillates between shrillness and bombast and shyness and tears. If, in the delicate move from familial to somewhat broader social endorsement, the young persons discover that a profound aspect of their personality is loathsome to the dominant majority, a painful crisis ensues. The discovery that one is a "queer," a "faggot," and a "pervert" is terrifying news to the delicate emergent ego. The news is so frightening that some self-protectively blind themselves to their own sexual identity in an amazing feat of denial. Others cope, often alone, with little or no solace or support. Even those on whom they have most depended up till now are normally of no help. Parents and siblings usually give clear witness to their detestation of homosexuality. Sexual awareness, then, brings the homosexual adolescent into a terrible loneliness. That so many of them bear this solitary suffering so well and arrive at such high levels of psychological adjustment is a striking tribute to the resilience of the human spirit. Heterosexual youths have their own tensions, but normally nothing comparable to the crushing rejection that greets the young gay person with the onset of puberty.

In view of all this, it is both arrogant and unjust for the heterosexual and dominant majority to perpetuate the myth that gay persons are psychologically unsound when these persons have passed more tests of psychological adjustment than many heterosexuals are ever required to do. There is simply no evidence that the psychological state of gays disqualifies them *as a class* from deeply committed and specifically conjugal relationships. The gratuitous assertion or assumption that they are lamed in this respect constitutes, in terms of traditional Catholic moral theology, a mortal sin of calumny. It is also a sin of injustice requiring restitution. Few of us heterosexuals are without sin in this regard, and so we are required by the virtues of justice and veracity to take the trouble to know better the actual situation of our gay brothers and sisters and to make appropriate reparatory responses to their needs.

The second objection to marital friendship for homosexual persons rests on their alleged preference for promiscuous sexual life-styles. Again, studies do not support these stereotypes. Lesbians are particularly prone to form lasting marriagelike relationships. Even among male homosexuals, where promiscuity is more common, prolonged "affairs" are common. The Bell-Weinberg study reaches this conclusion:

> Our data indicate that a relatively steady relationship with a love partner is a very meaningful event in the life of a homosexual man or woman. From our respondents' descriptions, these affairs are apt to involve an emotional exchange and commitment similar to the kinds that heterosexuals experience, and most of the homosexual respondents thought that they and their partners had benefited personally from their involvement and were at least somewhat unhappy when it was over. The fact that they generally went on to a subsequent affair with another partner seems to suggest a parallel with heterosexuals' remarriage after divorce rather than any particular emotional immaturity or maladjustment. In any case, most of our homosexual respondents spoke of these special relationships in positive terms and clearly were not content to limit their sexual contacts to impersonal sex.[25]

There is, of course, evidence that homosexual men are more promiscuous than any other group. This fact, however, must be put in context to be evaluated. A major factor is the high availability of sex in the male homosexual world, and homosexual men are men. As the psychologist, Dr. C. A. Tripp writes: "The variety of sex the heterosexual male usually longs for in fantasy is frequently realized in practice by the homosexual. . . . There is no indication that homosexual promiscuity is any greater than its heterosexual equivalent would be in the face of equal opportunity."[26] There are other reasons that account for the promiscuous pattern among many male homosexuals. Two men do not have the same social freedom to live together that women enjoy. It often amounts to revelation of one's orientation with all the hazards that entails in a biased society. The prejudice of the community and of traditional Catholic moral theology discourages stable relationships and indirectly opens the way to promiscuity. Homosexual unions also usually lack children. As the Vatican Council noted, "children contribute in their own way to making their parents holy."[27] Part of that holiness is the holiness of fidelity and stable, enduring love. By excluding any serious consideration of mature and stable gay couples adopting children, or of lesbian couples having children by artificial insemination, we block, without due ethical process, this inducement to healthy relationships among gays. Another factor that inclines to promiscuity among gays is the fact that they are more likely to find partners that are more culturally diverse, which makes for greater likelihood of incompatibility on the long haul.

Therefore, we may not simply look from a distance at the statistics of greater male homosexual promiscuity without distinguishing the various groupings of homosexuals and without recognizing the pressures against marital relationships in the life situation of many gays.

The Marriage Option and Solidly Probable Opinion

Within the confines of Roman Catholicism, there is division on the ethics of homosexual behavior. A number of moralists hold the traditional "be-but-don't-do" position and a number of others are open to humane expressions of gay sexual love. The hierarchical magisterium seems firm on the "be-but-don't-do" position. The theological magisterium is divided. The hierarchical position is admittedly noninfallible and is not an obstacle to open debate as long as there is due account of and study of that position. What tools for such a pluralistic situation did the Roman Catholic tradition provide? The answer is that the tradition provided an excellent moral system known as probabilism for precisely such a situation. The system has been in a state of disuse, and this represents a major loss of a traditional Catholic treasure.

Probabilism, like all good things, was abused, but the theological achievement that it represents was significant and, until we see how it relates to the charismatic theology of Paul and John and to the concept of the moral inspiration of the Holy Spirit in Augustine and Saint Thomas Aquinas, it has not been given its theological due. Another reason for bringing probabilism down from the Catholic attic is that after Vatican II's recognition of the truly ecclesial quality of Protestant Christian churches, neoprobabilism could be the test of ecumenism. Is our ecumenism merely ceremonial or can we really begin to take Protestant moral views into account in discussing liceity in doubtful matters? The older probabilism did not even face such a question.

The triumph of probabilism in the Church was an achievement of many of our long-suffering theological forebears and we do well to harken back to their work. Let me briefly repeat what probabilism is all about. Probabilism arose, and finally gained prominence over competing systems, as a way of solving practical doubt about the liceity of some kind of behavior. In practice, it confronted a situation in which a rigorous consensus claiming the immorality of certain behavior was challenged. The question was: At what point does the liberty-favoring opinion attain such respectability in the forum of conscience that a person could follow it in good faith? Those who said that even frivolous reasons would justify departure from rigorous orthodoxy were condemned as laxists by Popes Innocent XI and Alexander VII. At the other extreme were the absolute tutiorists who taught that you could never follow the liberal opinion unless it was strictly certain. Even being most probable (*probabilissima*) was not enough. In graph form the situation was like this:

A	/B

A represents the dominant rigorous opinion claiming that certain activity could never be moral. B represents the liberal dissent. Laxism claimed that the most tenuous B would override A. Absolute tutiorism claimed that until B replaced A and was beyond challenge, it could not be followed. The Jansenists found absolute tutiorism attractive, but Alexander VIII did not, and he condemned it on December 7, 1690. Thus between the two banned extremes of laxism and absolute tutiorism, the Catholic debate raged with probabilism gradually becoming dominant.

Probabilism proceeded from the twin insights that a doubtful obligation does not bind as though it were certain, and that where there is doubt there is freedom. It held that a solidly probable opinion could be followed even though more probable opinions existed. To be solidly probable, a liberal opinion had to rest upon cogent though not conclusive reasons (intrinsic probability) or upon reliable authority (extrinsic probability). As Tanquerey puts it in his manual of moral theology, to be probable, an opinion could not be opposed to a "definition of the Church" or to certain reason and should retain its probability when compared with opposing arguments.[28] Since there is no "definition of the Church" regarding homosexuality and since furthermore it is clear that the Church does not have the competence to define such issues infallibly,[29] that condition cannot stand in the way of using probabilism.

Intrinsic probability, where one followed one's own lights to a solidly probable opinion, was not stressed in the history of probabilism, but it was presented as a possibility. Stress fell upon extrinsic probability where one found "five or six" moralists known for their "authority, learning and prudence." Even one extraordinary preeminent teacher alone could constitute probability. What this meant is that minority B on our graph became solidly probable through private insight or through the insight of five or six learned experts even though the enormous majority of theologians disagreed. Note well that the basis of probabilism is insight—one's own or that of reliable experts. Insight is an achievement of moral intelligence. It cannot be forbidden, neither does it await permission to appear.

Note also that probabilism does not require a consensus or certitude. As Father Henry Davis writes, "when I act on the strength of a probable opinion, I am always conscious that though I am morally right in so acting, since I act prudently, nevertheless, the opinion of others who do not agree with me may be the true view of the case."[30] Obviously, the perennial debate will be between those who argue that the defenders of probability in a particular case are actually crypto-laxists and those who argue that the deniers of probability are disguised absolute tutiorists.

Probabilism was a remarkable development, and represents a high point in Catholic moral thought. It recognized that the apparent safety of absolute tutiorism was only apparent. The acceptance of such a rigorous position, as Father Tanquerey explained, would impose an impossible burden on the faithful contrary to the mind of the Gospel, which promises that the yoke will be sweet and the burden light; it would thus increase sins, generate despair, and drive many from the practice of religion.[31] Those reasons and probabilism itself are still relevant today.

To dismiss probabilism as the legalistic bickerings of the sixteenth and seventeenth centuries, is theologically shortsighted. In the heyday of the debate, extravagant claims were made. Caramuel, who became known as the "prince of the laxists," taught that Adam and Even used probabilism successfully to excuse themselves from many sins, until their wits and their probabilism failed them and they did fall. Vigorous efforts were made to trace the formal doctrine of probabilism to Augustine, Jerome, Ambrose, Gregory of Nazianzen, Basil, and Thomas Aquinas. One need not become party to such adventures to insist on and argue how compatible probabilism is with deep Christian traditions. The early Church was remarkably sanguine about the presence of the illumining Spirit in the hearts of the faithful. As Vatican II says:

> The Spirit dwells in the Church and in the hearts of the faithful as in a temple (cf. 1 Cor 3:16; 6:19). In them He prays and bears witness to the fact that they are adopted sons (cf. Gal 4:6; Rom 8:15–16, 26). The Spirit guides the Church into the fullness of truth (cf. Jn 16:13) and gives her a unity of fellowship and service. He furnishes and directs her with various gifts, both hierarchical and charismatic, and adorns her with the fruits of His grace (cf. Eph 4:11–12; 1 Cor 12:4; Gal 5:22).[32]

The Church has shared the confidence of Saint Paul when he said that the spiritual man "is able to judge the value of everything."[33] Augustine and Thomas manifest in strong theological language this exuberant confidence in the presence in all Christians of the illumining Spirit of God. Augustine asked: "What are the laws of God written by God in our hearts but the very presence of the Holy Spirit?"[34] And Thomas Aquinas, arguing that the new law is not anything written (including the New Testament), cites Jeremiah's promise that in the future testament God will put his law into the minds of his people and inscribe it on their hearts. In its primary meaning, then, the new law for Thomas is not the writings of biblical authors, Church officers, or theologians, all of which are secondary, but the instructive grace of the Holy Spirit.[35]

This, admittedly, is a heady doctrine which called for and did historically elicit a theology of the discernment of the Spirit. One must test one's claimed inspiration against all the witnesses to truth within the community. And yet this heady doctrine, with all of its perils, is not a private preserve of the current charismatic movement in the Church, but is rather *bona fide* mainstream Catholic thought. It is also, I believe, eminently congenial with the spirit of the debate that led to the championing of probabilism. The debate on probabilism in many ways seems a curious and stilted period piece, but it would be ungrateful and unconservative of us to reject this achievement of the Catholic tradition. And reject it, in effect, we did. Of course, it maintained its presence in the manuals, but in practice it was rendered nugatory. This was done by simply ignoring the genuine possibility of intrinsic probability and by controlling the theological enterprise in such ways that any theologians favoring a liberal opinion that did not square with the contemporary Vatican view were quickly deemed neither learned nor prudent. Thus did extrinsic probability pass. And thus were the doors thrown open to a juridical positivism based on the hierarchical magisterium.

The neoprobabilism for which I call would have to be extended to include Protestant witnesses to moral truth. Vatican II said of Protestant Christians that "in some real way they are joined with us in the Holy Spirit, for to them also He gives his gifts and graces, and is thereby operative among them with His sanctifying power."[36] It becomes unthinkable, therefore, if these words mean anything, that we accept that solid probability could not also be achieved through the witness of Protestant Christians, who are also subjects of the "gifts and graces" of our God. I submit that if that thought is unpalatable, our ecumenism is superficial and insincere.[37]

Obviously, within Protestant and Catholic Christianity, there is considerable support for the possibility of moral, humane, and humanizing sexual expression by gay persons. Extrinsic probability does obtain. Intrinsic probability is within the reaches of mature persons. There is no reason why this traditional tool of Catholic thought should not be used by pastoral counselors. Obviously the acceptance of the ideal of marriage for gay persons is not something that could be celebrated with public liturgy at this point in the history of the Church since such a celebration would imply a general consensus that as yet does not exist. The celebration of private liturgies, however, to conjoin two gays in permanent and committed love would seem commendable, and well within the realm of the principles and spirit of probabilism. The marital good of exclusive, committed, enduring, generous, and faithful love is a human good. We have no moral right to declare it off limits to persons whom God has made gay.

NOTES

1. On the negative qualities of the macho-masculine, see Daniel C. Maguire, "The Feminization of God and Ethics," *Christianity and Crisis* 42 (March 1983): 59–67.

2. See Walter M. Abbott, general ed., *The Documents of Vatican II* (New York: Herder and Herder, 1966), p. 447, in the *Decree on Priestly Formation*.

3. Ibid.

4. Ibid., p. 446.

5. Ibid., p. 71, in the *Dogmatic Constitution on the Church*. Emphasis added.

6. Ibid., pp. 71–72.

7. Ibid., p. 474, in the *Decree on the Appropriate Renewal of the Religious Life*.

8. Ibid., p. 475.

9. The phrase "human reality and saving mystery" is from Edward Schillebeeckx's book, *Marriage: Human Reality and Saving Mystery* (New York: Sheed and Ward, 1965).

10. Abbott, *Documents of Vatican II, The Church Today*, p. 255.

11. Ibid.

12. Ibid., p. 252.

13. Ibid., pp. 252–53.

14. Ibid., p. 253.

15. Ibid., pp. 250–51.

16. Ibid., p. 251.

17. Ibid., p. 253.

18. Ibid., p. 256.

19. Ibid., p. 255.

20. Alan P. Bell and Martin S. Weinberg, *Homosexualities: A Study of Diversity Among Men and Women* (New York: Simon & Schuster, 1978), pp. 229–30.

21. Ibid., pp. 230–31.

22. Ibid., p. 207.

23. Ibid., p. 208.

24. Ibid., p. 215.

25. Ibid., p. 102.

26. C. A. Tripp, *The Homosexual Matrix* (New York: McGraw 1975), p. 153.

27. Abbott, *Documents of Vatican II*, p. 252.

28. ". . . ei nec definitio Ecclesiae nec certa ratio adversetur. . . ." See Adolphe Tan-

querey, *Theologia moralis fundamentalis: De virtutibus et praeceptis* (Paris: Desclée, 1955), 2: 293.

29. See my "Moral Absolutes and the Magisterium," in which I argued that it is not meaningful to say that the Church is infallible in specific issues of morality, in *Absolutes in Moral Theology?* ed. C. Curran (Washington, D.C.: Corpus Books, 1968).

30. Henry Davis, *Moral and Pastoral Theology* (London and New York: Sheed and Ward, 1949), 1: 107.

31. See Tanquerey, *Theologia Moralis*, p. 287.

32. Abbott, *Documents of Vatican II*, p. 17.

33. 1 Cor 2:15.

34. *De spiritu et littera*, C 21, M.L. 44,222.

35. "Ed ideo dicendum est quod principaliter nova lex est lex indita, secundario autem est lex scripta," *Summa Theologica* I–II, q. 106, a. 1, in corp.

36. Abbott, *Documents of Vatican II*, p. 34.

37. See Daniel C. Maguire, *"Human Sexuality:* The Book and the Epiphenomenon," in *Proceedings of the Thirty-Third Annual Convention of the Catholic Theological Society of America* (June, 1978), ed. Luke Salm, F.S.C., pp. 71–75 from which this description of probabilism is taken.

MARY E. HUNT

Lovingly Lesbian:
Toward a Feminist Theology
of Friendship

"Two women sleeping together have more
than their sleep to defend."
Adrienne Rich, "The Images"

C atholic lesbian feminists are a growing group in and beyond the
institutional Church. We are a varied lot, with so many experiences
and stories that it would be hard to single out a defining characteristic.
But one is sure, namely, our potential to create new models of friendship.
In a patriarchal, heterosexist culture, love relationships are so circumscribed by the normative courtly marriage as to prevent the flowering of
friendships of any kind, much less same-sex ones. Thus it is imperative
that we contribute our insights that all might love in generations to come.

We do so in the face of increasing repression. The doors which swung
open with Vatican II now seem to be closing swiftly. That period of
experimentation and its liberalizing consequences are rapidly coming to
an end. With it goes much hope. But the urgency comes from a personal
or pastoral source as well as from this structural or political one. Catholic
lesbian feminists will soon become lesbian feminists if the institutional
Church, as well as the popular Church, including the substantial gay
male sector, do not begin to take seriously and reap the benefits of their
insights. It is to avoid this end, as well as to enrich the entire Christian
community's experience of friendship, that I offer the following reflections.

NOTE: This essay results from many women's experiences shared with care and confidence.
It results too from the hidden lives of women, which have had to be pieced together and
intuited. My friends and I thank our foresisters and their friends that our daughters and
their friends may love at all.

In this essay I will explore the background and experience of contemporary lesbian feminism, then look at it in its Catholic manifestation. Then I will look at the notion of friendship which lesbian feminists cultivate, and, finally, draw out some of its implications for an understanding of friendship adequate for the whole Christian family. Such is a prologue for a more sustained treatment of friendship, but it is a way of naming and clarifying in an initial way what has heretofore been only implicit or intuitive.

What is lesbian feminism? Where did it come from and why won't it go away? Why use the work *lesbian*? Can't women just be friends? Why isn't there a new word for it? These are the kind of first-level questions which need to be answered in order to move on to creative analysis.

The theopolitical reality of lesbian feminism is that it can only be understood in a particular social context. That context is both patriarchal and heterosexist. By patriarchal, I mean that the entire social fabric is so imbued with the normativity of male experience that female experience is excluded. This means that schools, churches, businesses, governments, etc. are arranged according to male principles of competition, aggression, and production to the extent that so-called female characteristics of cooperation, agreeability, and process are negated. Patriarchy expresses itself in sexism in the culture, and has been responded to in some initial ways by what is known as feminism. Feminism is the insight into the historical and contemporary oppression of women, and at the same time a movement dedicated to strategies for overcoming it. Major work has been done on sexism from a theological perspective by Sheila Collins, Mary Daly, Rosemary Ruether, and others, and from a theoretical angle by Charlotte Bunch, Susan Griffin, Adrienne Rich, and company. More recently however, we have come to understand that this same patriarchal context is heterosexist as well.

The insight into heterosexism is just beginning to be explored logically by a generation of scholars who have benefited from the work which has been done on sexism. Heterosexism means that normative value is given to heterosexual experience to the extent that legal and acceptable expression of homosexual experience is excluded. As in patriarchy, there is no claim that heterosexual experience as such (like maleness as such) is bad. Rather, its normativity to the exclusion of homosexuality (just as the exclusion of women) makes it oppressive. When all social relationships and social institutions are arranged according to heterosexist principles, i.e., male-female dating and marriages, child rearing in heterosexual families, and the presumption that all are heterosexual until proven otherwise, it is nearly impossible for healthy, good, and natural homosexual relationships to flourish. That they do is some proof of grace.

Women whose experiences do not conform to this model realize early on that the context in which definitions are born is patriarchal and heterosexist. They realize that all women are defined not only according to their gender but according to their sexual relationships with men as well. The litany is something like the following: married women sleep with men, divorced and widowed women used to, separated women might again, single women would like to, lesbian women do not, and nuns, well, they are not even supposed to talk about it. Thus the "normal" (*Webster's*) definition for a lesbian in this context is "a female homosexual," the word itself coming from "the reputed homosexual band associated with Sappho of Lesbos." Here it is clear that even a lesbian in heterosexist patriarchy is defined in male terms, that is, as homosexual who does not happen to be male. Even the word chosen for such women is defined in terms of male fantasies about Sappho's friends.

So it goes, but the confusions are even helpful for understanding what a lesbian is not. A lesbian is not defined by her sexual partner any more than she is defined by those with whom she does not sleep. This is to fall into the patriarchal trap of defining women according to sexuality, which only serves to divide us. What we need is to be united in order that our strength will free all of us. A lesbian is an outlaw in patriarchy. But she is the herald of the good news that partriarchy is in its decline. A lesbian is a woman who in the face of heterosexist patriarchal messages not to love women—the others, the outsiders, the despised—indeed not to love herself as woman, in fact does both. She loves other women as friends, that radical relationship of laying down one's life that has always been valued in Christianity. And by loving other women she comes to that authentic self-love which is, in the words of novelist Doris Grumbach, "It was the very opposite of narcissism—it was metamorphosis."[1] To be a lesbian is to take relationships with women radically seriously, opening oneself to befriend and be befriended, so that by loving, something new may be born. When all women are free to have this experience, then, and only then, can we say that any women are free.

This renewed definition of lesbian comes from a particular social context. Three social movements paved its way. They are: the so-called sexual revolution, the women's movement and the lesbian/gay movement. I will treat each one briefly so that we may see the backdrop for this new definition. Agreeing with these movements is not important, but being aware of them as forming part of our history in the evolution of a postpatriarchal, postheterosexist culture, is.

First is the sexual revolution, perhaps the most dubious of all three. This was the much heralded and mercifully short-lived revolt against puritanical ways in the sixties. It was made popular through such slogans

as "Free Love," "Abortion on Demand," "Make Love Not War," etc.
The very expressions themselves give away the patriarchal nature of this
movement. For men it meant license for sex wherever and whenever with
whomever, taking away from women the "nice girls don't" excuse. For
women it meant the need for more birth control, more abortions, and
ultimately less freedom to really choose. Heterosexual activity in and of
itself was seen as revolutionary, for still inexplicable reasons. But if anything positive did come out of this rather virulent period it was the fact
that people finally began to talk more freely about sexuality. This was no
small matter when we reflect that even to the present day, discussion of
sexuality is taboo in some circles, including most of theology.

The second and far more significant social movement to have an impact on the definition of lesbian was the women's movement. This movement recognized the class nature of women's oppression in the historical
and contemporary scenes. At the same time it began to use women's
experience as the starting point for developing strategies to overcome
oppression of all types. In consciousness-raising groups women not only
mentioned sexuality but took it as a major focus, seeing it as the mirror
which reflected all of women's treatment in the society. The woman who
was oppressed in bed, who was raped or beaten, whose husband or lover
did not use birth control, the woman who was called frigid, the postmen-
opausal woman, all of these are various facets of the same woman,
namely, the oppressed woman in patriarchy.

Lesbians were told to keep their voices down during the early years of
the women's movement. Betty Friedan and others (who later, happily,
repented publicly) referred to lesbians as the "lavender menace," and
made it clear that lesbians could cost all women their rights if lesbians
insisted upon theirs. So, dutifully the dykes closed their mouths, remained invisible, and worked on birth control, abortion rights, child care
etc. for what amounted to straight women's liberation. It was only with
the lesbian/straight split in the women's movement (1970–71) that feminists began to understand the politics of lesbianism. As Charlotte Bunch
indicated, "lesbian feminist politics is a political critique of the institution
and ideology of heterosexuality as a primary cornerstone of male su-
premacy."[2] Until this cornerstone is removed, the structures of patriarchy
will stand firm.

The point is not that every woman act in a particular way, but that
every woman be freed from the constraints that patriarchal heterosexism
places upon her. Then and only then can women make real choices
about relationships with particular people, not excluding a whole class of
people (women) from the beginning. This same dynamic of instant exclusion of whole classes of people is operative in racism, in classism, in

discrimination toward the differently able, those from Third World countries, etc. It is this dynamic that lesbian feminists seek to change in its many manifestations.

The third major social movement which set the stage for present thinking about lesbianism is the lesbian/gay movement itself. When gays first fought back against police at the Stonewall bar on New York's Christopher Street in 1969, they opened a new era for homosexuals. No longer were same-sex relationships simply the stuff of back rooms and Mafia-run bars. Homosexuals were persons with dignity and (eventually) legal rights equal to all others. The movement was primarily male in that the leadership, focus, and values were basically derived from male experience. But women, even women who were not feminists, could see their rights as well. And everyone was finally able to see the lives and contributions of lesbians and gay men throughout history, who could now be celebrated by the gay community.

Feminists quickly became aware that being part of the gay community was important but no panacea. *Gay* had become another false generic like *man*, referring to both male and female homosexuals. This symbolized the values of the movement as well, which were focused on making male homosexual expression valid, and little else. Feminists could not stop our analysis with the sexual, but always understood our sexuality within the complex constellation of racism, classism, sexism, etc. The "natural alliance" between lesbian feminists and gay men was not so natural after all. This is not to say that there are not some obvious and important links, but it is to say that very different emphases have been made from the two perspectives.

Gay males, for example, have emphasized their sexual lives as the locus of their liberation. But since *gay* is not a generic word we can conclude that the lesbian emphasis is quite different and not to be homogenized. Lesbian feminists have not defined ourselves according to sexuality, although that has been important. Rather, we have defined ourselves according to certain relational commitments to other women, or what I am calling female friendship. The nature of our relationships with regard to the specifically sexual aspect is quite simply no one else's business. This is not to say that lesbian feminists are in the closet about our sexuality, nor that we advocate continuing the hidden relational lives of our foresisters with the women they loved. Far from it. Rather, the goal from a lesbian feminist perspective is that persons eventually be allowed to love whom they will without current heterosexist gender restraints.

To achieve such a goal, we are reclaiming the word *lesbian* for what it has always meant, namely, women loving women without fixating on the presence or absence of genital activity to define it. What we are talking about is the basic feminist truism that the personal is political. This is important to distinguish from the private, which has never been claimed to be political. Concretely, that I take my relationships with women seriously is an important personal choice in patriarchy which has clear political implications. But that my friend and/or sexual partner is Susie and not Debby is private, therefore not political, though it is of course both public information in a certain way and something which we choose to share among our families and friends. This distinction is important because it allows lesbian feminists to have private lives like everyone else. We can live without having our sexuality politicized beyond what relationships can handle. At the same time, we can make claims about the political nature of loving women within a patriarchal, heterosexist culture without those claims being tied to one or another relationship. In short, sexuality is not privatized, but neither are specific relationships publicized, at least not beyond the usual small circle of friends who know, support, and critique any human relationships.

This analysis must be seen in the light of contemporary women's studies and what we might call lesbian feminist theory. Adrienne Rich has suggested that the cost of heterosexism has been so high as to erase the lives and loves of many lesbians from history.[3] The threat of lesbianism has served to divide women, alienating them and making them fearful of one another. The ultimate epithet for any women, regardless of her sexual preference, is *lesbian*. To diffuse this, Rich has suggested the notion of the lesbian continuum, placing all women somewhere on the continuum. This would include married women who take their relationships with women friends seriously on the one hand, and women who live together in primary affective relationships on the other, and everyone in between.

Rich's analysis suggests that when all women can embrace and celebrate the lesbian in them the distinctions between "who is" and "who is not" will finally fall away. It has been suggested that perhaps letting all women onto the continuum might degrade or de-emphasize the value and dignity of those relationships which are on the latter end of the spectrum, those which would traditionally be defined as lesbian anyway. However, it is clear that such a wholesale identification of women as lesbians is not about to happen, though for those few who do so identify there will undoubtedly be a warm welcome. The idea, rather, is that all women take seriously their friendships with women, and the only word which we have to indicate this revolutionary reality is *lesbian*. Thus, it is at our peril that we back off of the word. To do so is to deny the powerful women's reality which has gone before us and probably to short-circuit what is ahead. I feel for women who say that they agree with the concept—frightening as it is for many of them to think of the implications of taking relationships with women seriously—but only wish we could employ another word, please. As yet there is no word, so I simply remind them that there was a time not so long ago when the word *woman* had distinctly sexual overtones. All females were described as "girls" and "ladies." How quickly language and concepts change together. The point is that no one knows all of the implications of integrating sexuality into women's friendships. But we do know that the important thing is not that they necessarily do it, but that they do it lovingly and responsibly.

This is why we insist on reclaiming the word *lesbian*, wrenching it from its patriarchal context, à la Mary Daly, and giving it a content worthy of the lives of some great women friends throughout history. Inviting all women to share its richness, it is important that *lesbian* not be forced to carry the symbolic freight of sexuality for all women. Instead, we can insist on our self-identification as friends in a culture which tells all of us to keep our distance from one another. Thus *lesbian* takes on a new meaning. It becomes paradigmatic of all types of friendships in a culture which provides precious few structures for women and men, men and men, women and women to relate to each other as friends without the corruption of such unions with partial, distorted notions of heterosexism.

Throughout the country and in fact in many places in the world a women's community is emerging. This community is made up of women who understand and value the necessity of women's friendships for our collective survival. Here, female friendships can flourish in places and spaces where they go unquestioned in themselves and are subsequently evaluated according to the persons involved. Music, art, poetry, drama, dance etc. can be shared in the women's community without the annoyance of male objectifiers or the more subtle drain of liberal male hangers-on. The community is dynamic and shows its resourcefulness by great mobility and simple comfort. It is, however, almost completely white and middle class, something which limits its value, although women of color are beginning to make their voices heard as well in contributions which promise new life for all of us.[4] The women's community, however, is a tiny fraction of a percentage of the general culture where women's lives and friendships are trivialized unto death.

However, lesbian feminism and the women's community are having a significant impact in the culture if reports in popular news magazines can be taken seriously. For example, it seems that lesbians on campus are more visible than ever before, and that their visibility is both political as well as personal. They are not simply part of the larger male gay movement. They evidence instead a clear awareness of how relationships with women offer them more depth and possibilities for growth. There are even reports of some straight women wondering about themselves, whether they are whole persons or if indeed there is something wrong with them. While I have some sympathy for their confusion, I encourage their line of thinking. It points to what lesbian feminists are saying, namely, that loving other women, thus being free to love oneself, is good for every woman's health. This is nearly impossible under patriarchal, heterosexist influences.

Just as quickly as this insight into what we call woman identification out of lesbian feminism comes to consciousness, Hollywood and Madison Avenue are right there to counteract it. We can expect a spate of films of the *Personal Best* caliber which will capitalize on and trivialize women's friendships. These films play on male fears and fantasies about what the world would really be like if women loved women. Of course the results are predictably shallow, neurotic, one-dimensional, stereotypic, sexually focused relationships. These simply do not ring true about most lesbian feminist friendships, where it is not an instant attraction due to a compatibly toned body, but an attraction born of friendship with a sister in the struggle, and perhaps a sister in the snuggle too! These are the life-giving friendships which grace women even in a patriarchal, heterosexist culture, and which give some hope and role models for the next generation.

What about Catholic women? Has our experience been any different from the mainstream? Has our Catholic training kept us from such experiences? It is hard to find general samples because of the difficulties about coming out. The consequences of talking about friendships with women are often too great to allow women to survive and also be honest. This must be respected since the real costs for women in terms of jobs and possibilities far surpass those of gay men—another logical consequence of patriarchy. However, if my friends are any indication, there are a fair number of "good Catholic girls" who identify themselves as lesbian feminists. There are even more who would call themselves "women-identified" feminists, not having quite understood or internalized the political necessity of using *lesbian* but having grasped the basic insight into women's friendships as key to our survival. I am confident that this shift in terms will come about someday when it will no longer be necessary, due to a more massive shift in consciousness, but I do not expect to see that day.

Catholic women with experiences to share concerning all of this include not only young, single women reasonably fresh from campus, but nuns and even some married women as well. The divorced, widowed, and separated number among us, but the primary categories would be the first two mentioned. It is curious that in some other countries where the social movements mentioned above have not been as strong as in the

United States, there are still many Catholic women whose experiences fit the friendship bill being described. Their experiences, when shared with ours, appear to have some similar strains.

How would we characterize such experiences? It is difficult to say if Catholic women have different experiences from other women. But we do know that the Catholic emphasis on virginity before marriage and chastity during marriage, guarded over by the Virgin Mary, who made it all a tough act to follow (being simultaneously virgin and mother), produce some anxiety for many Catholic women. However, the lines are clear, the do's and don'ts quite explicit. At the same time, values like friendship and community are paramount. They are so stressed during the school years, which are often spent in same-sex environments, that it is a rare Catholic girl who does not grow up to have close women friends. From schools and camps to religious communities women live out their relational lives with women. Of course, mixed environments are not unavailable. But when one reads the literature about women's experiences one finds that Catholic women tend to speak of their same-sex environments as formative. This is not to say that same-sex environments create lesbians or the kind of friendships which I am arguing that feminists who are lesbians nurture. If it were so easy, I fear that the integration of every Catholic school and summer camp would occur overnight. Rather, I am suggesting that it is to those institutions with strong women-identified role models (mostly nuns and single women), where women's lives were valued, that most Catholic women trace their formation in female friendships.

This is an exciting contribution to the postpatriarchal, postheterosexist world we are trying to create. But it is ironic that in these same institutions where women are taught the values of friendship, loyalty, community, self-confidence, group reliance, etc., they are also taught the absolute taboo against sexual expression with women. Apparently, however, the friendship and community values are much stronger than the fabricated taboos against sexual expression. Once the taboos are perceived for what they are, namely, the product of patriarchal, heterosexist control over women, they can be overcome with amazing ease. Then sexuality can be integrated without tremendous guilt into already existing friendships and communities. This is not to say that automatic results are possible and easy. We have to learn to integrate sexuality responsibly, appropriately, judiciously, and deal with all of the resultant complexities, both social and relational. Nevertheless, it is gratifying to see how much healthier and stronger are the friendships and communities in which we are effecting this integration, often at great personal risk. One woman recently shared her excitement about the lifting of this taboo. She ex-

claimed that after some forty years of thinking that sexual expression
with women was unacceptable, she now was able, with the encouragement of her lesbian feminist friends, finally to love fully. That she might
have gone to her grave without this experience, like too many before her,
increases my sense of urgency.

I am not sure that Catholic women's experience is any different than
anyone else's. But I am sure that role models are easier to come by for
Catholic women vis-à-vis adult women's relationships. Here the richness
of having structural alternatives to heterosexual marriage becomes obvious and operative. Modern Catholicism has always taught that in addition to heterosexual marriage there were two other possible states for
women. "Single blessedness" and "the religious life" were options
women could choose and make sense of. Protestant and Jewish women,
by contrast, had no such structured alternatives. The closest Protestant
women could come to a religious state was being the pastor's wife. This
was of course until women could be ordained or commissioned for
church work, in which cases some of them went off two by two to the
missions. But in Catholic circles "single blessedness" was always assumed
to mean heterosexually single, i.e., without a man. Most of us knew such
people, and although their state was acceptable they were the poor things
who never married. Now we are beginning to read those situations a
different way. We now know that Aunt Kate and her friend Jenny were in
fact singly blessed, blessed in that they had each other!

Friendships between so-called single women were very usual and quite
socially acceptable as long as no one went into too many details. This is
not to say that there have not been some single women who have not
been in affective relationships with anyone. But it is to say that for some
single women it was not that way at all, and only heterosexist history
blurs the fact of their female friendships. For many, life was spent in a
coupled female relationship, a good friendship which lasted a lifetime.
For others such friendships were more communal and less focused on one
other person, but the fact is that such friendships did exist and women
lived quite happily in them. Women lived and worked and traveled together, sometimes spending holidays with aging parents and only in their
own later years giving full attention to their friends. Most of them never
spoke much about sexuality and, given the times, no one dared to raise
the question. But after the sexual revolution and the women's and les-
bian/gay movements, it is for us to integrate and express the sexuality
which sometimes blesses deep friendship, and only hope that they did
too. Our freedom to speak and celebrate that love flows from the painful
silence of their friendships. Like the Jews, we say, "Never Again."

Religious life has produced its share of women's friendships as well.

For generations, nuns lived in the fear of "particular friendships." They were evil-sounding liasons which no one ever fully defined but everyone knew were wrong. Women were moved or asked to leave their congregations when "particular friendships" came to light, practices which, unbelievably, continue to this day in less enlightened communities. But the fact is that some of the ladies protest too much about all of this. We are beginning to see from a feminist perspective what "particular friendships," another euphemism like "single blessedness," really mean. In congregations where the value on loving everyone and the myth of full-time availability for mission (a vocabulary set which is fraught with confusion) are considered normative, friendships are diffused lest the natural questions of commitment and sexuality might arise. Thus a "particular friendship" is not one with a man which would perhaps lead to marriage. Surely these, as it must be, general friendships, have existed and women have left their communities sensing that a heterosexual celibate commitment and a heterosexual marriage are on the face of it incompatible.

"Particular friendships" persisted in fact and in fantasy. Why? Because the basic healthy intuition of religious women is that wholesale love does not exist; we love concretely. Full time availability for work to the exclusion of love relationships creates only neurosis and burnout. Spirituality is no substitute for sexuality. And some nuns are even understanding that friendships are not friendships unless they are particular, that is, unless they are with another person (singular not group) who challenges, loves, and cares on an ongoing basis. In same-sex communities where women have cast their lots with other women it should come as no surprise to anyone that many friendships will arise with other women. And these, like all friendships between healthy mature adults, will demand some acknowledgment of the sexual component, and of course in the case of religious women, some sort of community-conscious decision about the nature of the friendship. The important point is, of course, that simply being in a religious community does not exempt women from having to deal with such matters, and there is some evidence to suggest that being in same-sex communities with the intensity of commitment which many find will increase the likelihood of such friendships.

What this means is that religious women are being invited (some might say pushed) by the sexual revolution and the women's and lesbian/gay movements, whether they are aware of them or not, to reexamine, redefine, and reaffirm their own woman identification. This is not an altogether comfortable process for some of them. It is a process which will have to be taught and refined like any other. But it will become part of the formation of every Catholic woman, nuns included, if sisterhood is to attain its much touted power. It is a process which will lead to deeper bonding and stronger ties in the long run, with communities finding even more energy unleashed for mission than ever before. It calls for new definitions of celibacy, new self-understandings as groups of women related in new ways to a patriarchal, heterosexist Church, and new bonding between women in religious communities with women not in such groups. Anything less will simply perpetuate the patriarchal pressures under which women religious have lived and deny the history from which they come.

This is not to say that all religious women are lesbian, at least not in the patriarchal sense of sleeping with women. This is simply not true, and no amount of revisionist history will make it so. But it is to say that religious women have a proud history of friendships among them, a history which in many cases goes back to the foundress and her friends. How this history translates into our own day and how the charism of friendship can be nurtured in our own time is the challenge for religious women. I can only hope that they will not be scared off by patriarchal definitions nor talked out of necessary explorations. I hope they will not be duped by those among them who will push off this task as the work of the new feminist foundresses, separating themselves and their resources once more over patriarchal definitions. Only the careful tending of women's friendships both within and beyond religious communities will make sure that Catholic women do our part for our daughters. Patriarchal patterns die hard. They do not dissolve overnight. And they are insidiously affecting all of us. Religious women have the special responsibility which comes with their at least pseudoprivilege in the institutional church, as well as with their poverty and education, which give them access to much real and symbolic capital.

This responsibility entails speaking what many of them know, namely, that healthy friendships between women can and do, thankfully, exist in many religious congregations. Some of these friendships include a sexual dimension; some do not. What we know is that the question of sexual expression is not determinative of anything in religious communities. What is important is how such relationships are conducive or divisive of community, and how such relationships energize and enspirit the people involved. Other questions are based on patriarchally conceived canons which most women religious when pressed would be forced to admit are inadequate. Nevertheless, too many neurotic, exclusive, nongenital relationships are celebrated in communities which will not even tolerate healthy, nonexclusive relationships which include sexual expression. We know that something is radically wrong and that mistaken criteria are being used to evaluate such relationships. Fortunately, however, the stories are beginning to emerge about the many religious women whose lives have been enriched immensely by female friendships. The many and varied dimensions of those friendships may now be seen in their true light. Much more delay in all of this can only keep religious women from their full potential as feminists. It may in fact signal that they have been so co-opted by the heterosexist, patriarchal Church as in the final analysis to be alienated from one another and from other women. Our woman's prayer is that this is not so. But tossing off the constraints of the institutional Church in this regard is among the tasks for leadership in religious communities today, just as shedding the habit and the rules of cloister challenged leaders in earlier generations.

We have looked at the background and experience of lesbian feminism, and explored Catholic women's particular experience. Now we turn our attention to the nature of this friendship itself as experienced by lesbian feminists. Then we will reflect on the meaning of friendship for the whole Church, that is, we will begin to sketch an adequate theology of friendship for the whole Christian community. The sketch will be filled out as time goes on, as more experiences are had in a postpatriarchal, postheterosexist Church.

Lesbian feminist friendships are known to us through a variety of sources. I look at my own experience and smile to think how blessed I have been with a very particular friendship, but also with a constellation of friendships which participate to one degree or another in the richness which is lesbian feminism. I look at my friends' experiences and the quality of relationships we share. It is astonishing how in the midst of our culture any women's friendships can flourish. But they do and we cultivate them like out-of-season flowers because we know all of the forces which mitigate against them.

We have other sources on women's friendships now. Finally the literature is coming to the fore. We have the formidable collection *Surpassing the Love of Men*, which details literary loves over the past centuries,[5] and few have missed the adventures of Molly Bolt, who made *Rubyfruit Jungle* the first feminist best seller.[6] This was a far cry from *The Well of Loneliness*, which convinced a whole generation that love between women had to be role-defined and tragic.[7] We learn about women's friendships from women's music, that growing group of compositions for, by, and about women. Meg Christian's "Ode to a Gym Teacher," sometimes referred to as the lesbian national anthem, provides a satirical look at the desparate search for role models prior to feminism. There are also the tender, powerful love songs of Holly Near and Chris Williamson, as well as the bawdy tunes of Teresa Trull, all celebrating the fact that women do love women. And there are the haunting melodies of Sweet

Honey in the Rock, assuring us that "Every woman who ever loved a woman you ought to stand up and call her name."[8]

All of these give us clues to women's friendships, clues earlier generations simply did not have. The clues are as varied as the friendships. But there are some general lines of agreement. Women are not to be possessed but to be shared. Friendship means support through the difficulties. Making love with a woman can be a delightful experience. Many women have loved women. These kinds of cultural affirmations allow women to see that their experiences are not unique, that the most natural feelings in the world have been distorted by patriarchy. This does not mean that solving the riddles of patriarchy will result in hassle-free relationships. But it does mean that the challenge of loving well is tough enough without having a whole layer of cultural negativity to make it even tougher.

These sources show that something new is struggling to be born in women's friendships. Perhaps it is that the cynicism and exploitation which mask love in straight society are finally being overcome. The mockery which has been made of love in patriarchy, the pain and prerequisites which prevent people from embracing one another in a deep, life-giving way are being put to rest. This is a major contribution to Christian culture, one which can model for relationships of all kinds the way into the future. No other contemporary source, neither the churches nor the gay male movement, nor even the straight women's movement, is making such a self-conscious effort to improve the quality of love.

Classical male qualities of friendship include such characteristics as care, responsibility, respect, and knowledge, according to such writers as Eric Fromm, etc. But for lesbian feminists it seems that some other characteristics come to the fore. The first of these is *mutuality,* that quality of a mature friendship when giving and taking are possible between equals, when one can truly complement the other not from role expectations but because of gifts. It is a rare, if existent, heterosexual relationship which is truly mutual. This is because in a heterosexist, patriarchal world women and men cannot be equal. This is the nature of patriarchy. Thus a friendship which is characterized by mutuality is possible only when a man and a woman live in contradiction with the prevailing culture. Living in this state of contradiction, conscious of all of its pressures, is usually more than most such friendships can take. However, friendships between women, on the other hand, can have this quality by their very nature. There can be an honest assessment of the strengths and liabilities of each one, and some sharing accordingly to each one's ability and each one's needs can be actualized. Then roles can be tossed aside and new possibilities emerge. Hence it is friendships between women which model mutuality for everyone.

A second characteristic of a woman–woman friendship is *community*. It seems that there is some urge in women to broaden, nurture and enlarge a friendship so that it will always exist in a network of relationships. This urge toward community is exactly the opposite of what happens in a male–female relationship in patriarchy when the urge to possess, to close off, and to protect seem to overpower even the most communally oriented of couples. Conversely, in women's friendship there seems to be a desire not to close off relationships but to join them with other similar friendships and create a kind of community. This may simply be a survival mechanism, a response to the fact that in patriarchy friendships between women are dangerous and need all of the support they can muster. But I like to think of it as a programmatic commitment on the part of women to give friendship a communal dimension. It seems also to guarantee a much healthier life-style, where neurotic minuets will be minimized and where groups in which ups and downs, holidays and tragedies may be shared will be the norm.

We are only beginning to structure friendships in this communal way. As noted above, it will be some time before those already in communities will be able to come out about the friendships which exist among them. But I submit that when both of these processes get under way, when communities are built intentionally on friendships and when communities make explicit their friendships, then the richness and power of women's friendships to transform the culture will really be felt. This kind of community building based on friendship will be the stuff of the ecclesia of women to which theologians refer when talking about the impact of feminism on the churches.[9] I support this move and only hope that the lessons of friendship and community building which will result from it can be broadened to include all members of the ecclesia.

A third aspect of women's friendships is a direct dealing with sexuality and the consequences of doing so, namely, *honesty*. This is perhaps the single greatest contribution of lesbians to all women, in that lesbians have urged upon all women an honest and forthright dealing with sexual dynamics which exist between them. It seems that up until very recently women functioned toward one another as if out of a completely heterosexist mind-set. Sexual dynamics were something one had to confront with men, always and everywhere, but friendships with women were cultivated without such complications. I have even heard straight women say that they do not confront sexuality with women because their experience with men is that when sex is no longer a part of the relationship the relationship itself is gone. They claim they do not want to risk this with their women friends, whose friendships are too important to them. The implications for their relationships with men are frightening. However, we have learned more recently that all mature, adult relationships have some kind of sexual component. We have found that it is better to face and deal with such dynamics then to let them stand in the way of quality relating.

This is not easy, given our socialization. But the rewards are many. What lesbian feminists have learned is that acknowledging and facing honestly the fact that in some friendships, for reasons which remain altogether mysterious, there may exist between two women sexual energy which calls for resolution. If the friendship is to flourish, this resolution is imperative. Otherwise, there is great risk of thwarting an otherwise good friendship.

Dealing directly with sexuality in any situation is simply a question of honesty. Failure to do so means introducing distrust into the relationship, distrust which will usually manifest itself in other aspects as well as the sexual one. What it means to be lesbian in a nonpatriarchal, nonhetero- sexist age is to take the risk which comes with acknowledging sexual energy and resolving it. The experience of many women is that not every friendship leads to the expression of sexuality. This is a myth created by the media to sell everything from liquor to paper towels. But it is equally women's experience that some kind of attraction often needs to be named, simply named. But in those cases where sexual dynamics do come into play there will often need to be some exploration between friends, which more often than not will result in a mutual decision that sexual expression will not enhance and might detract from the friendship. This is simply because we find that sexuality involves so much time and energy and emotion, participates on so many symbolic levels which for women are usually well integrated into the entire personality fabric (unlike men, who seem to have greater ease at distancing their sex life from the rest of their personalities), that we do not have the resources for too many such relationships in a lifetime, and rarely for more than one at a time.

In those few and cherished friendships in which the integration of sexuality is desired by both friends there is a symbolic signaling of a deepening of friendship and commitment. This is never a decision taken lightly. But it is one which involves the friends in each other's lives in ways that demand responsibility, ongoingness, nurture, etc. We are only beginning to see how such relationships, when encouraged and celebrated by families and friends, will transform the relational life of the Church.

Of course, the fact that women do not have to worry about birth control in their sexual explorations is no small incentive for greater hon- esty with women. Imagine if this same depth of honesty could be realized between women and men. Imagine the improved quality of friendships and even marriages which might result if the dynamics of dishonesty, which are so often set up at the sexual level and played out at every other level in relationships, were not in play.

Another characteristic of women's friendship is their *nonexclusivity*. Of course we can all think immediately of exclusive, clingy relationships between women which make the most possessive male-female relationships seem positively open. But contemporary lesbian feminist friendships simply are not that way. On the mixed side these were the result of male property orientation toward women, and on the female-female side a kind of shutting out of the world from that one little peaceful relational spot which women had found. Now we are creating a women's community in the broader culture so as to create the space that women's friendships need. The formation of solid bonds between and among women over generations and national boundaries is another attempt at creating womanspace adequate to the expansive nature of growing friendships. Thus friendships can be open and inviting, letting in the light of other friendships and sharing the goodness without fear of loss or trivialization. This invites women not to relational or sexual promiscuity but to the creation of friendships in a communal context which will in the long run mean added strength and richness for each one. The implications of this model for the entire Church remain to be spelled out, but it seems clear that opening the space for women will only lead to greater openness for women and men, as well as for men with men.

Another characteristic of female friendship is *flexibility*. Flexibility means the freedom to express oneself and grow with others in a variety of ways. It means letting go of the old role models which lesbians and gay men picked up from the only (heterosexual) model which existed. It means having to come up with new categories through which to explain and to nurture friendships, because the ones we have are simply inadequate. Are Susie and Cathy lovers? Well, Susie and Cathy are friends. Why do you need to know more, so that you can discriminate? This is the kind of response which comes when the categories are no longer adequate.

We are learning to be flexible about our loving. We are learning that we do not necessarily have to live in the twos of the nuclear family. We are learning that we can have intense, romantic friends but still live in the wider community or in fact even alone if that seems best. We are learning to develop the communities and networks of communities which multiply our options and spread out the energy of friendship where it is so badly needed.

Finally, female friendships are remarkable in their *other directedness*, the extent to which they point beyond themselves to something larger, something more beautiful, something more inclusive, some might even say something divine. This is something which male-female relationships in a patriarchal, heterosexist culture strive to attain but never reach. The reasons for this are historical in that female friendships have been forced outward, forced to understand and relate to the culture in order to survive. On the other hand the usual heterosexual relationship, which all too often is not even a friendship underneath it all, is focused in on itself, trying to reach some norm which patriarchy has established as the most effective way of stifling growth. Hence it is women's friendships which hold the key to transcendence, because they must transcend what *is* in order to be at all. This is a burden for women, but one which promises to make all things new if only women can survive long enough.

I have suggested that women's friendships are mutual, community seeking, honest about sexuality, nonexclusive, flexible, and other directed. These qualities, it seems to me, have tremendous potential not simply for relationships among women, though that potential has yet to be explored, but for the whole Church. It is these characteristics which will transform our culture and create the preconditions for the possibility of the reign of God. I am not arguing that all women's friendships participate in these qualities as yet. That is wishful thinking. Rather, by naming them I hope to make it so, or at least bring to consciousness what might be possible in women's lives so that our contribution to the whole Church can be forthcoming.

A theology adequate to this kind of friendship model is much more promising than the theology of sexuality which some of us have hinted at in the past. It is more adequate because it acknowledges that it is not sexuality per se but friendship which determines what the quality of life can be. In patriarchy it is certainly the sexuality dimension which makes the difference. But after patriarchy it is the entire relationship which makes the difference.

New constructive theologies are recognized as such by their saying something new about the fundamental theological categories God, humanity, and the world. This is done in a systematic way when some new insight, experience, or concept is used to illumine these basics. Friendship, it seems to me, is in its postpatriarchal, postheterosexist potential an insight, experience, and concept able to carry us to new heights in theology. Although I will save a full exploration of this possibility for a later essay when we have had more time to live into the idea, I offer now a few hints toward such a theology. To do so I will make certain Christian presuppositions which can be summarized by the normativity of love and justice as the essence of revelation. And of course since this constructive theology attempts to be systematic, the three concepts, God, humanity, and world, are each interdependent. They will be explored according to the six characteristics proposed for female friendships in hope that the specific new content about friendship can be brought to bear.

We begin by exploring who God is, what language and characteristics we can use for meaningful talk about God. The model of friendship, while not in and of itself adequate to exhaust the reality of God, is surprisingly helpful. No longer are we left with Father, Lord, Ruler, and King, nor even with Spirit and Mother Hen, which are often trotted out to balance the gender. But now we have the androgynous, unfettered notion of God as friend to add to the list.

Two of the characteristics gleaned from female friendships which are useful for understanding God as friend are mutuality and the urge toward community. Mutuality is suggested by process theologians who are concerned with how God is affected by humankind, and obviously vice versa. Mutuality is that quality of the otherness of God which is really God's oneness with us. To characterize otherness as mutuality is to say that God can only be understood in human terms, but that the very understanding is affected by our belief in God. In short, mutuality means that our relationship with God, like all friendships, is freely chosen on both sides (unlike family or government images like Father and Lord, in which the relationships are not necessarily intentional and gratuitous). More needs to be explored, of course, but it is clear that God as friend opens up a new paradigm for our understanding.

A second characteristic of female friendships, the urge toward community, is an essential aspect of the Christian God. The idea of the reign of God, the omega point, the gathering of all that is into a harmonious community, these are all Christian ways of talking about the God-human cooperation which will result in salvation. Jesus is the force in Christianity, the friend whose relationship with us is manifested by our being part of the Christian community. This membership is evidenced by the work of love and justice. This is not the pietistic "what a friend we have in Jesus." Rather it is the experience of being part of a historical group of friends. Jesus' friendships, especially the example of his particular friendship with the beloved disciple (Jn 13:23, 21:7, etc) as well as with his immediate community of women and men, are a model for contemporary Christian life. This is the community which derives its identity from the laying down of life for friends. Again, much remains to be explored, but we can conclude that the missionary urge which springs from Christianity is in fact to go and make friends in all nations.

Likewise the theological concept of humanity can be understood anew using friendship as the defining model. We have been developing what humanity will look like in a postpatriarchal, postheterosexist age, and we have looked at characteristics of female friendships. Focusing on two more of these, honesty and nonexclusivity, gives us a way to see the friendship model operating on the macro as well as the micro level.

The honesty which begins with direct dealing on sexuality questions in a relationship is the same habit of honesty which is needed for a renewed human family. It is the honesty which invites people to see our common heritage rather than stressing the accidental differences like age, race, nationality, sexual preference, physical handicap, etc. It is in the most optimistic of moments this honesty which could lead nations to face the nuclear threat and act like friends for once. It is a dream of course, but why not when options are limited?

Nonexclusivity as a characteristic of female friendship is helpful for imagining a renewed humanity. This could mean an end to preserving national boundaries at all costs while at the same time inviting international cooperation. Nothing would be seen as exclusively mine. Rather, things and people and ideas would be seen as here for the sharing not for the taking; they would be seen realistically as part of what is given to be enjoyed and given back. Nothing and no one would be seen as object or property, only as participating in a kind of cosmic subjectivity which encompasses all of creation. Needless to say, we are some distance from such values. But they give us goals against which to measure our collective progress as well as something toward which to aspire. This is, after all, the task of theology: to develop ethics and strategies to bring us closer to our goals.

Finally, the third theological basic, world, can be reunderstood in the light of a friendship model. World is a great abstraction, almost too great for meaningful discussion. But understood in terms of the earth and all nonhuman life, it is easy to see how flexibility and other-direction, characteristics of female friendships, are helpful lenses through which to examine it.

Flexibility means the freedom to develop a new relationship to the earth. In a nuclear age it means scaling down our grandiose notion of humanity and letting it come into line with the more modest role that was meant for us in creation. Likewise it means changing our attitudes toward the earth, understanding that our very future is tied up with our practices of ecology.

Other-directedness too helps us to see how the world is really oriented not for our pleasure but for our collective future. The pleasure of a few cannot be allowed to determine the future of everyone, or what will surely be no future at all at the rate we are going. This need for balance is critical over against the contemporary nuclear myopia, and it may be this insistence on balance which saves us from ourselves. To whom or to what we ought to be directed is not clear. But what is clear is that an orientation beyond what we know is the hallmark of faith, faith in a friendly future.

This treatment of lesbian feminist friendships, their Catholic particularities, and the beginnings of a theological sketch are an attempt to clarify some basic concepts, most of which have been previously misunderstood. Clarification is but a first step toward embracing the new, risking the friendship itself. It is that risk which will open the way for an enrichment of the God-human-world friendship in which we are all invited to participate.

NOTES

1. Doris Grumbach, *Chamber Music* (New York: Fawcett, 1979), p. 203.

2. Charlotte Bunch, *Lesbianism and the Women's Movement*, ed. Nancy Myron and Charlotte Bunch (Baltimore: Diana Press, 1975), p. 10.

3. Adrienne Rich, "Compulsory Heterosexuality and Lesbian Existence," *Signs: Journal of Women in Culture and Society 5*, no. 4 (Summer 1980): 631–60.

4. The best example of this emerging contribution is a collection entitled *This Bridge Called My Back: Writings by Radical Women of Color*, ed. Cherrie Moraga and Gloria Anzaldua (Watertown, Mass.: Persephone Press, 1981).

5. Lillian Faderman, *Surpassing the Love of Men: Love Between Women from the Renaissance to the Present* (New York: Morrow, 1981).

6. Rita Mae Brown, *Rubyfruit Jungle* (Plainfield, Vt.: Daughters 1973).

7. Radclyffe Hall, *The Well of Loneliness* (New York: Simon & Schuster, 1974). Original publication: Covici-Friede edition, 1928.

8. Lyrics from the popular song "Every Woman" by Bernice Johnson Reagon, recorded by Sweet Honey in the Rock on their album *B'lieve I'll Run On . . . See What the End's Gonna Be*, Redwood Records, Ukiah, California, 1978.

9. Elisabeth Schüssler Fiorenza, "Gather Together in My Name . . . Toward a Christian Feminist Spirituality," in *Women Moving Church*, ed. Diann Neu and Maria Riley (Washington, D.C.: Center of Concern, 1982), p. 11; reprinted as the epilogue to Elisabeth Schüssler Fiorenza's *In Memory of Her: A Feminist Theological Reconstruction of Early Christian Origins* (New York: Crossroad, 1983).

III
...

PASTORAL
PERSPECTIVES

GABRIEL MORAN

Education:
Sexual and Religious

My aim in this essay is to link contemporary discussion of homosexuality to both religious education and sex education. These two kinds of education tend to be disparate fields, often hostile to each other. I suspect that homosexuality is one of the missing links between sex education and religious education. I cannot prove that point here nor can I propose new curricula. What I would like to propose is that until the reality of homosexuality is calmly accepted throughout education, no one's education is adequately religious or healthily sexual.

Although I will say a few things about the sex education field, my primary approach is through religious education. I have worked professionally for the past quarter of a century in religious education and that is my main credential for writing this essay. I was hesitant about seeming to pretend that I am an expert on gay experience. I admit I am not an expert but that fact is not an excuse for saying nothing. Any of us who have access to public media have a duty to protest in the name of justice against the perpetuation of vicious stereotypes that surround homosexual reality.

The gay revolution seems still to be at that stage as was nineteenth-century feminism when Sarah Grimké said, "All that we ask is that you take your foot off our necks and allow us to stand upright on the ground God gave us." The calm acceptance I referred to above is not immediately available. A coolly dispassionate attitude will not clear away the destructive myths nor will it cure irrational fears. I agree with the 1963 Quaker document that said "one should no more deplore 'homosexuality' than left-handedness,"[1] but such eminently reasonable statements can shroud the mystery. The mystery I refer to is not the origin and cure of homosexuality but the origin and cure of homophobia, that is, the straight world's irrational fear of the "homosexual problem." The main audience for which I am writing is dictated by my agreement with Richard Woods: "The 'problem' of homosexuality is primarily one of *straight* liberation— liberation from the myths, stereotypical thinking and the consequent forms of discrimination that, in turn, engender defensive postures among gays."[2]

I

Sex education is a whole universe of its own with graduate degrees, professional organizations, and publishing houses. It is accompanied by controversy and resistance wherever it appears. To some people who are fighting for acceptance of the most elementary kind of sex education, talking out loud about homosexuality may seem unwise. School committees and parent groups are frightened enough by words like *masturbation* and *contraceptive*. Why bring up what is really scary to them? My answer in principle is that if we are going to have to fight for a program that educates sexually, then we may as well fight for an honest and comprehensive program.

Beyond this principle, something more has to be said about the specific topic within sex education. The resistance to a sex education establishment does not come exclusively from right wing reactionaries. To name just two examples, Bruno Bettelheim's *The Uses of Enchantment* and Neil Postman's *Teaching as a Conserving Activity*[3] have no kind words about sex education. My own resistance is linked to the peculiar combining of two nouns. Why is the concern sex education and not sexual education? The primary need as I see it is not an object called sex in the school curriculum but an examination of qualities and relationships throughout educational experience. How do father and mother interact in the home? Why are the vast majority of elementary school teachers women while college professors are usually men? What kind of affective life do teachers and students share in high schools? These are sexual questions about education not likely to show up in sex education.

The experts on sex who are determined to enlighten the rest of us can be as narrowly ideological as their right wing adversaries. A kind of nervous indoctrination creeps into many programs that are supposed to be sexually educative. Jacqueline Kasun complains that sex education programs vary from the "coyly sentimental to the grossly explicit."[4] Like politics and religion, sex does not fit comfortably in the modern school because so much of schooling consists in adults telling children what the truth is. Education in school should be but often is not an exploration into the meaning of things. The deficiency gets easily covered over in history, math, and chemistry classes. When school systems try the same thing with sex and religion they get a vocal opposition because the question of value becomes visible. The indoctrination that parents unfortunately put up with in so much of education suddenly becomes obvious in religious and sexual matters.

One reason for introducing the gay question into sex education is that it can give pause to the sex education establishment. Those who push very hard at their version of sexual enlightenment get a little nervous when homosexuality comes into the discussion. They may speak of "alternate life-styles"—one of the great banal phrases of the day—but not of the reality of lives of homosexual men and women. After all, if sex experts start "advocating" homosexuality as they have been advocating contraception, abortion, etc., people might begin to suspect they are gay. A more extensive examination of gay sexuality might help us reflect on what we mean by advocacy, instruction, and curriculum aims all through education.

My impression is that homosexuality is still the great absent topic in sex education. The word shows up but in carefully segregated treatments. I will cite only one example but a significant one. A *Festschrift* in honor of Dr. Mary Calderone, cofounder of SIECUS, was published in 1981 with the title *Sex Education in the Eighties: The Challenge of Healthy Sexual Evolution.*[5] One essay in the book on "Sex Education in Religious Settings" has two paragraphs at the end on homosexual "marriage" and ordination.[6] The entire book has four other passing references to homosexuality. I draw no sweeping conclusion from this fact. However, I do think that if there is a human race in 2081 and some group chooses the same ambitious title for a book, they will look back with amusement or astonishment at a book on sex education in the 1980s that had practically nothing to say on homosexuality.

II

When one turns from sex education to religious education, silence or condemnation would probably not surprise anyone. Actually, the picture is not that bleak. Until a dozen years ago no author would risk anything positive on the subject. Today there is some diversity. In general, Protestant denominations are fairly predictable according to where the denomination fits on the conservative to liberal spectrum. Catholic and Jewish publications have a wide split within their respective traditions. On a temporal continuum one might identify four stages. Until about 1970 there was almost total silence. With the emergence of a gay rights movement, one wing of Christianity turned vocally negative. The only difference today is that their condemnation has become more strident. A visitor from another planet listening to these preachers and reading this literature would assume that homosexuality is listed as the number one sin in the New Testament.

In the rest of Christianity much of the writing moved to a second stage. Here it is said that gays should not be badly treated or legally harassed—despite their acting contrary to God's will. A third stage that seems to have arrived in some quarters removes gay sex from the paragraph listing sexual problem. These books acknowledge that an aspect of some people's lives is their homosexual orientation. There is a fourth stage, which I find in no textbooks but which is suggested by some writers today. They would view homosexuality as a necessary corrective to present heterosexual attitudes. The human race will never understand power, love, and transcendence so long as it fails to embrace gay sexuality.

I will cite some examples that will give the flavor of my generalization about curricula. In a series of Southern Baptist books published in 1973 the word *gay* comes out into the open. The book for young adults has a chapter called "Sexual Inversion" that ends: "Gay people are the most unsure people ever. They are not really gay. They are sad, sad, sad. As one man has said, 'Show me a gay homosexual and I'll show you a gay corpse.' "[7] The book in this series for fifteen- to seventeen-year-olds is not as negative on the topic; it does say that if one is afflicted there is a cure.[8] A 1971 book from the Methodist Publishing House takes up homosexuality and the author says he does not want to add to all the nonsense written on the topic. In his own way he tries to be positive about "treating homosexuals with more dignity" and recognizing that "many live normal lives apart from their homosexual activity." He even tells students not to worry about homosexual feelings and experiences but to see a psychiatrist if they persist "before it becomes a way of life."[9]

What I have called the second stage—condemn the sin while opposing governmental persecution of the sinner—is evident in many church documents of the 1970s. A 1970 document of the United Presbyterians distinguishes homosexualism (what Saint Paul condemned) and homosexuality (a condition of personal existence). The document calls homosexuality "essentially incomplete in character." The authors favor some "enlightened legal measures" to govern public behavior and to protect children but they oppose governmental interference in the sexual lives of consenting adults.[10] Many churches began stressing the theme of "meaningful ministries to all persons as members of the 'Family of God' including those who are homosexual."[11] The compassionate attitude toward the person and the opposition to legal attacks are almost invariably followed by a sentiment of the kind: "We conclude that homosexuality is not God's wish for humanity."[12]

Jewish positions range from the condemnation of the first stage to the liberalizing attitude of the second stage and perhaps to simple acceptance in the third stage. Traditional Judaism, with its great stress on the family, has had few positive words on homosexuality. However, like liberal churches of the 1970s, some of Judaism was reexamining the issue. The General Assembly of American Hebrew Congregations in 1977 called for an end to governmental and other kinds of discrimination against gays. It also called for education "to provide greater understanding of the relation of Jewish values to the range of human sexuality." A 1979 course on human sexuality takes a straightforward approach. Among other things, it notes that the Union of American Hebrew Congregations' board in 1974 accepted a congregation that was predominantly homosexual.[13]

The most strikingly positive materials of the 1970s are from the Unitarian Universalist Association. In 1970 the General Assembly of the association called for education "with the particular aim to end all discrimination against homosexuals and bisexuals." In 1977 the UUA created an office of gay concerns staffed by gay people. The 1973 curriculum package includes such items as George Weinberg's *Society and the Healthy Homosexual* (Doubleday, 1973) and Phyllis Lyon and Del Martin's *Lesbian/Woman* (New Glide, 1972). The introductory notes to the text *About Your Sexuality* say that the intention of the material is to inquire into and change attitudes toward sexuality, including homosexuality. The syllabus has an entire booklet on *Same Sex Relationships*. Here we have decidedly moved from homosexuality as one of the problems to it being one of the possible developments within the positive context of friendship and love. The booklet states:

> The goal of this unit should be to emphasize the values of same-sex friendship, to help young people accept as natural the sexual feelings and/or overt sexual behavior which may be part of such relationships and to differentiate between exploratory same-sex experiences and a homosexual life-style in a manner which removes the guilt from the exploratory behavior but is also supportive of the homosexual life-style as a viable life pattern.[14]

I do not think that this Unitarian material is the perfect model. Many religious people would want advertence to evil, sin, and self-deception. Many gay people would find the approach too bland; the film strip in the syllabus is mild indeed. Nonetheless, as a step toward situating the question in a context of positive connotations, one can surely applaud the effort. The material implies the fourth stage named above, that is, examining homosexual love challenges the severe limits we place on the heterosexual person. The UUA syllabus suggests that we all need same-sex love in our lives and are suffocating because of the homophobic atmosphere.

III

As for the Catholic Church, you don't have to be a Catholic to know that this church puts great emphasis upon the procreative purpose of sexual activity. Only over a long period and with a change of larger pattern could the Catholic Church take a positive view of homosexuality. Nevertheless, the Catholic Church has always had more variety than outsiders assume. (John Boswell's fine book has documented that fact for the first thirteen centuries.)[15] Today the diversity may be greater than ever, and new thinking on sexual matters will continue with or without official approbation.

Catholicism has never maintained that the only vocation is marriage and family. Indeed, unlike Protestantism and Judaism, it located the word *vocation* with people who were not married. While a thorough reworking of this language must eventually occur, the solution is not simply to move the word *vocation* over to marriage. I will return below to the question of multiple religious vocations in the Church. Here I simply note that the Catholic Church has been a harbor of feminist activity and for similar reasons it may be generating considerable gay activity. A Church that does not assume that God's exclusive wish is heterosexual pairs is liable to give birth to a variety of sexual and political rebellions.

Two recent documents of the Catholic Church deserve mention here. The National Catechetical Directory has little to say about homosexuality.[16] However, when it does mention "persons with a homosexual orientation" it is to say that "the church is seriously obliged to provide catechesis suited to the special needs of these and other groups." Going one step further, the same section of the directory says: "Catechetical programs should, whenever possible, be developed in consultation with representatives of those for whom they are intended. The aim should be to help them overcome the obstacles they face and achieve as much integration as they can into the larger community of faith."[17] If that prescription is pursued it would carry Catholic catechetical practice beyond the second stage of ministering *to* the gay community into the third stage of accepting gays as people who speak for themselves. The issue of ordaining homosexual people is part of a more fundamental question of whether a church ministers not only to gay people but also by gay people. Churches will never develop adequate curriculum on the topic until gays and nongays devise curriculum together.

In 1981 the Education Department of the U.S. Catholic Conference published *Education in Human Sexuality for Christians.* The document tries to use a positive tone about all sexual education, including attitudes toward homosexuality. Like the NCD, it expresses concern for people who feel rejected by the Church, mentioning specifically divorced and homosexual people. It is most effective in talking about family life and the need to accept the child as she or he is. After noting of children ages nine to eleven that friendship is a prized possession, the text says: "This may also raise questions about homosexual feelings and acts, which the parents should discuss naturally and clearly in the context of Christian principles. It is common for persons of this age to develop an interest in the bodies of others who are of the same sex."[18]

The most interesting comment on the present topic is on page 40: "The person who is ostracized in his/her own church community because of a homosexual orientation finds little comfort that the church distinguishes between homosexual orientation and homosexual activity." One could call that a postliberal comment. The distinction of orientation/activity is a very recent one and the intent here, I presume, is not to reject it. The distinction has been helpful, for example, in interpreting biblical material. Nevertheless, a simple and complete separation of the two categories leads to new forms of intolerance. External homosexual behavior is not necessarily an expression of homosexual orientation. From the other side, however, homosexual orientation finds its natural, expected expression in homosexual behavior. Celibacy among homosexual people is presumably no more common than among heterosexual people.

Many Catholic textbooks of the present attempt to be positive about homosexuality. A 1981 book for senior high school is entitled *Lifestyles.*[18] That fashionable title might suggest a chapter on gay life. Actually only a few paragraphs are devoted to the topic. The life-styles turn out to be married, single, vowed religious, and ordained priest. After saying that most people pass in and out of a phase of homosexual desire, the text notes: "For some, however, homosexual orientation forms a more lasting part of their sexual identity." The student is assured "there is no conflict between being homosexually oriented and being a Catholic." But then the line is drawn: "Catholic teaching maintains that homosexual genital activity is morally wrong."[20]

That final sounding judgment may seem to slam the door. One could speculate, however, that this text achieves a kind of democratization. The reason why homosexual genital activity is forbidden is simply that gays are like everyone who is not married. The Catholic Church "asks its members who are homosexual in orientation to live as should the single, the widowed, the divorced, the celibate and the vowed religious." The word *celibate* in this list is redundant because all these people are required to be celibates. The interesting reversal that can occur, and which is certainly being discussed outside textbooks, is that an argument against the enforced celibacy of the divorced, widowed, and never married can be made an argument for "homosexual genital activity."

This kind of text is presumably what the USCC document means in saying gay people may find little comfort in the new solution of "praise the orientation, condemn the behavior." I do not suppose textbooks can lead the way in a rethinking of this area. In the hands of a sensitive and honest teacher more variety, openness, and flexibility can be expected. To its credit the text ends the section on that note. Nonetheless, unless a lot of statistics about "genital activity" are completely askew, the textbook treatment of heterosexual as well as homosexual activity is a long way from the world students are living in.

IV

From what has been said above and from what I think is realistically possible at this transition in history, I will now comment on family and school parts of a sexual education. I am looking to get us beyond the second stage identified above and into the third stage, where homosexuality is not a problem but a fact of ordinary life. In the last section I will comment briefly on Church vocation as one of the prerequisites to a fourth stage.

The first few years of a child's life are probably the most important years of her/his education. Strangely enough, our ways of referring to education more often than not exclude early childhood. For example, current interest in moral education is dominated by Piaget and Kohlberg. Both of these men explicitly say that moral education begins at age five or six; before that the child is premoral.[21] I think that this supposition about children invalidates their systems of moral education. A child's religious and moral attitudes are largely set in childhood. Whatever disagreement one may have with Freud, he surely demonstrated the importance of childhood for the development of our feelings, especially sexual feelings.

For about the first five years of life, education, sexual education, and religious education are the same thing. The acceptance of oneself as a bodily creature with limitless desires to know and to love is the central theme of this education. Whatever helps to make the infant bodily at home lays a foundation for both sexual and religious life.[22] Many recent studies show the importance of physical contact in infant life. The parent or another adult has to embrace, coddle, and rock the small child. The child who is held gains a sense of secure limits: there is a world beyond but is not about to destroy me; my body is a comfortable place from which to move beyond the body.[23]

Part of the confusion in educational language is our use of the word *teacher* when we mean *schoolteacher*. Although schoolteaching is important, it is a limit case of teaching. In a normal form of teaching, words are choreography; they refer to bodily movements. In schoolteaching, words refer mainly to other words. The place to examine the primary meaning of teaching is the relation of parent and child. To teach is to show someone how to do something. Parents teach all the time, most often without being aware that they are doing so. That fact should generally be encouraging to parents though it often makes them nervous.

Parents who have a positive outlook on life convey that feeling to their children. Parents need not imitate schoolteachers and give sophisticated explanations. When children begin asking questions, what they mostly want is a respect for their questioning mind and a response that makes some sense to them. Surveys still indicate that parents give little or no sex instruction to their children. While that is not the same as failing to give a sexual education, the phenomenon is nonetheless puzzling. If parents would even just acknowledge their awkwardness, the child could deal with that better than silence or evasion. I presume many parents imagine they will have a long talk when the child gets older and they discover too late that that's not the way it happens.

With a little help from counselors, schoolteachers, clergy, etc., parents might get past the first obstacles to dealing naturally with sexual matters. However, homosexuality may require specific attention. A crucial fact about homosexuality is that few parents are homosexual in orientation or if so they do not admit it. The result is that human attitudes toward homosexuality are mainly transmitted by heterosexual people or people who have to hide their homosexual orientation. The transmission of a positive attitude toward homosexuality will probably always have to contend with this situation.

The need, of course, is not to introduce infants or five-year-olds into details of gay life. The main thing is not to inculcate feelings of hatred and revulsion. It should hardly be surprising to find that many of today's parents have unconscious feelings of revulsion and anxiety. C. S. Lewis in recounting his life's story noted the presence of homosexuality among the young of his day. Lewis, no great liberal on this point, wondered why people get so exercised by homosexuality since, as he said, it is by no means the worst of sins. His explanation was that those who do not share the gay life "feel for it a certain nausea." He concluded that such feelings have little relevance to moral judgment.[24] Many people, including parents, who try to be liberal are influenced by this feeling of nausea. Getting that feeling into the open would be a big help.

On the conscious level parental fear is directed to their children being gay or to child molestation. On the first point there may be little parents can do to prevent their child being or becoming gay. In any case, instilling fear of gay people is not an effective tactic for that purpose. Parents need to be provided with this information. The molesting of children is indeed grounds for fear but the problem is mainly a heterosexual one. Child molesters show up in about the same percentage among gay people as straight. That means about 90 percent of child molesters are heterosexual.

With the homophobia in our culture such statistics alone will not be persuasive. Face-to-face conversations with counselors and, if possible, gay people is the way to allay parental fears. Statements in Church documents are fine but they will not get us very far if this prior question is not faced. "The church cannot move on this issue unless it is able to deal with the feelings and fears straight people have about their children in relation to gays."[25]

V

When the child reaches reflective self-consciousness and starts school, education necessarily develops a split. On one side religious education needs to take on the more specific form of a Christian (or Jewish) education. Children should be instructed in their religion and the religion of their forebears. On the sexual side children need instruction in factual matters of sex. Some temporary separation between Christian doctrines and basic sex information is helpful. Many Christian people protest such a separation, but I think it is useful for a while so that children can attend to some biological and psychological facts. The school can, without reducing sex to function and technique, helpfully demystify the whole area.

Getting some straightforward facts extends to a Christian form of religious education on the subject at issue that would include knowledge of what the Bible actually says about homosexuality. The fact is it says very little. In junior high school one cannot go into contemporary exegesis of Genesis, Leviticus, and Romans. Nevertheless, schoolteachers ought to be familiar with such material so that they do not convey the impression that the Bible is particularly concerned with condemning homosexuality. When students get to be older they can get some of the detail for themselves. If they can read the Gospels with clear eyes, they will find, as Boswell says, that Jesus "said nothing which bore any relation to homosexuality. The only sexual issue of importance to Jesus appears to have been fidelity."[26]

Many adults seem to hold the view that if children in school receive more and better sex information, the knowledge will lead to increased sexual activity. One cannot prove that such a thing never happens, but the general pattern is overwhelmingly the opposite. The children who engage in sex most promiscuously are the least knowledgeable in correct sexual information. Interviews with pregnant teenagers provide documentaries of this fact.

As for homosexuality, what can and should be done in school is to name it. Some people who are homosexually oriented apparently know that fact from early in life. What they have to hear repeatedly said aloud is: they are not sick, they are not crazy, they are not alone. They need to feel free enough to express their feelings to trusted adults. Most children go through a phase of desires and activities that are, broadly speaking, homosexual. While it is undoubtedly helpful to tell children of this age that "you are probably going through a phase," the word *probably* should never be omitted. A child who has been told that it is only a phase will have his/her anxieties deepened if the phase does not end.

This counseling issue leads me to the one obvious change needed in schools, namely, the presence of teachers and counselors who are openly gay. No curriculum reform can ever substitute for this one simple change. The homosexually oriented student needs a person to identify with; the family, as I have indicated, is deficient here. Quoting a schoolteacher, Jack Babuscio writes: "Many students grow up believing that none of the people they know are homosexual. They gay image is supplied by television comedians or the uninformed and often malicious gossip of the streets. . . . A teacher who is openly gay could therefore play a very positive role in the school."[27]

"Openly gay" is liable to connote to some people a public display of one's private sex life. That is not what is meant. The basic question is the right of the teacher to admit who he/she is. In most circumstances one is not interested in hearing the details of somebody else's sex life. Neither heterosexual nor homosexual sex in one's personal life is regular fare for the classroom. From the other side, however, any good teacher draws upon personal attitudes, friendships, and commitments. One should be able to make casual references to whom one lives with or whom one loves. A gay schoolteacher who lives in fear of being discovered is unduly limited in offering any kind of role model to students.

Schoolteaching is just that point where antigay forces gather their heaviest weaponry. Many parents are drawn into the opposition by the apocalyptic rhetoric in the area. I imagine antigays are right in their suspicions that tens of thousands of schoolteachers are gay and many of them have a great influence on the young. That influence does not extend to transforming heterosexual students into gay ones. If many teachers were openly gay, the number of known homosexual students would probably rise. That situation merely indicates how many people are hiding the facts. Reactionaries seem to have so little security in their own heterosexuality that they think in an open society millions of people would "convert" to homosexuality. I know of no evidence to support this belief.

VI

This last section is toward the future and the change of social forms that must precede a full change in attitude toward homosexuality. Ultimately, the issue is not homosexual orientation and homosexual behavior so much as homophile relations and gay (sub)culture. So much of the irrational homophobia springs from a fear that homosexual love threatens marriage and community. Given the sterility of much of today's communal and familial forms, the fears have a basis. Attacking homosexual life is a case of killing the messenger. What we should be doing is trying to reconstruct community forms in Church and secular society. If we did that, homosexual love would be seen as an ally to the family. A change of institutions may take generations; however, we can begin naming things better right now.

As a start, we can and should stop using the word *homosexual* as a noun. This clumsily contrived term of the nineteenth century helped to create the idea that some people belong to a stereotype called "the homosexual." In this essay I have used the word as an adjective, and even this with reluctance. I have tried to indicate that a characteristic of a diverse part of the population is a primary orientation to same-sex love. The key concern ought to be with the word *love* rather than a search for an explanation of "the homosexual." With the simple removal from usage of the noun *homosexual,* it becomes nearly impossible to offer up the myths, half-truths, and pseudoscience that abound in this area. Talking about homosexual people and homophile relations forces one to look at reality.

An example of further change of language is the Church's—especially the Roman Catholic Church's—use of community and religious community. I will not repeat here what I have written in other places about the naming of community forms.[28] Suffice it to say that homosexuality is an unavoidable part of the question. We need a clearly delineated familial form of community and we need several other nonfamilial forms of community. A person ought to be able to work out a Christian vocation in one or several of these religious communities.

My proposal refers to changes going on in contemporary society, for example, in the lengthening of life, the control of births, and the shift in the position of women. My proposal is also rooted in the early Christian Church. Stanley Hauerwas says that the early Church had two vocations that were complementary. One was the special vocation to the family; the other vocation he calls singleness, a commitment to the Church community in relation to endtime.[29] Hauerwas's language of parenthood/singleness is a big improvement over married/celibate, but it is not sufficiently descriptive of relations and communities. The contemporary Church has to spell out several communal forms, one of which is homophile relations. The main point of Christian vocation is not sexual behavior but personal commitment and loving service.

To clarify my suggestions, I will contrast them to a position that may sound similar to some people. Ronald Mazur in his book *The New Intimacy* proposes openness and variety in sexual life.[30] Mazur claims to have invented the category of "lifestyles." Even if he did not invent it, his usage reveals the dangerous softness in that term. Mazur proclaims that the human race has entered a new era in which there are thirteen forms of intimacy, and with a homosexual flip the ways of being intimate jump to twenty-six. Other people are passing instruments for one's individual pleasure and sexual liberation. I do not think any of what he describes deserves the name of familial or communal. Neither permanence nor children are highly valued in this kind of writing.

The language of "alternate life-styles" has crept into many Church documents. For the sake of clarity, commitment, and community I think the language should be resisted. Human beings are not infinitely malleable and they are not free of self-deception. Men, and more especially women, are not going to find liberation by having twenty-six ways of bed hopping. I am advocating the full emergence of homophile relations on conservative grounds, namely, that human love would become more stable and permanent. I have no sympathy with supposed liberation that is pressured by television marketing and is oblivious to the human problems of possessiveness and greed.

Familial love and homophile love are partners in conserving the ideals of community and vocation. When we get to open recognition of that partnership the need for exclusively gay communities will decrease.

Church groups like Dignity, Integrity, and Affirmation have been clear from the start. They are not attempts to start a homosexual Church but to provide temporary shelter in a Church and society not yet ready to face the issue. Such groups are indispensable right now. James Nelson, quoting a gay person, writes: "Usually for most gay women and men, coming out *in* the church has meant coming out *of* the church." For those who don't, "the church has meant more than just a closet . . . the church has become for them a giant tomb."[31]

An important educational function of these groups is to show that "coming out of the closet" is a crude metaphor whose useful days may be numbered. People in these support groups learn that there aren't "homosexuals" in and out of closets. There are human beings who reveal who they are in different ways to different people. One need not always be on display as an alternative to hiding in a closet. These gay groups, with their self-conscious attention to suffering members, can turn narrowly narcissistic. At their best, however, they, like feminist groups, bring a new meaning of power to political life and Church life. Such groups need the larger Church, but in turn the larger Church is in desperate need of their invigoration.

I presume no romantic vision of gays as the only healthy people. Like other oppressed minorities, gay experience suffers from the distortion that oppression causes. By the same token, individuals who survive the ordeal are probably healthier than the average straight person. That is not really the point. The Church, along with the secular world, has lived with deformed notions of sexuality. We today are not faced with taking the first steps toward sexual reform, nor can we take the last. Our humble task is to name the reality more clearly than has the past and begin cultivating the social forms which the future will need.

NOTES

1. Alastair Heron, ed., *Toward a Quaker View of Sex* (London: Friends Home Service Committee, 1963), p. 21.
2. Richard Woods, *Another Kind of Love* (Garden City, N.Y.: Doubleday, Image, 1978), p. 60.
3. New York: Knopf, 1976; New York: Delacorte, 1979.
4. Jacqueline Kasun, "Turning Children Into Sex Experts," *The Public Interest*, no. 55 (Spring 1979), p. 4.
5. Lorna Brown, ed., *Sex Education in the Eighties* (New York: Plenum Press, 1981).
6. Ibid., p. 134.
7. John Drakeford, *Made for Each Other* (Nashville: Broadman, 1973), p. 142.
8. Andrew Lester, *Sex is More than a Word* (Nashville: Broadman, 1973), pp. 83–89.

9. Ellis Johnson, *Youth Views Sexuality* (Nashville: Methodist Publishing House, 1971), pp. 78–80.

10. *Sexuality and the Human Community* (Philadelphia: United Presbyterian Church in the U.S.A., 1970), pp. 18–20.

11. American Baptist Church in *A Synoptic of Recent Denominational Statements on Sexuality*, 2d ed. (New York: National Council of Churches, 1975).

12. *Homosexuality and the Church: A Position Paper* (Atlanta: Presbyterian Church of the United States, 1979), p. 5.

13. Annette Daum and Barbara Strongin, *Course on Human Sexuality* (New York: Federation of Reform Synagogues, 1979), Session II, pp. 4–5.

14. Deryck Calderwood, *About Your Sexuality*, rev. ed. (New York: Unitarian Universalist Association, 1973).

15. John Boswell, *Christianity, Social Tolerance and Homosexuality*, (Chicago: University of Chicago Press, 1980).

16. *Sharing the Light of Faith: National Catechetical Directory for Catholics of the United States* (Washington, D.C.: USCC, 1979).

17. Ibid., par. 196.

18. *Education in Human Sexuality for Christians* (Washington, D.C.: USCC, 1981), p. 29.

19. Eugene Tozzi and Suellen Koelsch Tozzi, *Lifestyles* (New York: Sadlier, 1981).

20. Ibid., pp. 54–55.

21. Jean Piaget, *The Moral Judgment of the Child* (New York: Macmillan, Collier, 1962); Lawrence Kohlberg, *The Philosophy of Moral Development: Essays in Moral Development,* vol. 1 (San Francisco: Harper & Row, 1981).

22. William McCready and Nancy McCready, "Socialization and the Persistence of Religion," in *The Persistence of Religion,* ed. Andrew Greeley and Gregory Baum (New York, Herder and Herder, 1973), pp. 58–68.

23. For a summary of the research, see Rudolph Schafer, *Mothering* (Cambridge: Harvard University Press, 1977).

24. C. S. Lewis, *Surprised By Joy* (New York: Harcourt, Brace and World, 1955), pp. 108–9.

25. Peggy Way, "Homosexual Counseling as a Learning Ministry," *Christianity and Crisis,* 30 May 1979, p. 125.

26. Boswell, op. cit., p. 115.

27. Jack Babuscio, *We Speak for Ourselves: Experiences in Homosexual Counseling* (Philadelphia: Fortress, 1977), p. 107.

28. For example, *Religious Body* (New York: Seabury, 1974), chapter 4; *Education Toward Adulthood* (New York: Paulist Press, 1979), chapter 5.

29. Stanley Hauerwas, *A Community of Character* (Notre Dame: University of Notre Dame, 1981), chapter 10.

30. Ronald Mazur, *The New Intimacy* (Boston: Beacon Press, 1973).

31. James Nelson, *Embodiment* (Minneapolis: Augsburg, 1978), p. 209.

JAMES D. WHITEHEAD

and EVELYN EATON WHITEHEAD

Three Passages of Maturity

Journey and Passage

A major metaphor of Christian life, vigorously reclaimed since Vatican II, is that of journey. More than a figment of romantic imagination, this image captures our sense of being on the way and of being accompanied and guided by Someone.

Journey, as a metaphor of religious living, suggests the necessary mobility and peril, the discoveries and losses that pattern our Christian lives. As a people, our religious travels began with Abraham leaving home. This image of journey has been even more strongly imprinted on our souls since the Exodus—that generation of desert travel during which it began to be revealed where we were going and with whom. The Israelite experience of journey—in the Exodus, Exile, and Diaspora—was echoed in Jesus' itinerant movement: "When Jesus had finished instructing his twelve disciples he moved on from there to teach and preach in their towns" (Mt 11:1). Christian history, like that of the Jews, is patterned by a deep ambivalence. A desire to settle down, sink roots, establish a stable life is experienced over against the need to move on, following a Revelation with endless surprises and turns. The metaphors of Christian life display this ambivalence: "pilgrimage" is countered by Augustine's image of a "City of God," a stable, well-boundaried municipality. An awareness of the continuing journey of the "people of God" exists alongside the sturdier conviction that "a mighty fortress is our God." We yearn for a secure, well-defended place to be with each other and with God. But each construction site ("Let us build three tents here"—Lk 9:33) tends to become in time an archaeological site—a place where God once had been. We Christians are settlers and builders, but our fidelity is pledged, since Abraham and Moses, to a mobile God whose revelations require uprooting and repeated departures.

If we Christians recognize our lives as journeys, we also believe them to be excursions with a direction and purpose. But what is this direction? Where are we going? The metaphor of journey contains another image which reveals something about the direction and the dynamic of our movement as a people. This is the image of passage. Since this notion was reintroduced by the Dutch anthropologist Arnold Van Gennep at the beginning of this century, Christian scholars have been exploring the passages which pattern modern religious maturing.[1] Apart from the classic passages of birth, adult initiation, marriage, and death, other perilous transitions appear in our lives. Each of these passages, as a critical period of opportunity and danger, shapes the direction of our life journey.

In this essay we will examine three passages that homosexual Christians may face in the movement of their lives. Before doing that, it may be helpful to examine the peculiar dynamic of a passage by recalling two transitions common in adult life: the death of a parent and the establishment of a deep friendship. The central paradox of a passage is always loss and gain: it is a time of peril and possibility. During a passage we become vulnerable to both personal loss and unexpected grace. In the death of a parent we lose our beginnings and our security. That buffer between us and the world, that guarantor of meaning and security (which we may have experienced as often in conflict as in affection) is taken from us. We are, at last, orphaned. Stripped gradually or suddenly of this important person—this part of myself—I may well become disoriented, alone on my life journey in a new and frightening way.

In the very different experience of a beginning friendship, a similar dynamic is at play: amid the excitment and enthusiasm of a deepening relationship we may feel a growing threat. If I admit this person into my heart, I will have to change. This is not because I am selfish or shallow, but simply because my heart will have a new occupant. Most threatened, perhaps, is my sense of independence: to allow you into my life I will have to let go of some of how I have been until now. Some part of who— and how—I have been will have to be let go if this new friendship and love is to grow. Naturally, then, I may hesitate. I may step back and choose not to undergo the threat of this passage of intimacy. In the face of the threat of a passage, then, we may resist. Our parent's death we cannot prevent, though we can deny its happening and refuse the passage that it instigates. And we can refuse the passage of friendship, feeling the risk to be too severe.

A passage begins, then, in disorientation and the threat of loss. It matures into a second stage as we allow ourselves to fully experience and to name this loss. This middle part of a passage may endure for several months or even a year or more. In the reluctant, gradual letting go of a parent or the slow, gingerly admittance of a friend, we are losing ourselves and finding ourselves. But the terror of a passage appears in this in-between time: How do I know I can survive without the security and dependability of my parent (even an antagonistic parent)? How can I be sure that this growing friendship will be better than my well-defended independence? In the disorientation and darkness of a passage, I cannot see the other side. I cannot be sure, cannot control, where this journey leads.

The imagery of passage being used here is that favored by anthropologist Victor Turner and others: passage as a narrow, dark subterranean journey. It is something that we "under go"; Turner speaks of it as "cunicular" or tunnellike. In exercises of guided fantasy, people often picture their life transitions in a very different fashion: a passage as an oceangoing voyage, as a leaving home and a setting out into uncharted waters. While this imagery of voyage includes the peril and unknown of the tunnel, it is strikingly different in its sense of openness, fresh air, and adventure. The nature of a specific crisis may dispose us toward certain imagery. The death of a child is likely to be experienced as a dark passage, a "valley of death" that must be gone through. A career change may be experienced as a frightening but exciting launching out into unknown waters. Both "passages" include leaving the familiar, traveling for a time while uncertain about the destination, and—for the Christian—expecting to meet God along the way.

The peculiar dynamic of a passage becomes clear in this movement of loss and discovery. Psychologically, we grow by letting go of parts of ourselves no longer necessary for our journey; we are purified of parts of ourselves that do not fit the future. The reliance on parents, once so necessary, and the personal independence we develop in young adulthood must both eventually be let go of if we are to grow into the authority of our own adult lives and into mature intimacy. But the reordering of our life that a passage promotes is also a disordering. The British anthropologist Mary Douglas writes about the "potency of disorder." And this potency is not only psychological, but religious. This time of vulnerability and loss is also a time of potential grace. In the threat and even chaos of a life passage, we experience the opportunity for extraordinary growth. We find unsuspected strengths; we are startled by our ability to risk and to trust. And often it is only with hindsight that we identify the gracefulness of a time of passage. From that threat and loss, we emerged not just different—and wounded—but stronger. In the darkness of that passage (or in the uncharted waters of our voyage) we found a new direction to or confidence in our life.

This experience of the grace of a passage illumines its third stage: emergence and reincorporation into the community. In the course of a passage we are likely to feel ourselves removed from the community. The disorientation makes us feel different; we withdraw and want to be left alone. Only gradually do we come to a renewed sense of ourselves—as able to go on without a loved one, or as able to sustain the strains and excitement of intimacy. This renewal and reordering invites us out of the passage, bringing us back to the community, changed and matured. Traditionally, rites of passage have celebrated this newness—the adolescent is now an adult; these two individuals are a new community in marriage.

Some human passages we anticipate and celebrate more easily in rites and rituals. Other passages are less expected and may remain hidden and disguised. When unexpected and hidden, a transition may be deprived of the rites of passage which identify and celebrate this movement. The three passages of homosexual maturing are of this type.

As we explore these passages further below, we will examine how the Church might more gracefully structure rites of passage to facilitate these challenging life transitions. Whatever the passage, both human wisdom and Christian conviction tell us these transitions are not to be navigated alone. A central function of a believing community is to protect and guide its members through these harrowing and graceful periods.

Three Passages of Maturing

A major challenge of any crisis or passage is to be able to imagine it. We search for metaphors and images which can give shape and direction to the confusing movements of our heart. We have already available to us an image of perilous transition for maturing homosexuals: coming out of the closet. This movement shares many characteristics of a traditional passage. Before examining how coming out may entail three different movements, we might recall the origin of this transition.

The closet is the starting point for the passage of coming out. This space shares many features of a womb: protective and dark, it is an excellent hiding place. It is at once secure and confining. Both womb and closet are important developmental havens meant to be outgrown. But to venture out of such secure confinement is to initiate a dangerous and exciting lifelong journey.

The psychological and religious development of the gay and lesbian adult may invite three different passages, from three distinct closets. In examining the features of these transitions, we may find clues to the rites of passage through which the Christian community will minister more effectively to maturing homosexuals.

1. An Interior Passage

This first passage is more like a revolution and conversion. A lesbian Christian, gradually or suddenly, comes to understand and embrace herself for who she is. This is a passage from the closet of ignorance or denial to the light of self-acceptance. After perhaps years of avoiding the inner movements of affection and attraction, I feel myself invited to let go the charade I have been playing with myself, and to accept and befriend my own sexual identity. This is a passage of identity and vocation—coming to admit and love who I am and who I am being called to be.

This passage will, expectably, be terrifying for many adults. Our culture and our Church have reinforced the self-denial that keeps gay persons in the dark, even to themselves. To listen to and to own the movements of affection in my heart places me in great jeopardy. Here we see again the peculiar paradox of a passage: I am invited to let go of some cherished or accustomed part of myself, but will I survive the loss? If I admit to myself the direction of my desires do I enter a passage or a dead end? In the midst of this passage—the only route to the maturing of my adult identity and vocation—I know the doubts experienced by our religious ancestors in the Sinai Desert. Nostalgia for the security of my former life (even if it was slavery) struggles against an insistence toward an insecure freedom of a new life.

This interior passage is a movement to self-intimacy. I am invited to acknowledge and embrace the person I am, with the enduring affections, desires, and feelings which constitute my self. This passage is interior in two senses: it takes place *within* the individual (though often spurred or threatened by social events) and it can take place apart from questions of interpersonal expressions of affection and commitment. Whatever decisions I will come to concerning the expression of my affection, I am invited in this first passage to befriend myself as *this* homosexual person created and loved by God.

This first passage differs from the later transitions in its foundational and nonnegotiable aspects. All of our adult love and work hinge on the self-knowledge and self-intimacy released in this passage. Those Christians who over many years find themselves to be predominantly and enduringly homosexual must come to accept and love this important part of themselves. To refuse this passage, to turn back because of the terror of this transition, is to choose a self-denial of a most un-Christian form. To deny the existence and goodness of my affections and of my affective orientation must necessarily twist my adult efforts of love and work, and thus must diminish my vocation.

This statement may seem too strong. Do we humans not survive with all kinds of strange strategies and compromises? The force of our insistence here is on the *interior* aspect of this passage: religious maturity means nothing if it does not include self-awareness and self-intimacy, a loving if mellow embracing of this person I am finding myself to be. In the closet of self-rejection we can be obedient children, fulfilling every Church law, but we cannot become adult believers.

If this passage is so crucial, what about its timing and its possible failures? Both psychological research and pastoral experience suggest that this passage of identity is for many Christians a delayed passage. Kimmel[2] suggests that a self-identification as homosexual often occurs in one's early twenties; pastoral experience might adjust this timing for many Catholics into their middle or late twenties.

This delay in coming to a (somewhat) clear self-recognition as homosexual has both positive and problematic features. Problems can arise for young gay and lesbian Christians making life choices before they have negotiated this passage of sexual identity. The timing of this passage—and for some it is delayed until their thirties or even later—does not necessarily precipitate disaster, but it does mean that some important life experiences and commitments will demand later reappraisal and reintegration in light of this delayed passage.

But this delay may also have positive aspects. A danger for the adolescent or young adult, noted by many psychologists and counselors, is that of identity foreclosure: several homosexual experiences in the middle or late teens may convince a young person whose sexual identity is still fluid and in formation that he or she is constitutionally homosexual. Such a person may move into an explicitly gay life-style, prematurely closing off or "foreclosing" an identity that is, in fact, still unclear and developing. The accumulated experience required to recognize and to begin to accept my sexual identity as predominantly and enduringly homosexual usually requires some years of adult living. Daniel Levinson's research into patterns of early adult development, circumscribed though his study is, suggests convincingly that many people today require most of the decade of their twenties to come to a sense of their adult identity. Increasingly, religious counselors are inviting young Catholics to take the time required to come to a firm sense of their sexual identity. The timing of this movement of identity is crucial but varies greatly. Some must confront this initial passage in their late teens, others not until a decade or more later. And this timing can be frustrated by both foreclosure (judging prematurely that I am gay or straight) and denial (refusing to accept the accumulating experience which reveals me to myself).

The notion of timing brings us to the question of rites of passage, reminding us that such an event is a potentially sacred time. This time of self-examination and loss is also a period of opportunity and grace. Here, in the recognition of this passage as graceful, the Church's ministry to homosexual maturing begins. So frightened have we been of the homosexual members of our mystical body that we have ignored the graces that have accompanied the quiet interior passage to self-acceptance of so many homosexual Christians. In the place of rites of passage we have isolated our ministry in the private, often hidden, caring that was given in such closetlike settings as the confessional. A complication here is that "rites of passage" are generally public events in which we acknowledge, invoke, and celebrate the action of God's grace, while this first passage as we have been considering it is essentially interior and individual. How shall we protect its privacy without rendering it secretive? We do make this passage public when we sponsor community discussions of homosexual maturing; we give this crisis visibility when we recognize it as one of the patterned modes of grace and maturity within the Christian community. This book itself is a kind of rite in which this first interior passage and other graceful events in the lives of our lesbian and gay members are brought to light and celebrated. Public discussions of the patterns of homosexual religious maturing are rites that "routinize" gay Christian life—making it less exceptional or even "bizarre" and more a variant route among the many journeys we undertake with and toward God.

Finally, the recognition of this passage as a crucial period of grace in young-adult life has a developmental value. When we negotiate a crisis successfully we not only survive, we grow stronger. We are strengthened for the journey and its subsequent challenges. Psychologically speaking, our growth in our sense of identity strengthens us to love well and work effectively. Religiously speaking, our graceful embrace of our identity becomes the strength of our vocation as we come to know and love who we are and who we are being called to be. This confidence in our religious identity, our vocation, supports all our subsequent efforts of Christian intimacy and our life work.

2. A Passage of Intimacy

A second passage appears in the life journey of homosexuals when they experience an invitation or challenge to share themselves with others. In the interior passage I am being invited to a deeper acceptance and love of *myself*; in this second passage I am being led to a mode of presence with *others* where I am known for who I am. These passages may occur at the same time, yet we can distinguish these two different challenges: in the one, self-acceptance, and in the other, the need and desire to be known and loved for who I am. The danger and ambiguity of this second passage appears in the conflict between a growing desire to share myself and the apprehension that such sharing might mean rejection and humiliation. As the desire to share myself grows, the question arises—with whom will I do this sharing? Dare I tell my friend of many years this secret, vulnerable part of who I am? A woman religious wonders whether to share this part of her heart with her spiritual director. A gay priest wants to share his sexual identity with other priests in his support group but hesitates to do so. A young adult would like to share this part of herself with her family.

In the traversing of this passage I gradually let go of the safety of not being known, the security of sexual anonymity. Strengthened by a growing comfort with myself (the fruit of the first passage), I am encouraged to depart from this protective anonymity and enter the risk, and excitement, of being known as I am. I am invited out of a second closet.

The timing of this passage merits special scrutiny. For many gay and lesbian Christians the first tentative steps of social intimacy (as distinguished from self-intimacy) happen in the middle or late twenties. The delay of this passage of intimacy, like that of the first passage, has both problematic and positive features. One problematic aspect is the accumulated experience of *not* being known by my closest friends and colleagues. This history of sexual anonymity, as it grows, may make it more difficult to "come out" in any interpersonal way. A positive aspect of this delay is that it may allow for a steadily increasing comfort with and love of myself. This returns us to the interrelationship of these two passages. We learn about our loveliness, whatever our sexual inclinations, by being loved. It is most often others who first announce to us the surprising news of our goodness and attractiveness. Yet our adult ability to love well— that is, to share our lives and bodies in honest and nonmanipulative ways—rests on an enduring confidence in our own loveliness. Convincing myself that God loves me when I do not love myself is a most difficult task. The lessons of my loveliness, learned from others and from God, must take root in me as a dependable conviction: this is the meaning of virtue.

A commonplace in both gay and straight experience is the plunge into the second passage of interpersonal intimacy without first traversing the interior passage of self-acceptance. We announce ourselves, uncover ourselves to others in the hope that if they love us, we may be brought to accept ourselves. Often such efforts arise from a too powerful dependence on others and a deep distrust of ourselves. The busy, if not frenzied, activity of the narcissistic person parodies this second passage: revealing myself to others again and again I hope to learn who I am. Having sidestepped the earlier passage, and lacking its fruit of a confidence in and comfort with oneself, the narcissistic person deals in facile self-revelation and instant intimacy. But this activity of self-disclosure and sharing, which at first appears to be the work of this second passage, never takes hold. The fruit of this passage—a sustained and enduring relationship—never occurs, because such persons do not love themselves.

We have described this passage as one of intimacy. By this we mean the psychological and religious resources which allow us to sustain the ambiguities, excitement, and strain of being up close to others. A passage of intimacy is a period for both testing and developing these strengths. This passage is necessary for so many homosexuals today precisely because it is so difficult to continually come up close in friendship and work while keeping this important part of oneself closeted. These strengths of intimacy, tested and released in this passage, rescue us from a too intense privacy. Decisions about sexual and genital expressions of intimacy are separable from this movement of intimacy; whether Christian adults choose a celibate or a sexually active life-style, they must face this passage. In this deepest sense of the word, intimacy is not optional.

If the timing of this passage and its relationship to the prior passage are important, so is the context in which it occurs. "Context" returns us to the question of rites of passage. What environments support or endanger this passage? Can we imagine rites by which our Church might more gracefully minister to this expectable crisis or passage in the life journey of its members?

This passage happens for some Catholics in the context of spiritual direction. As this context itself continues to be transformed (from a sin-oriented exchange between priest and "penitent" to a development-oriented exchange between the adult Christian and a religious guide), this sharing of one's homosexual identity occurs in a more supportive environment. The growth of Dignity, Integrity, and similar organizations within Christian denominations over the past decade has offered an explicitly religious context in which gay and lesbian Christians can meet others. The increase of retreats available for homosexual Christians adds another social context for this passage of psychological and religious intimacy. Since this second passage remains a somewhat private movement, the sharing of one's sexual identity with close friends or special intimates, the rites of passage will expectably take place at this level of supportive contexts, rather than in the more public settings implied in the more traditional use of this term.

We can come to a greater clarity about the subtle but crucial effects of rites of passage by reflecting on their dual purpose: to protect and to predict. Rites represent the community's concern to protect individuals at critical periods of life. Thus the rite of baptism protects the new Christian at the critical point of dying to a former way of life and being born to a Christian style of life. The rites of puberty in many social groups are intended to protect the young person in the dangerous transition toward

adult responsibility. Through organizations such as Dignity, through retreats and other support groups, the believing community protects gay
and lesbian Catholics who are struggling to let themselves be known and
to develop a style of intimacy at once homosexual and Christian. These
rites protect individuals from the culture's scorn and they protect them
from isolation, from having to experience this transition alone and in
private.

As rites of passage protect, they also predict. They help the individual
focus on the challenge being faced, and announce that the person will
survive. Here the accumulated wisdom of the community ministers to an
individual's experience: "This passage which you experience as unique
and special has happened before. God is at work here." The community's
care and attention tell us we will come through. The community witnesses to what God is about in such passages. God is stripping us of a
once necessary anonymity and calling us to share ourselves with some
others. In its rites a community encourages us to let go and to trust this
process of purification and growth. This contribution of the community is
crucial because our individual experiences are so limited. If I let go part of
myself—such as the security of being unknown—how can I trust that
this will lead to a better, more mature way of living? This is a question
that my community is able to, or should be able to, answer. Over the past
three thousand years and more, we have learned the patterns of God's
action: life from death, gain from loss, grace from crisis. An ungraceful
part of our recent religious history has been the community's denial of
homosexual maturing. With such a denial, the believing community for-
feits its role of protecting and predicting this pattern of religious growth.
Thus has homosexual Christian maturity remained closeted, hidden.
Thus "darkened," it could not perform its generative function: to witness
to the next generation the shape, both its perils and its graces, of this
Christian journey. This brings us to the third passage.

3. A Public Passage

For some gay and lesbian Christians a third passage appears in their life
journey. This is the transition into being recognized as homosexual and
Christian in the public world. This public passage is religious when it
includes coming out as homosexual *and Christian*. While the interior
passage cannot be ignored, this public passage need not be undertaken by
all homosexual Christians. There are perils that attend the public acknowledgment of oneself as gay. Recriminations from society and from
our Church still make it unadvisable for many homosexuals to be publicly known as such. Most Christians who have matured through the first
passage of self-acceptance and have risked the second passage of intimacy

with a few others continue to grow in the ways of Christ without coming out publicly. But for some, this third passage demands attention.

What are the possible motives inclining one to make this passage? One obvious motive is an exhibitionistic one: a compulsive desire to be seen and recognized. While exhibitionism is not a motive reserved for gay life, what often lingers in the public mind is the outrageous costumes and intentionally shocking display of some gay-rights demonstrations. And although judgments about the political usefulness of these demonstrations differ, one disservice of such display is to distract public view from others who bear more realistic and less ostentatious witness to the gay life-style.

A very different motive may impel other gays and lesbians whose public actions, whether in settings of work or politics or community discussion, disclose their sexual identity. At the other pole of the motivational continuum from exhibitionism is the motive of generativitiy. By this word, borrowed from Erik Erikson, we mean the impulse, often released especially at mid-life, to care for and contribute to the next generation. The most common example of this dynamic and its strength is, of course, parenting. From our twenties through our fifties we are especially concerned, as parents, with providing a livable future for our children. As this strength matures into a virtue, we come to care not only for "our own" but for the children of the world.

But this human instinct and Christian virtue is not biologically bound. The maturing of the celibate and unmarried Christian invites attention to this same impulse. And so this virtuous instinct will lead some lesbian and gay Christians to come out publicly. In so doing, their life and vocation become a public witness of homosexual and Christian maturing and a gift to the next generation. Such a life provides for both homosexual and heterosexual Christians an image of what it is to mature as Catholic and gay. Such a witness is generative since it provides a publicly observable model of homosexual Christian life. This is not a model in a legal or normative sense—"this is how lesbian or gay Christians *must* act"—it is a model in a more heuristic sense. Where there was once a void ("do *you* know any gay Catholics?"), patterns of Christian homosexual maturing begin to appear. It is possible! It becomes publicly imaginable to be both homosexual and a mature Christian. Many believers have known this for some time, but it was information not publicly available; it was not part of the Church's social imagination. Closeted lives, however holy, cannot provide images and models of religious maturing. A certain public exposure and light is required for this virtue of generativity to have its effect.

Some Catholics will feel called to make this third passage of maturity.

The very real dangers of this transition require an extraordinary personal resilience developed in the previous passages. Again, timing is crucial, as a negative example may best illustrate. A young homosexual may, after some years of denying his sexual identity, suddenly burst out of this repression. Attempting all three passages simultaneously, he joins several gay groups, declaring his identity to anyone who will listen. In a single, emphatic coming out he pursues the tasks of three passages: public witness, interpersonal intimacy, self-acceptance. In his public self-disclosure, he is hoping to be accepted—by society, by his family and friends, and by himself. The special challenge of this third passage argues that we enter it only when strengthened by the awareness and support gained over the years that are usually involved in making the earlier passages.

How can a person decide about this third passage? How do I know if I am being called to this more public transition? In the first, interior, passage it is the strength and virtue of my vocation that is released: I come to accept and love this particular person who I am and the life journey which is my own. During the months or years of this passage I come to a greater confidence in what God is about in my life. During the second passage another virtue is treated, Christian intimacy. I learn gradually to risk myself in coming close to others and I begin to construct the style of intimacy and interpersonal commitment that fits my vocation. These virtues of vocation and intimacy will be crucial to see the Christian through the public passage of coming out. One cannot enter this passage simply because it is "the thing to do" or because others have made it. A Christian enters it because she is invited to do so, because he senses himself so called. Many Christians are not asked to make this public passage. Others, because of the particular circumstances and special graces of their lives, will be invited, lured, goaded into this passage. What rites of passage can the believing community provide to assist this transition?

The rites for this public passage will also be of a contextual nature, rather than more specific public rituals. Few of us at this point in the life of the Church can imagine a ritual celebration at a parish coming-out party. A rite that is beginning to appear, however, is the establishment of parish and diocesan committees for ministry to and with homosexual Catholics. Such a structural event is a rite in that it publicly announces (and so, to some extent, authorizes) the existence of these members of the believing community. An example of such a rite was the recent establishment in the Archdiocese of Baltimore of a task force concerned with ministry to lesbian and gay Catholics. The report of this official task force, which received national attention,[3] "made public" the gay and lesbian members of the Catholic community. In so doing, it begins the process of protecting and predicting this public passage. Practically, it becomes more possible now for gay and lesbian Catholics to serve, publicly, on this task force. In acknowledging the existence of and then creating public space for homosexual Catholics to stand in the community, the Church facilitates this third, public passage. In doing this the Church senses, though not without some anxiety and self-doubt, that it is these maturing gay and lesbian Christians who will witness to believers the shape of homosexual holiness.

Conclusion: Passages and Exits

The journey of Christian maturing is patterned with many different passages. We are a people in movement, pledged to and in pursuit of a not always discernible God. Movement and change, then, are of the essence of religious growth. Grace (hints of God's presence and pleasure) breaks into our lives in periods of crisis and loss. In the passages into marriage, at the death of a loved one, approaching retirement, or in coming out, we are stripped of some previously important part of ourselves. Forced to let go of what once seemed so essential, we discover new parts of ourselves. We stumble onto strengths, resources we had not suspected. We are invited to leave home again and again; we find ourselves with fewer possessions and more flexibility as we travel with our sometimes elusive God. And in the repeated purifications of our life, we begin to learn that this is how we grow into the maturity of Jesus Christ. We thought (we had been taught!) that the journey would be more "normal," more orthodox. But it hardly ever is. As we gradually recognize the astounding variegation in our journeys with God, we also come to identify the common elements in our different passages.

Becoming more adept at our shared journey, we are beginning to see that some human movements we had named "exits" are more often passages of grace. Two such exits are the movements of divorce and of coming out. In a Church suspicious of adult change as likely to be tainted by error or sin, these movements were interpreted as exits. Divorce appeared to be, in essence, a chosen religious infidelity. As such, it could not be a passage of grace. Homosexuality was seen as a chosen unnatural disposition; as such, to be homosexual meant to be unholy. Like divorce, it was a necessary departure or exit from faith and grace.

Gradually we believers have been confronted with the evidence: mature members of our communities of faith divorce (most often with much pain and regret and guilt), but they do not by that event leave their faith or their maturity. Sometimes they seem to grow more mature and holy.

They seem (dare we say it?) to be graced by their divorce. Likewise gay and lesbian Christians: coming to cherish themselves and strengthened to pursue responsible lives of love and commitment, many become more mature believers as well. Embracing their sexual identity leads them not out of the Church but more deeply into it. We are finally seeing, then, that these life experiences need not be exits but may often be passages of grace. If these have become passages of grace for many despite the deafening silence of the Church's official ministry, how graceful might they become in a Church bold enough to confess the movement of God in these crises?

Finally it might be instructive to observe some parallels between these three passages and the maturing of the Church itself in its ministry to its homosexual members. The Church's gradual movement from a denial of the Christian homosexual maturing to a private acceptance (in the confessional and individual counseling) of the gay and lesbian Christian represents a kind of interior passage. In an exercise of self-intimacy, the Church acknowledged—at least individually and privately—the holiness of some of its lesbian and gay members. A typical approach during this period of the Church's maturing ministry was to affirm God's love for the homosexual while counseling a celibate life-style.

As the Church itself matured, growing more aware of and comfortable with different parts of its own body, its ministry began to more enthusiastically endorse the goodness of human intimacy, even for homosexual Christians. Now it began to bless, though in a very private and hidden way, the life of the homosexual couple. Here the theological logic was that such a life was a lesser evil than its alternatives. The public statements of the Church at this stage conflicted with its maturing "private practice." The parallels are not strong, but we may see this stage of the Church's ministry as representing a second passage. Responsible intimacy was recognized as an important part of maturing for the homosexual Christian, but this recognition was not public.

The establishment of organizations such as Dignity, the planning of pastoral conferences on the topic, the scheduling of retreats of lesbian and gay Christians—these efforts have begun to push the Church toward a new stage of ministerial maturity. Tentatively the Church is now approaching this third passage. Its public statements are more sophisticated and graceful; generalizations and homophobic overtones are diminishing. We are beginning to acknowledge that our own body, the body of Christ, is in part gay. Nor are these homosexual parts of the Christian body now seen only as immature or a cause of shame. As the Church itself matures, as it becomes more in touch with its own body, with all this body's wounds and strengths, it makes possible the public witness of those life-styles that can reveal to all of us the shape of homosexual holiness and maturity.

NOTES

1. For especially fruitful explorations of this metaphor see Victor Turner's *The Ritual Process* (New York: Cornell University Press, 1969) and his "Passages, Margins and Poverty: Religious Symbols of Communitas," *Worship* 46 (1972): 390–412, 482–94. Connections between passages and developmental crises are examined in chapter 2: "Adult Crises: Psychological Structure and Religious Meaning," in our *Christian Life Patterns: The Psychological Challenges and Religious Invitations of Adult Life* (New York: Doubleday, Image, 1982. Van Gennep's work is available in his *The Rites of Passage* (Chicago: University of Chicago Press, 1960), a translation of *Les Rites de Passage* (Paris: E. Nourry, 1908). For discussions of relationships between developmental passages and Christian sacraments, see *Liturgy and Human Passage*, ed. David Powers and Luis Maldonado (New York: Seabury, 1978).

2. Douglas C. Kimmel, in "Adult Development and Aging: A Gay Perspective" (*Journal of Social Issues* 34, no. 3 [1978]: 113–30), reports on his own research ("an exploratory study of 14 gay men, all over the age of 55") and on a "study of gay male and lesbian members of the American Psychological Association." Findings of this latter study (see Kimmel, p. 116) give evidence of three transitions which parallel the passages we are examining. The gays and lesbians of that study "considered themselves homosexual" at age 21 and 23, respectively; they "disclosed identity to parent" at 28 and 30 respectively (roughly paralleling our second passage); these psychologists "disclosed identity professionally" at 31 and 32 respectively (our third, public passage). This and other research on homosexual maturing is generally on very small groups, often a privileged status. Without giving such studies too much weight, we may discover in them some fruitful hints about the patterns of psychological and religious maturing among homosexual Christians.

3. The Task Force's statement, dated 5 October 1981, appeared in the 11 February 1982 issue of *Origins* (11, no. 35: 549–53), a publication of the National Catholic News Service.

MATTHEW FOX

The Spiritual Journey
of the Homosexual . . .
and Just About Everyone Else

This past summer I had the privilege of teaching with Sister Jose Hobday, a Franciscan sister and a Native American. One day she took me aside with great seriousness and said she had a question she had to put to me as a representative of white society. "I cannot understand," she began, "the hang-up in white culture and Church towards the homosexual. In our native traditions we don't even have a word for 'homosexual.' And it is well known among us that often the homosexual was the most spiritual member of a tribe, who played powerful roles as counselors to some of our most important chiefs." She went on to explain how in her ministry of retreat-giving, the people she encountered who were "the most beautiful Christians of all" were very often homosexual men and women. This had been my experience as well.

Obviously, what Sister Jose was experiencing as an outsider in the white person's world was homophobia. If we lived in a society or a Church that was not homophobic we would need no article on the topic I have chosen to write on and no book like the present book. If our society and our churches accepted the homosexual for what he and she is there would be no wagging of tongues and lifting of eyebrows about "Homosexuality and Spirituality." In itself the homosexual's spirituality is not different from anyone else's—however, here lies the rub. All spirituality is incarnational, i.e., grounded in the locality of subcultures and culture. Sadly, churches can become too much like the world and can fall into sins like homophobia in bending over to imitate the world and its ways. For this reason the experience of the homosexual growing up in Western culture and most Christian denominations has indeed affected his or her spirituality or way of life. It has, for example, profoundly affected such a person's self-image. It has profoundly affected his or her relationships—how many homosexuals, for example, have felt the need to either (1) keep the "deep, dark secret" from their parents and siblings, thus introducing a basic dishonesty to one's family relationships; or (2) had to, by coming out, cut ties altogether with parents or other family members; or (3) hide their own sexual orientation even from themselves until after marriage, thus hurting other innocent people? Self-knowledge and self-discovery is the first step along the spiritual way according to the teachings of the mystics, yet self-discovery regarding one's sexuality has seldom been endorsed in the churches.

This lack of self-esteem that the homosexual growing up in a homophobic society or Church suffers is of inestimable significance for one's ongoing spiritual growth or lack thereof. For without trust, which includes trust in oneself and in one's body and in nature, there can be no full development of a psychological or spiritual kind. The pain and suffering that a homosexual in a homophobic culture undergoes can be either redemptive or alienating. It redeems when it leads to a sensitive vulnerability that allows the homosexual to identify with the sufferings of other oppressed persons—the Jew, the black person, the Native American, women in a patriarchal society, the *anawim* of any description. When the homosexual can grow *through* her or his suffering a great spiritual richness is attained. Compassion is gained. When, however, for any number of reasons a homosexual cannot pass through the pain that homophobic cultures rain on him or her, then a psychospiritual arrest can happen and the homosexual becomes a scapegoat, a self-fulfilling prophecy of a homophobic society, a broken and essentially lonely person who, in his or her alienation, truly feels like an alien, a stranger in a sick society. In the alien's effort to please that society he or she falls prey to its own worst sins: power over, power under, sadomasochism, consumerism, hatred of body, inability to sustain relationships, adolescent arrest, and egoistic quests for perfectionism and immortality. Like the slave who has imbibed the ideology of his slave master, the homosexual then fulfills the prophecy of the heterosexual, plays out the worst stereotypes of the repressed homophobic conscience, and gives to the sexist homophobic society a weapon of great strength: "See," he will say, "what I warned you about the homosexual."

Suppositions Regarding Spirituality and the Homosexual

In this essay on Spirituality and the Homosexual I wish to make explicit three suppositions:

1. In using the term *the homosexual*, I do not mean to negate the uniqueness, the decision making, the diversity of persons both women and men who are homosexual. Just as there is not one life-style of "a black" or "a woman," so too homosexuals come in great varieties of colors, vocations, life-styles, talents, woundedness, journeys. Nevertheless, to be homosexual in a culture that is excessively conscious of sexuality in the first place and that is excessively heterosexual and therefore homophobic, does create a common ground for speaking of that emergent movement of persons demanding their sexual liberation and who call themselves gay and lesbian. Carter Heyward, speaking of her experience of coming out, writes:

> I knew that coming out was, for me, not first a statement about who I sleep with but rather a statement about what I value in human and divine life: learning to stand on common ground; a process at once sexual, political, spiritual, economic; a relational journey both individual and collective.[1]

As stated earlier, I do not believe the homosexual has a spirituality distinct from that of a heterosexual, a bisexual, or anyone else. Yet because the cultural situation is so different for a homosexual there is an urgency about his or her finding and living out a spirituality that often escapes the more comfortable life-style of the heterosexual. Because the homosexual has often encountered deep pain and personal anguish earlier in life than the heterosexual, it is very likely that the homosexual has fallen more deeply and sooner either into divine grace or into demoniclike compulsions. An example of the latter would be the high rate of alcoholism among homosexuals, especially among homosexual men.

2. In saying that the homosexual's spirituality does not differ significantly from the heterosexual's I am not saying that differences in spirituality do not per se exist. But the most basic difference in spirituality is *not* that between homosexual/heterosexual—it is between Fall/Redemption spiritual theologies and Creation-centered spiritualities. The Fall/Redemption tradition begins with the doctrine of original sin and sees all of salvation history through those glasses. Jesus, in this tradition, came primarily to wipe away original sin. This tradition, represented by Augustine in the West, is essentially dualistic and noncosmic—there is no cosmic Christ in Augustine's spirituality. In this regard it is important to point out that the homosexual has been a special victim of the Fall/Redemption spiritual tradition. Indeed, all oppressed groups have been. For in this tradition an awesome silence prevails about prophecy, social justice, and human liberation. Essentially introspective,[2] this tradition begins its theology with sin and personal guilt. It has proven an invalu-

able tool for maintaining the status quo and especially as regards the human propensity in the West for equating guilt with sexuality. It should never be forgotten that Augustine, who named the term *original sin* by mistranslating Romans 5:12,[3] actually posited that original sin was passed on in the sexual act by the male's sperm. Christian theology ought to meditate long and hard on the subtle implications of this sexual/original sin philosophy for the homosexual who in a real sense is taught very early in society and Church that his/her sexual feelings and orientation are inherently sinful from the start, i.e., originally. Of all people, the homosexual must let go of the Fall/Redemption spiritual tradition and the sooner the better.

The homosexual will recognize in the Creation-centered spiritual tradition the kind of liberation with discipline that he or she needs to live a spiritual life, one that culminates in transformation of self and society into compassionate human celebrators and justice makers. This tradition, which is the oldest spiritual tradition of the Bible, for the Yahwist author of the Hebrew Bible wrote in these terms, begins not with original sin but with original blessing.[4] Can you and I, can the homosexual and the heterosexual, believe that he or she is an original blessing? There is where authentic faith lies—in learning to trust the gift and beauty of one's own unique and original existence. An existence that is itself gratuitous and does not need justifications of a moral kind to earn a blessing. This tradition is a cosmic tradition and sees salvation history as integral to history of the universe, of nature, of human history, of our bodies. The whole cosmic body and the body of Christ are in process of healing, redeeming, forgiving, releasing. Trust is the basic psychology of this tradition and not guilt. Learning to trust the cosmos, oneself, God, and others while remaining vulnerable, childlike, mystical, and beauty oriented— here lies the steps on such a spiritual journey. It alone, psychologist William Eckhardt teaches, can lead to a way of life that is compassionate.[5] Lack of trust, his seven-year study on compassion demonstrates, cannot lead to compassion. Self-love leads to compassion, not self-hatred. "Have compassion toward yourself" says Meister Eckhart, the great spokesperson of the Creation-centered spiritual tradition. For how will Christians ever manage to fulfill Jesus' injunction to love others as we love ourselves if we have not learned to love ourselves?

3. Homosexuals, like heterosexuals, like all saints, sin too; but being homosexual is not one of these sins nor is it the "original sin." Homosexual sins are no different from any one else's sins, for the fact of being homosexual is not one of these sins. Otherwise the Creator, who as far as we now know has created approximately 10 percent of the human race homosexual, would be a sadistic and vicious God. And that, we know,

cannot be the truth since faith teaches us how delighted, how thrilled, how exuberant She was and is with creation and its ongoing blessings. And among those blessings human beings, whether heterosexual or homosexual, especially delight God. "God finds joy and rapture in us,"[6] says Meister Eckhart writing out of a profound absorption with the Wisdom tradition or the Scriptures.

While the sins of homosexuals are in themselves no different from those of heterosexuals, bisexuals, etc., nevertheless, because sin—like language and all else that is human and incarnational—is to an extent culturally determined, the homosexual, by being driven into underground and marginal living situations, may find temptations to some sins more prevalent than in so-called straight society. For example, the sin of consumerism. There is a general dictum of economics that reads: The more you make, the more you spend. This "law" seems to hold rather valid among middle-class persons in a consumer society. To the extent that the homosexual finds himself or herself in (1) a middle-class situation and (2) in consumer society, a special access to the sin of consumerism exists. Why? Because the homosexual *qua* homosexual is not a parent and to that extent is spared the financial burdens, many of which are joys, that parents have in providing for their children's needs and upbringing. This kind of economic independence sets the middle-class gay person up as an easy victim to advertisers, who are the missionaries of consumer religion in our time. The insatiable greed for the latest fashion and consumer product must be resisted by the homosexual of the middle class.

The sin of self-hatred is easier for a person to fall into if one has had to deny his or her sexual identity for years even with those friends and relatives who are closest to one. The sin of self-hatred is easier to succumb to when bad theology teaches a person that in effect God loves you less because of your sexual identity or even that God loves you only on condition that your being not lead to action—a horrible dualism that a true Scholastic could never countenance since even that intellectual tradition instructs that *agere sequitur esse,* "we will act according to our being."

Another sin that the homosexual may be especially tempted by is the sin of ersatz immortalities. Because the homosexual *qua* homosexual has not parented children and because children for centuries have represented immortality in the West, the homosexual is thrown into a very profound and significant search for immortality, for a gift to leave behind, as Rank puts it.[7] Rank points out that in healthy persons this gift often takes the form of art and creativity. But in an unhealthy and materialistic society the first temptation is to look at material goods or their amassing as a sign

of immortality. In this respect the sin of clinging, the fear of letting go, the
sin of pyramid building, of excessive pursuit of material security, or of
prolongation of the idol of youthfulness, would seem to hit the homosexual subculture with particular vengeance and would need to be resisted
strongly.

The Homosexual as *Anawim*

Liberation theologians have raised the consciousness of the People of
God as to how the biblical God works through the lowly and how the
Spirit of God works through these people, bringing about divine salvation in a battered and sinful human world. Mary, the mother of Jesus,
sings of this relationship in Luke's Gospel when she declares:

> He has scattered the proud in the imagination of
> their hearts,
> He has put down the mighty from their thrones,
> and exalted those of low degree;
> He has filled the hungry with good things,
> and the rich he has sent empty away.
>
> (Lk 1:51–53)

Gustavo Gutíerrez, commenting on this passage, writes: "The future of
history belongs to the poor and exploited. True liberation will be the
work of the oppressed themselves; in them, the Lord saves history. The
spirituality of liberation will have as its basis the spirituality of the *anawim*."[8] The early Church was a scandal to the Jews—as was the cross
itself to Greek and Jew alike—because the oppressed would henceforth
be in charge of their own lives. Mary represented such a scandal, since
she called herself a "handmaid." Scriptural scholar Raymond Brown
writes: "In the early dialogue between Christians and Jews, one of the
objections against Christianity is that God would never have had His
Messiah come into the world without fitting honor and glory, born of a
woman who admitted that she was no more than a handmaid, a female
slave."[9]

I maintain that the homosexual is indeed a representative of the sexual
anawim, of the dark or shadow side, the underside, the dispossessed side,
the persecuted side of the Western consciousness as regards sexuality.
Culture knows very little about sexuality and even less about homosexuality and what causes it—after all it was only in the last century that
humanity learned that women contribute an ovum to the process of
human fertilization and thus are not merely passive receptors of the male

seed. But instead of maintaining a respectful silence about the mystery of homosexuality, society and very often religious believers too have felt themselves annointed to pontificate on the morality or immorality, the "naturalness" and "unnaturalness" of homosexual activity. This presumption on the part of a clear majority that it can judge the morality of a 10 percent minority constitutes a social scandal from a theological point of view. We know for certain that the God of the Bible—while we do not know Her reason for creating so varied a species as humankind—*is biased in favor of the anawim.*

The Good News that breaks through for the believer in the Gospel of Jesus is that, strange to tell, it is right here in the space of oppression where God is to be heard. That God is indeed among the poorest and the least in a special way and that it would behoove the majority to listen to the minority. Writes Latin American theologian Segundo Galilea: "The 'least' are not only individual persons in Latin America, but human groups—marginal subcultures, social classes or sectors. There is in them a collective presence of Jesus, the experience of which constitutes a true contemplative act."[10] In other words, when Jesus announces in Matthew's Gospel that we are to relieve the suffering of the little ones, and in the process we will find God in and among the little ones, he is announcing Good News to the homosexual. And Good News for the heterosexual—which Good News consists of the dominant society being still and learning from the oppressed (and therefore learning wisdom and compassion) and of letting go of repression and object making of persons different from oneself. This Good News in turn brings the Good News of celebration—for when letting go occurs celebration among all persons, homosexual and heterosexual, can happen once again; it also brings the Good News of justice making, for only when those in power let go of their claims to unjust social structures are the poor let free.

And it brings the good news of creativity, for as psychologist Otto Rank demonstrates,[11] creativity is only possible when diversity is allowed. When diversity of sexual orientation is admitted by the public as a whole, then authentic creativity can emerge from both heterosexual and homosexual worlds alike. A case in point is John Boswell's study, which demonstrates that the most fertile of all Christian periods in the West occurred during the 100-year period from 1050 to 1150 when homosexuality was allowed its space and time and place in society and Church alike.[12] Tolerance becomes the key to creativity not because it is a pious virtue to practice but because its presence indicates a willingness by all citizens of society or Church to *let be*. By letting homosexuals be homosexual, the heterosexual is freed from homophobia and can channel her or his energies into creativity at the same time that the oppressed homosexual is freed to let himself or herself contribute what she/he can to culture's growth and development. Since grace builds on nature and since recent studies of homosexuality indicate that fully 10 percent of a culture is homosexual, then it is imperative that we let nature be nature and let homosexuals be homosexuals. When this is allowed to happen grace may break through in many forms for all persons of culture and Church. And homosexual and heterosexual alike will be able to bless and not curse one another. But for this to happen it must be emphasized that a majority (90 percent) has no right to dictate the private morality of a 10 percent minority any more than a minority has a right to forgo all moral responsibility and interconnection with the majority. The Gospel—which announces that the *anawim* bear special gifts to the people of God at large—must be allowed to break through society's projections on gay and lesbian people in order to set all peoples and the Spirit itself free.

With this freedom goes increased responsibility. Ernest Becker warns that the opposite of guilt is not innocence but responsibility.[13] When the homosexual is freed to be himself or herself what are some particular areas of responsibility that one is called to? One such area would be the liberation of other sexually oppressed peoples. It should be remembered, advertisers notwithstanding, that the majority of the human race does not find itself in a sexually fulfilling life-style. This is the case with prisoners and members of institutions such as mental hospitals; with handicapped, with widows, widowers, divorced, and sometimes other single persons. A good test of the homosexual's spiritual liberation, since it is "by their fruits that you will know them," will be that person's dedication to the liberation of other persons. This liberation and compassion may take the form of active organizing or of simply being with and offering affection, time, and presence to the lonely of society. If compassion is not the result of gay and lesbian liberation then that liberation has not been at all radical, at all spiritual. It has been merely an ego or personal liberation and not a liberation of the Self, which is by nature bound to all selves, human and others, of our holy universe.

The Spiritual Journey of the Homosexual . . . and Just About Everyone Else

The Creation-centered spiritual journey rejects the three-fold and all-too-familiar path of the Neoplatonic tradition, which is named as Purgation, Illumination, Union. Instead, it offers a four-fold path, which is named in the following manner: (1) Creation: the *via positiva*; (2) Letting Go and Letting Be: the *via negativa*; (3) Birthing and Creativity: the *via creativa*; (4) New Creation: Compassion and Social Justice: the *via trans-formativa*.[14] Since I have already stated that in my opinion the homosexual's spiritual journey and task is no different essentially from any other loved creature of God, I do not intend to demonstrate that the Creation-centered spiritual journey is that of the homosexual or vice versa. What I would like to ask is this, however: Given the unique cultural context and milieu in a homophobic culture for the homosexual, is it possible that, emerging from the depths of such a journey, the homosexual or sexual *anawim* is indeed graced with a special insight as to the stages of the Creation-centered spiritual journey? Might indeed this insight be one way in which the grace of God is breaking through the *anawim*'s experience to enlighten the rest of society in our time? I shall answer this question in regard to each experience of the four paths.

1. The Homosexual and the Via Positiva

Inherent in the *via positiva* is a theology of blessing, of experiencing the ecstacy and blessing that all life is. "Isness is God" said Meister Eckhart—and here lies the great miracle of existence. The goodness of creation, its essential trustworthiness and voluptuousness, is praised by the psalmist and other writers of the wisdom tradition of Scripture. Ours "is a world thoroughly worthy of trust" writes Wisdom scholar Von Rad.[15] Beauty overwhelms us at every turn toward creation and nature—it is awesome, it is frightening, and since, as Simone Weil observed, beauty has everything to do with terror, it is beautiful and not merely pretty or nice. The ecstacies of creation—nature, friendship, art, poetry, dance, work that is noncompulsive, non-competitive sport, sexuality[16]—all these are available to heterosexual and homosexual alike.

But a question arises: Is it possible that the homosexual has experienced a unique challenge to his or her trust of nature and creation and this at a rather early and prelogical age precisely when it came to his or her sexual orientation? Here, all of a sudden, the gay or lesbian person must face the question whether creation is "very good" (Gn 1:31)—*except for his or her creation*. But one does not "choose" one's sexual preference. It is part of creation—indeed, of nature. Homosexuality is "unnatural," as the Greeks and Scholastics called it, only to the heterosexual. The homosexual undergoes a deep crisis regarding creation. This crisis may result in behavior that is immature and ego-oriented; or it may go the other route—it may begin the deepening and hallowing route that true spiritual depths are made of. It may result in greater, not lesser, trust of self, body, nature, cosmos, and God. If that be the case—and my pastoral experience has taught me it often has been—then the homosexual will bring a hard-won and deeper appreciation of beauty and grati-

tude to the banquet of life and will be able to pronounce from the depths
the words of Meister Eckhart: "If the only prayer you say in your whole
life is 'Thank You,' that will suffice."

The struggle for self-trust that the homosexual embarks on is a profound one that culminates in the recovery of a theological theme that
brings Good News to all persons: That every child of God is a *royal
person*, that is, a person endowed with divine dignity and with divine
responsibility.[17] Until persons—whether heterosexual or homosexual is
of no consequence here—come to grips with their royal personhood with
all the beauty and responsibility that it contains, they will not work so
that others who are different from them can also attain their dignity and
nobility.[18]

2. The Homosexual and the Via Negativa

Like any member of an oppressed group, the homosexual will know a
lot about darkness, loneliness, nothingness. And about letting go and
letting be. The homosexual child must let go earlier than most children of
the parental, social, or psychological role models that society gives one in
the sexual sphere. Such a person will have to let go of the exclusive option
of marriage as a life-style. The sacrament of "coming out" is a kind of
letting go: a letting go of the images of personhood, sexuality, and self-
hood that society has put on one in favor of trusting oneself enough to let
oneself be oneself. Just as the slave had to empty himself or herself of the
slave master's language and thinking and value system, so too the homosexual undergoes emptying of a profound personal and social kind of
projects and projections that heterosexual society has insisted on. This
emptying and letting go and letting be can lead either to a deeper and
more vulnerable, more compassionate sense of belonging with others
who suffer unjustly—or it can lead to a cynicism, a rage, a hoarding of
consumer idols including sexual consumerism on the part of the homosexual. If it leads to the former it is certainly a blessing in disguise, a
school of wisdom learned by suffering, a theology of the apophatic God,
the God of darkness, whom the straight world needs so desperately to
hear more about.

Part of the profound letting-go process that all people must undergo in
their spiritual growing is the letting go of pain, of enemies, of hurt, and of
guilt. The choice to wallow in one's pain or in one's guilt is a deliberate
choice—as can be the deeper option, which is to let go and move on. Of
course, before one can let go of pain one must first admit to the pain,
cease denying it, and allow pain to be pain for a while. The homosexual
who has allowed pain to be pain and then let go of it brings healing to
others, for all persons suffer pain. Yet, judging from our culture's con-

stant flight from pain, straight society is not terribly adept at moving beyond it. Those who have undergone deep experiences of the *via negativa*, such as many homosexuals have done, can bring prophetic insight about pain and letting go to the greater society.

3. The Homosexual and the Via Creativa

Creativity is always *ex nihilo*. It is always from nothing and from our experiences of nothingness. It is out of the dark. The darkness of letting go and letting be are precursor to the energy of birth and rebirth. People as astute as Otto Rank put the question: Why are so many homosexuals in the arts? I would reply that the first reason is that such a high percentage of homosexuals have undergone the *via negativa*, having to let go of parents and families and self-archetypes so early, that they have been emptied and hallowed out for the great birthing that follows. Rank's own answer, that homosexuals by not having children search for other expressions of immortality and art is one of them, does not contradict my observation. For in fact the birthing of beauty and truth in all the ways that art can do so—dance, pottery, music, poetry, drama, to name a few—is in fact the birthing of alternative children. These are the gifts the creative person wishes to leave behind. Both heterosexual and homosexual persons are creative—*all* after all are made as "images of God" the Creator—but the homosexual is driven to birth continually by a powerful experience of the *via negativa* as well as by the need to create a different life-style for oneself. Living marginal existences is conducive to creativity, while comfort seldom is. One is reminded of Eckhart's image, which he derives from the prophet Isaiah: "From eternity God lies on a maternity bed giving birth . . . . What does God do all day long? God gives birth."

4. The Homosexual and the Via Transformativa

Hopefully, the direction in which the homosexual takes his or her love of beauty and creation, wisdom from suffering, and creative possibilities is not just the direction of creating more trivia for a consumer-oriented society. Hopefully, this ever-deepening spiral of the spiritual journey will culminate and crescendo where Jesus told us it ought always to crescendo—in compassion. "Be you compassionate as your Creator in heaven is compassionate" said Jesus at the end of the Sermon on the Mount in Luke's Gospel (6:36). Compassion does not mean to feel sorry for people or to treat them as superior/inferior, as the English language has come to mean by the word. "Compassion means justice," declares Meister Eckhart, and that is precisely the biblical tradition. But compassion also means celebration. Both justice *and* celebration rejuvenate society and transform it. Without celebration, justice workers become too serious, exhausted, and without a taste of the future. In short, in a capitalist and consumer society they become like capitalism itself, joyless and imageless. Without justice making, on the other hand, celebrators become bored at their own parties, incestuous, consumers. And celebration, ✗ instead of a return to the simple gifts of creation reexperienced with the art of savoring, becomes one more consumer expense—boring, violent, expensive.

While heterosexuals as much as homosexuals are called to the justice making and the celebration that compassion is about, still it can be said that a movement of *anawim* who have themselves experienced the oppression of injustice boasts a unique capacity to understand the journey of other victims of injustice whether of a racial, economic, or sexual kind. While all persons are called to recovering the art of celebration, who can teach us more about celebration that those who have learned to celebrate in the midst of sadness and oppression? Who will know more about the value and the purposelessness of savoring pleasure than those who have had to face the critical question of whether life is beautiful or not? Who know more about the beauty of creation and New Creation than those who have been told verbally and nonverbally by religion and society that the way they were created was a mistake or even sinful?

Additional Gifts from the Homosexual

If it is true that the homosexual represents a certain form of the *anawim* and if it is true that the homosexual has often been involved in an ever-deepening journey along the Creation-centered spiritual pathway, then it must follow that the Spirit of God wants to bestow gifts on the nonhomosexual People of God by way of the homosexual. The pity of dualism and sexism that keeps the homosexual underground is that the majority of God's people become deprived. And often depraved. The slave master suffered as much from the system of slavery as did the slave—but, alas, imagined he did not. At least the slave knew he was not free. How many homophobic persons and institutions know what they are missing by oppressing gay and lesbian persons? In addition to driving such persons to what is sometimes an exaggerated system of segregation and life-style, a homophobic culture banishes healthy role models for the one out of ten children who are homosexual.

In addition to gifts from the homosexual that have been alluded to in this essay I would like to conclude with some others that deserve our attention and meditation. Jesus taught us to "love our enemies"—if, as

Sister Jose Hobday has observed, white culture has made a special enemy of the homosexual, then it is time to start meditating on what kinds of graces and blessings might come our way if we were to embrace instead of condemn the sexual *anawim* in our midst.

1. Sexual relativity. I think that it is more than coincidence that the gay and lesbian liberation movement is occuring in a time and culture which is passing from a scientific myth of Newtonian absoluteness to that of Einsteinian relativity. There is a relativity about sexuality that is not well served by those who, like Newton, feel they can know the unbending "laws" of nature. Plato said that homosexuality is unnatural because animals don't do it—the problem is that he did not know what animals do and do not do when it comes to sex. One prophetic gift from the homosexual will be to teach *humility* to those who, like Plato, presume to know exactly what is and is not "natural." And that what is natural varies with different groups. As Alfred North Whitehead, working out of an Einsteinian and not a Newtonian world view put it, "the laws of nature develop together with societies which constitute an epoch."[19] Part of the Einsteinian epoch we are moving into will be an acceptance of the relativity of sexual life-styles. And with this acceptance an awareness will occur as to how the essence of sexuality is relationship and the quality of relationships—not absolutist laws and principles à la Newton. Eckhart taught that "relation is the essence of a thing." This corresponds beautifully with Einstein's teaching on the theory of relativity.[20]

2. A faith built more on relationship than on institution. Because the homosexual has not been welcomed *qua* homosexual into ecclesiastical institutions, that gay or lesbian person who has remained active in any ecclesial community has had to look deeper than institutionally for the questions of faith: What matters? Does anything matter? There is a well of creativity to be tapped from persons who have learned to live marginally in institutions; they could be a powerful force in revitalizing those very institutions.

3. A witness to the power of difference as a basis for creativity. The homosexual stands as a witness to how people can indeed be different. Otto Rank criticizes the West and America in particular for equating equality with sameness, whereas in fact authentic equality consists in admitting one's difference and thereby allowing others their uniqueness and difference. And, Rank insists, creativity comes from differences and not from sameness. Minority groups, the *anawim*, are more creative because they have touched nothingness in their being emptied, but also because they have been made painfully aware of their being different. When a society can allow for differences it will, as Boswell demonstrates the medieval Church did, celebrate creative rejuvenation.

4. Recovery of the body as spirit, of sensual spirituality, of nonproductive love. Behind the dualism of body versus soul or of spirit versus matter that has heinously infiltrated Christianity from Hellenism lies the dualism that spirit is about soul and not body. That is not the case in biblical teaching, where the word too often translated as "soul," *nepesh*, indeed means all of the following: throat, neck, desire, life, person.[21] The homosexual, by not equating sexuality exclusively with procreation, as Augustine did, allows for the energies of Spirit to flow once again, to overcome dualisms that neither Jesus nor the prophets ever imagined, to allow passion its proper place so that compassion might be born.[22] Furthermore, by removing sexual expression from a dominantly productive motif, as if sexual love needs to be justified by having babies, the homosexual—like the author of the *Song of Songs*—teaches society to pause long enough to savor life and its divine delights. In this way homosexual love is an affront to capitalism, which is per se production oriented and has never developed an art of celebration.[23] Otto Rank believes that humanity is emerging from the "Sexual Era" when the quest for immortality or soul was expressed in an exaggeration of Family or of its opposite, Celibacy. In this era sexuality was in fact taken too seriously by all of us. As we emerge from the sexual era we need those who can teach us the lighter, more playful, less serious, and less goal-oriented side to sexuality—the mystical side. Here, as Masters and Johnson have found, the homosexual offers a gift to the heterosexual community and society as a whole.

If it is true, as Gutíerrez writes, that "the spirituality of liberation will have as its basis the spirituality of the *anawim*," then the issue of First and Third World liberation, of feminist and male liberation, of North American as well as Latin American liberation, of white as well as black, brown, red liberation cannot be joined without the sexual *anawim* being listened to.

I wish to conclude this essay with portions of a letter that I received from a gay man who was part of a Dignity retreat I gave recently.

> It is only by finally coming to terms with being gay—and letting myself be gay that I have begun to see the incredible pain and magnificent pleasures of being a living person . . . . That struggle—which I fought the whole time—is opening my life in a way I never thought possible. It has given me the chance to work at my whole life and to say I don't have to be like everyone else in the rest of my life's aspects either.
>
> Living as a gay man has let me feel love and passion and pain I didn't know I was capable of. But it *all* makes life an experience worth living.

I wonder if I can now translate some of that into my work life. I'm struggling to put passion into what I do for a living. (In my work as a lawyer) I am outraged and feel great helplessness. They don't understand human needs and don't seem to care.

So I struggle with vocation—but thanks to being gay I can honestly say that I am becoming "awake."

It is my experience that the broken world in which we live and which is so overtly heterosexual needs all the awakening that it can get. Perhaps it is not too late to begin to listen to the *anawim* in our midst.

NOTES

1. Carter Heyward, " 'In the Beginning Is the Relation': Toward a Christian Ethic of Sexuality," *Integrity Forum*, Lent 1981, p. 3.

2. See Krister Stendahl, "Paul and the Introspective Conscience of the West," in Krister Stendahl, *Paul among Jews and Gentiles* (Philadelphia: Fortress, 1978), pp. 78–96 for an important critique of how Augustine's introspective conscience has distorted Western theology's reading of the Bible.

3. Herbert Haag, *Is Original Sin in Scripture?* (New York: Sheed and Ward, 1969). His conclusion is no.

4. See Claus Westermann, *Blessing in the Bible and the Life of the Church* (Philadelphia: Fortress, 1978).

5. William Eckhardt, *Compassion: Toward a Science of Value* (Toronto: CPRI Press, 1973).

6. These and other sayings from Meister Eckhart can be found in the following books: Matthew Fox, *Breakthrough: Meister Eckhart's Creation Spirituality in New Translation* (Garden City, N.Y.: Doubleday, Image, 1980); and Matthew Fox, *Meditations with Meister Eckhart* (Santa Fe: Bear & Co., 1982).

7. Otto Rank, *Art and Artist* (New York: Agathon Press, 1975).

8. Gustavo Gutíerrez, *A Theology of Liberation: History, Politics, and Salvation*, trans. Sr. Caridad Inda and John Eagleson (Maryknoll, N.Y.: Orbis Books, 1973), pp. 207f.

9. Raymond E. Brown, *The Birth of the Messiah* (Garden City, N.Y.: Doublday, 1977), p. 364.

10. Segundo Galilea, "Liberation as an Encounter with Politics and Contemplation," in Richard Woods, ed., *Understanding Mysticism* (Garden City, N.Y.: Doubleday, 1980), p. 533.

11. Otto Rank, *Beyond Psychology* (New York: Dover, 1958), pp. 54ff.

12. John Boswell, *Christianity, Social Tolerance, and Homosexuality* (Chicago: University of Chicago Press, 1980).

13. Ernest Becker, *The Denial of Death* (New York: Free Press, 1973).

14. I have outlined these paths in the following works: Matthew Fox, "Meister Eckhart on the 4-Fold Path in the Creation-Centered Spiritual Tradition," in Matthew Fox, ed., *Western Spirituality: Historical Roots, Ecumenical Routes* (Santa Fe: Bear & Co., 1981), pp. 215–48; and in Fox, *Breakthrough*, passim; and in Fox, *Meditations*, "Introduction."

15. Gerhard Von Rad, *Wisdom in Israel* (Nashville: Abingdon, 1978), p. 306.

16. I have dealt with these natural ecstacies as the basis of our mystical experience in Matthew Fox, *Whee! We, wee All the Way Home* (Santa Fe: Bear & Co., 1981), pp. 45–54 and passim.

17. See Helen Kenik, "Toward a Biblical Basis for Creation Theology," in Fox, *Western Spirituality*, pp. 39–68.

18. The prophetic responsibility of royal personhood is laid out in Meister Eckhart's sermon "Everyone an Aristocrat, Everyone a Royal Person" in Fox, *Breakthrough*, pp. 510–30. Such themes of liberation had much to do with Eckhart's condemnation. See Matthew Fox, "Meister and Eckhart and Karl Marx: The Mystic as Political Theologian," in Woods, *Understanding Mysticism*, pp. 541–63.

19. Cited in Donald W. Sherburne, *A Key to Whitehead's Process and Reality* (New York: Macmillan, 1966), p. 93.

20. Cf. Matthew Fox and Brian Swimme, *Manifesto for a Global Civilization* (Santa Fe: Bear & Co., 1982).

21. Hans Walter Wolff, *Anthropology of the Old Testament* (Philadelphia: Fortress, 1981), pp. 11–26.

22. See Fox, *Whee! We, wee*, pp. 1–28.

23. Norman O. Brown, *Life Against Death: The Psychoanalytical Meaning of History* (Middletown, Conn.: Wesleyan University Press, 1970), pp. 234–322.

BRUCE A. WILLIAMS

Gay Catholics and Eucharistic Communion: Theological Parameters

C an actively gay Catholics fruitfully receive the Eucharist in any circumstances? To answer this affirmatively would one have to be
rejecting official Church teaching concerning homosexual conduct, or at
least the authoritative force of that teaching? Or equivalently, must adherence to the Church's moral teaching in this matter necessarily entail
the absolute exclusion of actively gay Catholics from full participation in
the eucharistic community?

Unavoidably this is a key question for gay Catholics themselves, as well
as for Catholic Church leaders attempting to determine a responsible
pastoral policy toward gay members of their flock. Among Protestants,
meanwhile, several authors have recently been endeavoring to articulate
a theologically traditional but pastorally sensitive response to the challenge of homosexuality within their churches.[1] Predictably, in light of
their ecclesiological and sacramental perspectives, none of these authors
discusses the situation of self-affirmed and practicing homosexuals vis-à-
vis the Eucharist. Nevertheless, they do identify some of the very same
fundamental issues which must be confronted in determining eucharistic
policy for gay Catholics within the perspective of authentic magisterial
teaching. Complementary insights from two representative Protestant
sources may shed some light on the Catholic eucharist question.

I

Lewis Smedes, professor of systematic theology and ethics at Fuller
Theological Seminary (Pasadena, California) and an editor of the *Re-*

formed Journal, discerns a "dual-focused" responsibility for the Church in relation to homosexuality: to uphold the biblical teaching and "clearly proclaim the ethical unacceptability of homosexual relationships," on the one hand; and on the other, to "make plain the fullness of grace to homosexual persons, not only in reference to their condition but to their acts as well." The Church, he says, "is called on to set creative compassion in the vanguard of moral law," and to do this it "must be willing to live with ambivalence." The Church "cannot make believe that the homosexual person is simply a member of a sexual minority group," but at the same time "it cannot fulfill its ministry simply by demanding chastity." Above all, the Christian community needs to reveal God's great love of homosexuals as people by being itself "a community of personal acceptance and support" for such people, and offering them realistic but confident hope for "divine healing" from sinful habits and/or tendencies. In dealing with the homosexual believer who proves capable of neither heterosexual reorientation nor celibacy, the Church faces an apparent dilemma between its sexual moral standards and its compassion. Smedes leaves the resolution up to each individual church, but clearly enough indicates his own leanings:

> . . . What does the church do? Does it drop its compassionate embrace and send him on his reprobate way? Does it imitate God, as Paul described him in Romans 1:26—that is, does it abandon him to his unnatural passion? Or does it, in the face of a life unacceptable to the church, quietly urge the optimum moral life *within* his sexually abnormal practice? Does it in effect say, Since you are unable to opt for the better, at least avoid the worst? And does it help him to avoid the worst while it continues to embrace him as a person? These are questions each community must answer for itself.[2]

The same author, in a later article, emphasizes that the Church necessarily "embraces as members people who are less than ideal models of the Christian way" on the principle that "we are a fellowship of persons in constant need of mercy." At the same time, he admits that "a church may make certain minimal demands on its members" and holds that "in certain minimal ways" which he does not specify, "church members must at least not be *anti-models* of what God requires of Christian disciples."[3]

Presbyterian scholar Richard Lovelace, of Gordon-Conwell Seminary (North Hamilton, Massachusetts), is equally insistent on the need for compassion alongside traditional moral conviction in shaping the Church's pastoral policy toward homosexual people. In a forceful passage with implications perhaps more far-reaching than he himself intends (we shall return to this later), Lovelace writes:

> . . . The inability of church people to maintain an attitude of compassionate concern for homosexuals while disapproving of the active homosexual life-style may indicate a serious lack of depth of conviction of sin in their own lives, and possibly a failure to understand and appropriate the Gospel. It should not be difficult for a person who is aware of our common frailty to empathize with the agony, the self-rejection, the guilt, and the loneliness which the exclusive homosexual may suffer because of a condition which is rarely the result of voluntary choice. If we compare Jesus' attitude toward an uncompassionate pharisaism with His response to sexual sinners, we cannot doubt that He would prefer a congregation of homosexual believers struggling toward a principled religious answer to their condition to a congregation of judgmental homophobes.
>
> This does not mean, however, that the theological and biblical arguments advanced to persuade the church to change its traditional attitude toward the active homosexual life-style are persuasive. . . .[4]

According to Lovelace, evidently disagreeing with Smedes's tentative overture quoted above, pastoral compassion should not include the readiness to tolerate a sexually active life-style on the part of gay Church members whose inclinations appear insusceptible to either reorientation or complete restraint. Such an approach, in Lovelace's view, would deprive gay believers of the needed motivation to repent and would demean the power of grace to transform their lives. In a more general context, he sees the notions of "cheap grace" and "powerless grace" as operative in much of the current progay apologetic. The former, he warns, would effectively nullify "any call for repentance or discipline within the church."[5] Against the latter, he offers this suggestive observation (again, as will be noted below, possibly even more suggestive than he thinks):

> Meanwhile, we should recognize that if the church accepts the notion of powerless grace, it will not only short-circuit its message and deny that the Gospel is "the power of God for deliverance," but it should logically be prepared to tolerate many other forms of sin within the church which might cause neuroses if repressed: compulsive adultery and fornication, compulsive racism and other forms of hatred acted out in physical hostility, compulsive disobedience to authority, compulsive theft, and so on. . . .[6]

Notwithstanding his own uncompromising rejection of homosexual activity as a permissible Christian option, Lovelace deals cautiously with the *de facto* plurality of opinions now afloat in the Church regarding this subject. He affirms the need for a healthy balance between pluralism and discipline, and notes that the Church's life can be threatened by too much discipline—as in *lupus,* where "the body's own defenses mistakenly attack its vital organs"—as well as by the cancer of "an unlimited pluralism of opinions and life-styles." He cites the ancient maxim: "Unity in essentials; freedom in doubtful matters; but in all things, love." Approaching the homosexual issue in this spirit, he asks: "Should it be an issue in which Christians respect one another's varying theological convictions and resolve to live together in peaceful pluralism?"[7] The answer that he reaches is basically negative, but not without nuance.

The biblically based conviction that homosexual behavior is sin indicates for Lovelace the conclusion that this behavior should be "challenged and disciplined in the church, rather than tolerated or encouraged." This applies specifically to "those who publicly announce their own practice"; but the Church "need not make an effort to locate and discipline active homosexual members and leaders, and it should not discourage further dialogue and debate at lower levels concerning the legitimacy of some forms of homosexual practice." Remarking that "some cures are worse than the disease," Lovelace grants that sometimes "a positively unhealthy degree of pluralism must be tolerated in the church, because it would be even unhealthier to try to get rid of it or separate from it." Paul thus counseled the Ephesians "that cleaving together, not separation, is the antidote for being carried about by every wind of doctrine, because through 'speaking the truth in love' every member can then contribute its essential enzyme for the health and unity of the body (*see* Eph 4:14–16)."[8] Hence we ought "not only to condemn heresy where we see its danger to the church, but to deal compassionately with those who are gripped by it, 'with gentleness correcting those who are in opposition, if perhaps God may grant them repentance leading to the knowledge of the truth' (2 Timothy 2:25 NAS)."[9]

Lovelace accordingly recommends that Christians who are practicing homosexuals, and who are not publicly forcing the issue in a way that undermines the peace of the Church, should not be the targets of specific disciplinary action but should instead be issued "a general challenge . . . to search their consciences and to repent from sin."[10] In order to be credible, this call to repentance must be clearly placed in the context of a broader summons to Church and society "for a *comprehensive repentance* which includes the return to social justice, a turning from adultery and other personal forms of sin, and the abandonment of false religion."[11]

II

The above reflections offered by Protestant scholars, although not advanced in the context of Sacrament or Eucharist, are of basic importance for Catholics who do think in a sacramental and (particularly) eucharistic framework as they ask how gay believers can participate fruitfully in the life of the Church. Granting the traditional teaching maintained by the magisterium on the wrongness of homosexual activity, the basic issues raised by Smedes and Lovelace may be translated into Catholic sacramental terms as follows:

1. How might the Church's eucharistic discipline be applied so as to minister most effectively and compassionately to erring believers, while at the same time giving integral witness to her authentic doctrine and morals?

2. To what extent can the Church's unity in faith and charity, which the Eucharist preeminently signifies, accommodate a pluralism of convictions and life-styles among those who share that sacrament?

These questions do not envisage believers who are involved in moral error due to a conscious willingness to embrace grave sin; obviously such persons cannot fruitfully receive the Eucharist as long as they remain unrepentant. Likewise excluded from the scope of this discussion are believers prone to a given sin but striving against it in the face of repeated failure; such persons are essentially willing to live by the teaching of the magisterium, and are in fact officially encouraged to frequent the Eucharist (along with sacramental confession) for their strengthening.[12] The problem, as posed by the above questions, concerns believers who are (*a*) regularly willing to engage in conduct which they know is regarded as gravely sinful by the magisterium, and (*b*) conscientiously unpersuaded that their conduct is in fact sinful. By "conscientiously unpersuaded," we presuppose that the nonconformity of their thinking and behavior to magisterial teaching does not itself arise from gravely sinful dispositions such as contempt or crass ignorance. In other words, these believers (unlike the first group excluded above) do not, formally, have "a conscious willingness to embrace grave sin"; yet they are pursuing a course of conduct at variance with clearly known moral teaching of the Church.[13]

The situation of such people, even granted that it is not formally sinful (or at least not gravely so), is nonetheless anomalous in terms of the eucharistic signification of "one mind and heart" among Christ's members—a unity which is uniquely safeguarded by the magisterium. It is apparently on this ground that Archbishop John R. Quinn of San Fran-

cisco, in a pastoral letter on homosexuality (May 1980), judged it necessary to discourage actively gay Catholics from the Eucharist notwithstanding his unmistakably genuine pastoral concern for these people,
which was clearly expressed throughout his letter. "Despite the difficulties," he insisted, "homosexual persons who wish to receive the eucharist
must be honestly following the moral teaching of the church or at least
seriously striving to live up to that teaching." The archbishop based this
determination on a twofold principle:

> In order to receive the eucharist one must be in the state of grace,
> that is, in a living union with Christ characterized by the absence of
> grave sin. One must *also* be living in harmony with the moral and
> doctrinal teaching of the church. [Emphasis added.][14]

The implication here seems to be that actively gay Catholics, even though
possibly excused from formal grievous sin, are not apt recipients of the
Eucharist because of the objective contradiction between their sexual life-
style and the Church's authentic moral standards.

In several of Smedes's and Lovelace's remarks quoted above, strong
support can be found for this policy. By refusing to offer the Eucharist
generally to her errant gay members, even without necessarily imputing
formal mortal sin to such people, the Catholic Church can forcefully
uphold the requirement of "unity in essentials." Arguably, noncompliance with the Church's authoritative moral standards constitutes an evident "anti-model of what God requires of Christian disciples" and therefore contradicts the eucharistic signification of oneness in Christ. To share
the Lord's table with members who persist in conduct abhorrent to her
teaching could seem to involve the Church's acceptance of the notion of
"cheap grace," or else of "powerless grace," and in any case it could
render meaningless "any call for repentance or discipline within the
church." Finally, relaxing the stipulation of doctrinal and moral conformity for reception of the Eucharist might appear tantamount to en-
dorsing an "unlimited pluralism of opinions and life-styles."

Nevertheless, certain problems with a totally prohibitive position are
indicated by other observations of these Protestant authors as well as
elements of Catholic teaching. There are, first of all, those two Lovelace
passages previously marked as "suggestive." If "judgmental homophobes" in the Church are, as he says, undoubtedly less acceptable to
Jesus than "homosexual believers struggling toward a principled religious answer to their condition"—and if some who qualify in the latter
category are nonetheless conscientiously unpersuaded that they can and
must renounce the active gay life-style—these gay believers might well

wonder why they, but not their pharisaical brothers and sisters, are told *in globo* that they should not approach the Eucharist. Even if it were granted that a more lenient sacramental policy toward practicing homosexuals could imply a more tolerant attitude toward their conduct, and that this would logically entail that we "tolerate many other forms of sin within the church" including racism and social injustice (along with the pharisaism just mentioned), it might be argued that these other forms of sin are already tolerated in practice—albeit not in moral teaching—inasmuch as they are not systematically disciplined by withholding of the Eucharist. Of course these observations can be met with appropriate rejoinders, e.g., that sins involving pharisaism and various kinds of social injustice cannot be defined and targeted with the same precision as sins involving sexual misbehavior. Be that as it may, gay Catholics are not so easily dissuaded from the notion that they are victims of a double standard.

It must indeed be acknowledged that common Catholic usage in the matter of admittance to eucharistic Communion has shown a considerable "willingness to live with ambivalence" as regards people in a variety of objectively sinful situations, and this not only in the internal or quasi-internal forum but even at the level of publicly accepted practice (though not generally involving formal ecclesiastical legislation). If some are prepared to dismiss the social-injustice category as an insufficiently tangible example, a more apt illustration may be found in the sexual realm, viz., the contraception problem. Archbishop Quinn himself, speaking as NCCB president, told the World Synod of Bishops in Rome (September 1980) that in regard to contraception, "the moral issue as such has been resolved by many" American Catholics who regularly receive the Eucharist while refusing to observe papal teaching. While he expressed great apprehension at the ecclesiological implications of this situation, he clearly indicated that he considered the eucharistic Communion of these nonconforming Catholics to be in good faith. The archbishop emphasized that a large number of these people are "good and faithful Catholics" who cannot reasonably be charged with "obduracy, ignorance or bad will," and he evinced no inclination to regard their noncompliance with authentic Church teaching as grounds for discouraging them from frequenting the Eucharist.[15]

An additional instance of "ambivalence," and one that is formally accepted at the highest level of the magisterium, may be seen in the qualified approval of eucharistic Communion in the Catholic Church for non-Catholic Christians. The restrictive conditions legislated for this practice sufficiently attest to the ecclesiological ambivalence which it involves, and to the Church's concern to minimize that ambivalence as far as possible. Still, in the Vatican II *Decree on Ecumenism* (no. 8), the basic premise on which this *communicatio in sacris* can be legitimated at all (despite some unavoidable element of ambivalence) is clearly stated:

> . . . There are two main principles upon which the practice of such *communicatio in sacris*[16] depends: first, that of the unity of the Church which ought to be expressed; and second, that of the sharing in the means of grace. The expression of unity very generally forbids *communicationem*. Grace to be obtained sometimes commends it.[17]

The point which is stated here in reference to separated Christians seems applicable at least as easily, albeit in an analogical way, to Catholics in certain situations of objectively (not formally) grave sin. Put simply: if it can sometimes be desirable to make eucharistic grace available to non-Catholic Christians, who are in good faith despite their lack of full incorporation in to the Church's faith and government (and these are objectively serious deficiencies, are they not?), surely it can be no less desirable in principle for eucharistic grace to be shared by Catholic believers who are in good faith despite their nonconformity to the Church's authoritative teaching in some serious moral matter.[18] According to this principle, theological justification can be shown for the above-mentioned leniency of pastors in not generally discouraging eucharistic communion by sincere Catholics who practice contraception, or who are involved in various forms of social injustice. Is there any good reason, consistent with the same principle, why homosexuality should be treated differently?

This line of thought should not be misconstrued as a warrant for gay believers to cultivate a "victim mentality," whereby they would feel automatically entitled to the Eucharist simply because the Sacrament is frequently shared by Catholics who practice contraception or militarism or racial discrimination or pharisaical bigotry—and even to some extent by non-Catholics. (Such an attitude can easily engender its own kind of pharisaism, viz., the celebrated "pharisaism of the publican.") Nor are we proposing a back-door route to "cheap grace" by invoking the truism, "We're all sinners." Neither eucharistic grace nor magisterial teaching are to be trivialized; and therefore the Church's doctrine and sacramental discipline must continue to uphold the norm that participation in Catholic sacraments should express commitment to Catholic teaching and practice. All believers, gays equally included, must submit their attitudes and conduct to the challenge of God's word as proclaimed by the Church and discover in what ways they may be living as "anti-models of what God requires of Christian disciples."

What is being argued here is that gay Catholics should be held to the same norms as other believers as regards formation of conscience in reference to saramental participation. All believers—gays and everyone else—are obliged to take seriously Paul's admonition to examine themselves lest they eat and drink the Sacrament of Communion to their condemnation, not discerning the Body (1 Cor 11:28–29). But gay Catholics must likewise be included in the common recognition that believers can be alive in Christ, through baptismal faith and charity, even though certain impediments (subjective, cultural, etc.) may at least temporarily prevent them from fully appropriating and responding to some significant element of the Gospel as authoritatively presented by the magisterium. Such believers, who upon honest examination do find themselves in good conscience, can receive the Eucharist fruitfully despite the objective inadequacy of their conformity to the Church.

Speaking to U.S. and Canadian bishops assembled in Dallas for a workshop on sexuality (February 1981), the Dominican Benedict Ashley insisted that the Church "ought to continue to preach from the house-tops" her perennial moral principles on this subject, "patiently educating the Christian people in the biblical truth that true sexual fulfillment is to be found only in faithful and fruitful marriage." He then noted: "At the same time the magisterium must not reject nor neglect those persons whose subjective conscience does not permit them as yet to see the practical truth of the Church's teachings on these difficult matters."[19] Father Ashley was not specifically addressing the subject of homosexuality or the position of gay believers in relation to the Eucharist, but his remarks just quoted seem applicable.

If either divine law or the overall good of the Christian community is deemed to necessitate a less accommodating attitude toward actively gay Catholics than toward most other deficient believers, the reasons compelling this judgment should be clearly manifested by ecclesiastical authorities. Up to the present, no such reasons have been demonstrated. Meanwhile it must be recalled that Christians, as Smedes says, constitute "a fellowship of persons in constant need of mercy"—a mercy which must be experienced in the Church as "a community of personal acceptance and support" offering "divine healing"—and that Catholic faith sees the spiritual nourishment of the Eucharist as the foremost source of grace to meet this very need. Precisely in view of the singular importance of the Eucharist for the strengthening of imperfect Christians, as repeatedly underlined by the Church, gay Catholics involved in a life-style they honestly do not recognize as sinful should not be discouraged from this unique means of grace any more severely than other seriously errant believers who are presumably in good faith. This would seem to be the very least that is entailed in the American bishops' collective acknowledgement that homosexual persons require "a special degree of pastoral understanding and care" from the Church.[20]

NOTES

1. These efforts are studied in detail in the present writer's dissertation, *American Protestantism and Homosexuality: Recent Neo-Traditional Approaches* (Rome: Pontifical University of St. Thomas Aquinas, 1981).

2. Lewis B. Smedes, *Sex for Christians* (Grand Rapids: Eerdmans, 1976), pp. 73–74. (Emphasis original.)

3. Idem, "Homosexuality: Sorting Out the Issues," *Reformed Journal,* January 1978, p. 12. (Emphasis original.)

4. Richard F. Lovelace, *Homosexuality and the Church* (Old Tappan, N.J.: Revell, 1978), pp. 66–67.

5. Ibid., p. 96.

6. Ibid., p. 75.

7. Ibid., pp. 118–19.

8. Ibid., pp. 121–23.

9. Ibid., p. 126.

10. Ibid., p. 121.

11. Ibid., p. 124. (Emphasis original.)

12. Cf. Paul VI, *Humanae Vitae,* n. 25.

13. For an effort to interpret this phenomenon according to a considerably expanded notion of the traditional impediment of "invincible ignorance," see Louis Monden, S. J., *Sin, Liberty and Law,* trans. J. Donceel (New York: Sheed and Ward, 1965), pp. 137–38.

14. *Origins* X, no. 7 (July 1980): 112. Cf. *Principles to Guide Confessors in Questions of Homosexuality* (NCCB, 1973), final section, "The Overt Homosexual and the Reception of the Eucharist."

15. *Origins* X, no. 17 (October 1980): 264.

16. This term, usually translated as "common worship" (as in Flannery, below), technically refers to liturgical worship which involves sharing of the sacraments; it is distinguished from the more general term *communicatio in spiritualibus,* which can include the above but also extends to common prayer in paraliturgical and nonliturgical contexts.

17. Translation from *Vatican II: The Conciliar and Post-Conciliar Documents,* ed. Austin Flannery (Collegeville, Minn.: Liturgical Press, 1975), p. 461. Cf. *Decree on the Catholic Eastern Churches,* nn. 26–29. Postconciliar implementing documents available in the Flannery volume; see #37 (esp. pp. 495–99), #38 (pp. 502–7), #43 (pp. 554–59). Cf. Robert I. Bradley, S. J., "Discerning the Body of the Lord," in *The Sacrament of the Eucharist in Our Time,* ed. G. Kelly (Boston: Daughters of St. Paul, 1978), pp. 59–77.

18. Cf. Richard A. McCormick, S. J., "Indissolubility and the Right to the Eucharist—Separate Issues or One?" in *Proceedings of the Canon Law Society of America* (1975), pp. 26–37; reprinted in *Ministering to the Divorced Catholic,* ed. J. Young (New York: Paulist Press, 1979), pp. 65–84. See also McCormick's "Notes on Moral Theology," *Theological Studies* 43 no. 1 (March 1982): 119–24. McCormick, drawing the ecumenical analogy much more closely than the present essay intends to do, suggests the desirability of revising ecclesiastical law so as to allow for a qualified permission of some divorced-remarried Catholics to receive the Eucharist. Whatever its possible merits, McCormick's proposal must contend with complications which fortunately do not pertain to the present discussion. In the case of divorced-remarried couples, as with Orthodox and Protestant Christians, the

people involved have a legal-juridical status which needs to be addressed formally by ecclesiastical legislation. Gay Catholics do not present this problem; the pastoral leniency proposed for them in this essay does not require a change of Church law but only a consistently generous application of commonly accepted principles, as argued in the text.

19. Benedict M. Ashley, O. P., "The Use of Moral Theory by the Church," in *Human Sexuality and Personhood: Proceedings of the Workshop for the Hierarchies of the United States and Canada . . . Dallas, Texas, February 2–6, 1981* (St. Louis: Pope John Center, 1981), p. 239.

20. NCCB Pastoral Letter, *To Live in Christ Jesus,* 11 November 1976 (Washington, D.C.: USCC, 1976), part II, sec. 1, "The Family."

IV

VOCATIONAL
PERSPECTIVES

PAUL K. THOMAS

Gay and Lesbian Ministry During Marital Breakdown and the Annulment Process

> Because heterosexuals can usually look forward
> to marriage and homosexuals, while their
> orientation continues, might not, the Christian
> community should provide them a special degree
> of pastoral understanding and care.
>
> (U.S. Catholic Bishops, *To Live In*
> *Christ Jesus,* Pastoral Letter of 1976)

A well-known passage from the Book of Ruth, often chosen for the celebration of a marriage by either the officiating priest or even the couple themselves, forms one of the most beautiful pledges of love ever made by one individual to another.

> Wherever you go, I will go; wherever you live, I will live.
> Wherever you die, I will die, and there I will be buried.
> May the Lord's just punishment come upon me,
> if I let anything—even death—separate me from you!
> (Ru 1: 16–17; cf. 4, 15)

Few if any of the participants at a wedding ceremony consciously reflect that the extraordinary and exciting words were made between persons of the same gender. Yet, in truth, not only will the two share their lives together, even after death they will lie inseparably side by side![1]

Marriage, between woman and man, is indeed a unique interpersonal relationship of consenting parties, who promise to "love and honor each

NOTE: *Marriage* refers throughout the article to a heterosexual relationship between man and woman. Alternate terminology needs to evolve within the homophile community for lesbian and gay male couples.

other for the rest of their lives" (Rite of Marriage, no. 24). It is a heterosexual commitment to spend their entire future together in as intimate a way as possible. Through a covenanted bond, the spouses assume loving responsibility to encourage each other's full human potential as husband and wife.

The Church endeavors to safeguard the integrity of a marital relationship through its pastoral guidelines and canonical legislation, not only for the benefit of the individuals themselves, but also for the well-being of society as a whole. Ecclesiastical authorities, therefore, establish norms for the preparation of marriage and determine impediments for liceity and validity.[2]

The last few decades have seen a growing awareness on the part of the Church that certain people are psychologically impeded from entering matrimony either with any one at all (absolute incompetence) or, more usually, with a specific partner (relative incompetence). In other words, we now realize that, just as some persons are *physically incapable* of conjugal union (the invalidating grounds of impotence), so other individuals are *psychically incapable* of marriage (lack of "due discretion" or "due competence").

Thus, as the chapter will shortly explain, recent canonical jurisprudence has increasingly recognized among many causes of nullity that a homosexual orientation, by its very nature, can render a person unable to assume and sustain a valid conjugal relationship, *provided there exist the predominance of homosexual makeup and an exclusivity in homosexual attraction.*[3] In fact, some authors have advocated that homosexuality in itself be named as an invalidating impediment by Canon Law.[4] Just as a Catholic cannot validly marry a nonbaptized party or an aunt is unable to wed her nephew (without dispensation in each instance), so a homosexual person would be prohibited from entering a valid marriage with a heterosexual spouse (unless dispensed through justifiable circumstances).[5]

Although such jurisprudential concepts may seem homophobic at times, canonists themselves are not necessarily perpetuating the Church's past homosexual oppression. In fact, far from assigning any moral blame, the pastoral interpreter wishes to protect lesbian or gay persons, as well as their potential spouses, from the possible tragedy of marital breakdown. *At any rate, individuals must be judged within their own situations and in light of the total personality. Any tendency to categorize or generalize in specific cases must be carefully avoided.*

Homosexuality and Marriage

Even from early recorded history, homosexually oriented persons (e.g. Jonathan, Sappho) have entered marriage and raised families. In today's society of changing attitudes, many gay women and men do not choose so-called "connubial bliss," while their wedded gay friends indeed often lead lives of quiet desperation and fear. They suffer from a recurrent anxiety that, if their real affectional preference became known, they might lose the respect of their partners and the affection of their children.

A spouse's homosexuality, once revealed, might elicit responses ranging from aversion or contempt to confusion and misunderstanding but very seldom—at least in the beginning—concern or love. Few disclosures of a person's own deepest feelings generate in loved ones such vast ignorance and primitive emotions. "It is small wonder," says a formerly married gay author, "that most gay husbands and wives choose the lonely pain of the secret rather than risk the possible seemingly catastrophic consequences."[6]

According to several studies, nearly 20 percent of homosexual persons have married at least once,[7] though a rare few have had multiple heterosexual unions. The incidence of matrimony appears higher among lesbians than among gay males. (Parenthetically, homosexual men and homosexual women seldom espouse each other.) Of course, the actual number of any such marriages is nearly impossible to ascertain, since still-wedded homosexual individuals are perhaps least likely to participate in any surveys. Probably no aspect of gay life is quite so difficult to investigate and so deeply enshrouded in secrecy.

Nevertheless, approximately 4 million gay women and men in the United States are projected to have entered matrimony, if we accept the general estimate of homosexually oriented people as at least 10 percent of the total population. When we count their heterosexual spouses (and children if any), we discern a significantly large group whose wedded lives have been touched in a very real way by homosexuality.

Of course, gay persons have made a decision about marriage for many different reasons. Probably they act from several conflicting motives at the same time, though not always easily defined and hardly in their own consciousness. Edward Sagarin, who as a gay husband wrote under the pseudonym of Donald Webster Cory, discusses such attractions as "a desire to have children . . . a 'front,' an artificial facade . . . a desire to please one's family . . ."[8] Some seek to hide, deny, or vanquish their homosexuality. Others long for the stability of marriage as an institution (despite the high rate of divorce among the general populace!). Perhaps most people only half suspect, if at all, their true orientation and in all good faith discount same-sex emotions as just an insignificant phase, an adolescent infatuation, which a loving heterosexual relationship will "cure."

Not surprisingly, such conjugal unions are often unhappy and relatively short-lived. Sometimes sexual problems, such as indifference or outright aversion, arise from the start. Other times a gradual awareness of one's own gayness entails a sense of stigma, the strain of pretense or concealment, and a struggle for self-acceptance in the face of cruel jokes by unthinking companions.

Obviously, both spouses suffer (as well as any children) until the marriage dissolves heartbreakingly in separation and divorce. The nongay party may either come to desire more sexual fulfillment than the other has been able to provide or, upon learning of the partner's homosexuality, find it so intolerable as to terminate their union. The lesbian or gay spouse may experience guilt over same-sex feelings (even without genital contact) and decide to end the anxieties of an artificial relationship. In the words of Jane Austen, "Nothing can be compared to the misery of being bound without love, bound to one, and preferring another!"[9]

Tribunal Procedures

Even as the Church has a pastoral obligation to prepare couples for marriage and to support them in their commitment, it has no less a pastoral responsibility to help those who suffer through marital breakdown to rebuild their lives. As part of a vital and growing ministry to divorced persons,[10] the Catholic community has recourse to a tribunal system of ecclesiastical courts, through which spouses can find healing reassurance after broken relationships.

The word *tribunal* at first glance might bring to mind a cold, impersonal forum, which involves laws, lawyers, and judges. However, that forum, principally through the granting of annulments, helps divorced individuals to attain renewed peace of mind and/or the possibility of remarriage in a Catholic ceremony.

Briefly, an annulment is a formal declaration by a Church court that an essential requirement of a valid bond—for example, a genuine interpersonal relationship[11]—has been lacking from the very beginning of conjugal union. In fact, "a marriage annulment is a legitimate right that should be accorded any person whom the law finds to be deserving."[12]

Each diocese follows somewhat different policies in carrying out the required canonical process. Typically, the *Petitioner* (spouse who "petitions" for nullity) first fills out general questionnaires with important data on backgrounds and salient factors of possible nullity. Later the party makes her or his full declaration during an interview, usually at the tribunal offices. Meanwhile, the *Respondent* (spouse who "responds" to citation) also provides sworn evidence about the marriage and its failure, to assure a balanced point of view. His or her active cooperation helps the tribunal to arrive at a final determination, although a refusal does not necessarily subvert or hinder the process. Shortly afterward, two or three acknowledgeable *Witnesses* (relatives or friends of the spouses) add to the information or simply corroborate the essential problems in the relationship. They give their testimony individually and privately, to maintain the strictest confidentiality.

Ordinarily, an *Auditor* obtains all the depositions, unless they are submitted by mail under extenuating circumstances. Eventually, an *Advocate* offers the reasons for nullity of the marriage, while a *Defender of the Bond* indicates any factors in favor of validity. Ultimately, the *Judge* renders a decision by stating "the facts" of the case, invoking "the law" as applicable and drawing up "the argument" with moral certitude.

Many different factors prevent a tribunal from completing the essential procedures as quickly as everyone would desire. Additionally, financial realities necessitate a request for at least partial payment of court expenses, whenever possible. Finally, a declaration of nullity, if granted, does not affect the legitimacy of any children born to a marriage.

Homosexuality and Annulment

Few of the issues which confront tribunal personnel are more sensitive and complex than those connected with homosexuality! Few subjects evoke such hostility or misunderstanding as to defy proper considerations of reason, research, or religious solicitude!

And yet, in investigating the possibility of annulment, ecclesiastical courts focus directly (and refreshingly for once among Church authorities!) on sexual orientation rather than on overt genital behavior in itself.[13] Wherefore, when confirmed homosexual persons attempt a heterosexual union, the canonist reflects on their *lack of necessary discretion* in failing to perceive the true dimension of marriage as adverse to their own basic orientation, or (increasingly today) the canonist concentrates on their *lack of requisite competence* in fulfilling on an enduring basis the affectional and emotional needs of a heterosexual community of life.

Canon law states that "marriage is effected by the legitimately expressed consent of two parties who are capable according to law" (Can. 1081 of 1918 Code, Can. 1010 of new Code). Since natural law would be included, though not specified, the Code recognizes—at least generically—that a person might lack a natural capacity or competence for nuptial union.

The Second Vatican Council, by whose illumination we now interpret the Code, spoke of marriage as "the intimate partnership of life and love . . . established by the Creator and qualified by His laws . . . rooted in a conjugal covenant of personal consent . . ." (*The Church Today*, no. 48). The Council thus fostered development in the theology of marriage by emphasizing the interpersonal relationship of the spouses as an essential quality.[14]

Accordingly, Church canonists have evolved new insights for appraising the conjugal bond and its requisite elements for validity. In particular, today's behavioral sciences have helped to clarify both the psychological demands of a marital partnership and the capacity of individuals to assume and sustain its inherent responsibilities.

At the same time, modern research has provided a deeper understanding of heterosexuality and homosexuality, even though they remain complex in characterological structure and multidimensional in behavior patterns. Dr. Jean-Marc Bordeleau, a *peritus* ("expert") with the Montreal Tribunal, wrote as early as 1968 that same-sex "attraction may be exclusive or merely preponderant, it may be episodical and not exclude heterosexual activities. . . . The present definition differs very much from the one given hardly ten years ago, which considered homosexuality a perversion."[15] Thus, in deciding the nullity of a marriage, the updated canonist no longer refers to so-called abnormal inclinations but simply focalizes on the degree of affectional orientation. Often, for example, the predominantly homosexual person is repelled by the idea of genital relations with the opposite gender, much as an avowed heterosexual individual is revolted at any thought of relations with the same sex.[16]

In arriving at a final decision, therefore, the Judge determines whether or not the particular homosexual person of a specific marriage lacked the necessary competence to fulfill the requirements of an "intimate (heterosexual) partnership of life and love." Such marital incapacity must be, in canonical terms, both antecedent and perpetual.

Antecedent. Today's social scientists are virtually unanimous in the opinion that homosexuality, like heterosexuality, originates long before puberty, in the earliest experiences of the very young child. They also generally agree that no single factor causes a particular orientation, whether heterosexual or homosexual, but that multiple biological, psychological, and sociological circumstances determine one's constitutional makeup.

Perpetual. Nearly all contemporary experts likewise believe that a genuine homosexual or heterosexual orientation is basically irreversible. Indeed, historians have found through the centuries that a person's homosexuality remained unchanged, despite marriage or abstention; despite imprisonment, torture, and mutilation; despite electroshocks, lobotomies, psychoanalysis, or aversion therapy; and finally even despite the Church's threats of damnation, its charismatic blessings, and one's own lifetime of prayer! (The lack of adequate objective follow-up studies compromises the vaunted claims of successful reorientation by some therapists, who at any rate may have truly helped pseudohomosexual or bisexual individuals.) Homosexual or heterosexual behavior can be modified, of course, by any number of methods, but one's affectional orientation continues the same, notwithstanding the moral outrage of attempted alterations in one's basic personality!

Pastoral Reflections for Tribunal Personnel

Tribunal personnel, who in some dioceses still consider homosexuality a disorder or at least a symptom of an underlying pathology, need to update themselves with recent perceptions.[17] Thus, the latest Kinsey Institute report (1981) overwhelmingly concluded, after a ten-year study, that homosexuality is as natural as heterosexuality.[18] In the continuing absence of valid scientific evidence to the contrary, homosexuality *per se,* like heterosexuality *per se,* cannot be regarded as a disturbance of any kind.[19] In fact, the research of such leading experts as Dr. Evelyn Hooker even shows no greater incidence of mental illness among homosexual persons than among heterosexual individuals.[20]

Consequently, each member of a tribunal staff might examine whether he or she evinces an insensitivity that causes gay and lesbian persons needless pain. Jesus himself said that no unnecessarily heavy burdens are to be imposed on persons. The law is for the sake of people and not people for the sake of the law (cf. Mk 2: 27). "Alas for you lawyers, who lay unendurable burdens on others and will not lift a finger to lighten them!" (Lk 11: 46; cf. Mt 23: 4).

Auditors. In taking testimony, for instance, we need to use sensitive language about sexual orientation and to probe no further than needed into overt activity, which is a matter of conscience before God. The U.S. Catholic Conference pointed out, particularly to priests: "Obviously, our culture is changing. A priest fixed on an earlier plane of personal development will find cultural change painful. Instead of exerting prophetic leadership, he will withdraw or strike out against the changes. . . ."[21]

Advocates, Defenders, Judges. In stating "the facts" of a case, we could utilize—for example—the Kinsey scale as to whether a Petitioner or Respondent is homosexual in orientation or bisexual or heterosexual with same-sex inclinations.[22] In drawing up "the law" section, we might rely not only on past jurisprudence concerning homosexuality but also show a willingness to go beyond that already developed.[23] Finally, in formulating "the argument," we should render a decision without recourse to such expressions as "abnormal," "incurable defect of personality," and—perhaps worse of all—"basic perversion," used in a recently summarized case.[24] All of us can profitably recall the words of the Second Vatican Council: "In pastoral care, appropriate use must be made, not only of theological principles, but also of the findings of the secular sciences, especially of psychology and sociology" (*The Church Today,* no. 62).

A specific statement is necessary about female homosexuality, since lesbians can be often largely ignored in our sexist society. Present-day tribunal personnel, mostly male, "may be reluctant, psychologically, to recognize" (as canonist Clara Henning says) "that women can find sexual gratification without men!"[25] In fact, we must counteract any undue influence from our far greater knowledge of male homosexuality and at the same time realize that Church law itself reflects the masculine mind which has made and still administers it.

In conclusion, "The challenge is the same for every Judge. He must know his own culture and his own times. He must be able to perceive, and to weigh, and to create suitable, enlightened norms, by which justice can be rendered. . . . He must, above all, show forth the ability of the Church to treat people as individual persons of the community and not just cases or stereotypes. . . ."[26] The same words might be addressed to every member of the tribunal, whether male or female; only by following such advice can we adequately help gay persons and their former spouses to find the healing touch of Christ in their often shattered lives.

Single or Married Gay Persons

Gay individuals who are now contemplating or have already entered marriage need to explore the entire question, in depth and at leisure, with an objective and understanding counselor. Certainly, from the outset, each person must determine the preponderance of homosexual attraction before making any decisions about the future.

Gay and single. In the past, many people, including priests, often encouraged homosexual persons to marry. Donald Webster Cory (i.e., Edward Sagarin) felt years ago that "if it is possible to do so with a mate who understands your nature and who will not consider it a threat, the possibilities of a successful marriage are not at all remote."[27]

Today only the ill-informed counselor could urge a predominantly homosexual individual to consider matrimony, with an assurance that the so-called problem would work itself out. The idea that wedded life can "cure" true homosexuality in any way is an outright fallacy! Therefore, "the exclusive homosexual, as a rule, should be strongly advised against marriage, no matter how greatly he (or she) seems to long for the comforts of a conventional home or for a child."[28]

Gay and married. A relationship which exercises so important a role as marriage in the life of an individual ought not to be set aside without lengthy and serious reflection. Besides, no person should ever assume that matrimony is an easy commitment for anybody and thus can be simply nullified in the face of conjugal difficulties. Church tribunals are neither divorce mills nor annulment factories.

Indeed, particularly during previous generations, many homosexually oriented people—with the obvious exception of gay clergy and lesbian religious—were married and raised children. The Church itself has had a long history of insisting upon interior adaptation rather than allowing the personal assertion of individual difference.

However, as earlier indicated, lesbian and gay spouses adjust to a heterosexual relationship only on the surface and in the narrowest sense. Sometimes, they are wrongly tempted to believe that, with a more caring and loving mate, gay feelings would never have surfaced as an issue. Other times, knowingly unable to satisfy a partner's needs, they make a tentative decision to terminate the marriage.

Under such circumstances, the counselor might cautiously and sensibly support, if not separation and divorce, at least an affirmation of identity ("coming out"). Homosexual persons become much more healthy and happy when they accept and acknowledge their gayness and speak about themselves in a positive way. Secrecy and pretense only increase a false sense of shame and guilt over normal same-sex attractions. Radclyffe Hall, in her now classic portrayal of lesbian love, decries "that wilfully selfish tyranny of silence evolved by a crafty old ostrich of a world for its own well-being and comfort. The world hides its head in the sands of convention, so that seeing nothing it might avoid Truth."[29]

Finally, some gay individuals who remain married[30] may be concerned about the validity of their unions in the context of previous canonical reflections. The counselor might point out that, according to Church legislation, "Marriage enjoys the favor of the law; hence, in case of doubt, the marriage is to be considered valid, until the contrary is proved" (Can. 1014 of 1918 Code, Can. 1013 of new Code). In defense of what may seem a double standard, the Christian community should afford *maximum reassurance* to persons still married and *maximum relief* to those later divorced.

Divorced Nongay Spouses

Ordinarily, you will be the Petitioner before the Tribunal in an annulment procedure, particularly if you desire the freedom to remarry in a Catholic ceremony. Although the experience can be sometimes (but not necessarily) humiliating and painful, the process itself usually demands little effort to obtain great peace of mind. Meanwhile, focus on the good consequences of the past and redirect your energies toward an even better future.

When you first learned of a spouse's gayness, your self-esteem may have been threatened or even damaged. Hopefully, by now, you appreciate your own self-worth, that you are not less man or woman for having "failed" to satisfy your partner's needs. At the same time, you must recognize, without guilt, that you did not cause your spouse to "turn" gay, either by not providing enough sex or instead by demanding too much!

In fact, some of you may possibly suspect that you yourselves unwittingly chose gay wives and husbands, due to their lack of heterosexual aggressiveness and/or your own sexual inhibitions. Else, perhaps fully aware of another's gay feelings, you had hoped to change ("cure") the affectional preference.

Likewise, some of you now possibly grasp the underlying reason for certain qualities that attracted you from the beginning. For example, maybe you found in your lesbian or gay spouses a heightened sensitivity toward those who were different. Or perhaps you admired their special concern for the rights of other minority groups in society. Consequently, the "coming out" process has revealed to you, not a completely new individual, but another facet of his or her personality, with its appealing attributes.[31]

Continually, you need to root out any prejudices or stereotypes, with which we all have been raised, particularly in regard to homosexuality. Your own initial aversion, if any, may in fact endow you with a personal insight into a homosexual partner's sense of rejection and alienation within a hostile and unsympathetic world. Assuredly, your heartbreaking marriage to a gay or lesbian spouse can at least give you a positive appreciation of differences in others, whatever those differences might be.[32]

Divorced Gay and Lesbian Persons

If your marital relationship has ended in civil divorce, you yourself may not have any obvious reason to request a Catholic annulment. However, should your former spouse seek to remarry, certainly give cooperation to the Tribunal with honesty and integrity. In the face of any unjustifiable hostility, calmly affirm your own personal worth and your right to pastoral understanding.

Now that you are no longer hiding behind a mask, you need not conform to a role that others would have you play. By finally acknowledging your own distinctive nature, you begin to appreciate that gay women and men have "the ability to see with different eyes, that is, to disengage themselves from the value-systems uncritically accepted in society at large."[33]

Furthermore, you realize more fully that "closets" stunt their inhabitants not only psychologically but also spiritually. The homosexual Christian, writes John McNeill, "is usually well aware that it is most often selfish fear and a desire to escape personal humiliation, suffering, and loss that motivates the desire to hide one's identity."[34] Through openness about your true same-sex temperament, you leave behind a deception and falsehood unworthy of Christ's followers.

From a spiritual point of view, then, your "coming out" represents a fundamental option toward ultimate integrity and well-being as a human person and as a child of God. The ever deepening inner acceptance of your gayness, in the presence of the Lord, confers a basic moral assurance that you can follow your conscience to lasting self-respect and Christian maturity.

Finally, although every individual should avoid totally identifying personhood with his or her sexual orientation,[35] nevertheless at the same time you need to affirm homosexuality as an integral component of your personality structure. Otherwise, by discounting important sensibilities in a variant nature or by trivializing the different perceptions of a same-sex temperament, you hinder yourself from becoming the best possible lesbian or gay person God has called you to be!

> Do not model yourselves on the behavior of the world around you, but be transformed by the renewal of your mind, so that you may judge what is God's will, what is good, pleasing, and perfect. . . . We have gifts that differ in accordance with the favor that God has bestowed on each of us. . . . Let your love be completely without dissimulation. . . .
>
> (Rom 12: 2, 6, 9)

NOTES

1. Jeannette Foster believed that "this great short story (of Ruth and Naomi), long acclaimed as a masterpiece of narrative art, is the first of a thin line of delicate portrayals, by authors seemingly blind to their full significance, of an attachment which, however innocent, is nevertheless still basically variant" (*Sex Variant Women in Literature*, 2d ed. [Baltimore: Diana Press, 1975], p. 22).

2. Ecclesiastical authorities would undoubtedly propose norms and guidelines for the benefit of lesbian and gay male relationships if the Catholic Church ever differentiated its well-known official teaching about same-sex genital behavior (e.g., by qualifying *homosexual* relations as immoral only for *heterosexual* persons, not for *homosexual* couples). Even now some moral theologians, such as Philip Keane, have tentatively suggested that "the Church and society should be open to finding other ways of supporting stable homosexual unions" (*Sexual Morality: A Catholic Perspective* [New York: Paulist Press, 1977], p. 89).

3. The relevant Rotal decisions, which consider homosexuality as an independent basis for nullity of marriage, include those by Charles Lefebvre (2 December 1967), Heinrich Ewers (22 June 1968), Lucien Anné (25 February 1969), Nicola Ferraro (14 March 1969), Mario Pompedda (6 October 1969), Dario-Marie Huot (28 January 1974), and José Serrano (30 April 1974).

4. Canonical reflections on homosexuality, as a possible impediment to marriage, range

from Vincent Coburn in the *Jurist* (1960) to Thomas Green in *Linacre Quarterly* (1976), especially three articles by John Schmidt in the *Catholic Lawyer* (1973, 1975).

5. Just as Christians have always believed that nongay individuals "pervert" *their own basic nature* through homosexual behavior, so we have begun to understand that gay and lesbian people act contrary to *their own true orientation* by entering heterosexual relationships.

6. Don Clark, *Loving Someone Gay* (Millbrae, Calif.: Celestial Arts, 1977), p. 128.

7. Alan Bell and Martin Weinberg, *Homosexualities: A Study of Diversity Among Men and Women* (New York: Simon & Schuster, 1978), p. 160.

8. Donald Webster Cory, *The Homosexual in America: A Subjective Approach,* 2d ed. (New York: Castle Books, 1960), pp. 201, 205, 206.

9. Jane Austen, letter to her neice (1815).

10. Divorce ministry is described from multiple perspectives in James Young, ed., *Ministering to the Divorced Catholic* (New York: Paulist Press, 1979).

11. José Serrano, who stands among Rotal Judges as a great exponent of the interpersonal nature of marriage, affirmed: "Though it must be granted that the interpersonal relationship can reach greater or lesser perfection in different couples, yet in no way can it be said that this relationship completely belongs only to the 'more perfect' or 'desirable' ideal marriage, since in fact it constitutes an essential property of any marriage consent" (5 April 1973).

12. Terence Tierney, *Annulment: Do You Have A Case?* (New York: Alba House, 1978), p. v. Father Tierney's short book, intended for the lay person, is a useful guide to the annulment process. Unfortunately, he writes of homosexuality as "sexual confusion" and "haunting problem" (pp. 23, 66).

13. José Serrano, in his Rotal decision on homosexuality, said that same-sex activity in itself or in its frequency must not be the main focus of marriage cases (30 April 1974). Obviously, both heterosexual and homosexual persons can indulge in homosexual genital behavior. Besides, individuals are genuinely identified as gay or lesbian when their *strongest "emotional" and "sexual" responses* are aroused by people of the same gender, and (despite some popular opinion) independent of whether or not they engage in *"genital" relations* with the same sex.

14. Lucien Anné, in a widely applicable and now famous decision concerning lesbianism, wrote: "The statement of the Vatican Council (i.e. *The Church Today,* no. 48) has a juridical significance. It does not consider just *the mere fact* of the establishment of the community of life but considers *the right and obligation* to this intimate partnership of life . . ." (February 25, 1969).

15. Jean-Marc Bordeleau, "Homosexualité et Nullité du Marriage," *Studia Canonica* 2, no. 2 (1968): 225, 227.

16. Homosexual individuals, contrary to stereotype, usually relate to the opposite sex with sufficient ease *on a social level.* Lesbians do not experience repugnance towards men, nor do gay males have contempt for women, at least not as often or as much as nongay men do! (Two-thirds of heterosexual men, according to Kinsey, do not "like" women, while a significant number of women "feel" more warmth from gay males.)

17. The real sickness in people is not *homosexuality* (a natural variant of sexuality) but *homophobia* (an unhealthy irrational fear, anxiety, or aversion towards homosexuality).

18. Alan Bell, Martin Weinberg, and Sue Hammersmith, *Sexual Preference: Its Development in Men and Women* (Bloomington, Ind.: Indiana University Press, 1981).

19. The American Psychiatric Association removed homosexuality from the list of sexual deviations in 1973. Its latest manual clearly affirms that "homosexuality itself is not considered a mental disorder" (*Diagnostic and Statistical Manual of Mental Disorders,* 3rd ed. [Washington, D.C.: American Psychiatric Association, 1980], p. 282).

20. Dr. Evelyn Hooker, who was (for example) an original member of the National Institute of Mental Health Task Force on Homosexuality, found no significant psychological variations to distinguish the homosexual person from the heterosexual individual, al-

though she used the best testing tools available (Rorschach, MAPS, TAT) in a comparative study with random selection.

21. United States Catholic Conference, *The Program of Continuing Education of Priests* (Washington, D.C.: USCC, 1973), note 14.

22. Alfred Kinsey, whose studies were the first comprehensive report on sexual orientation and whose findings have been repeatedly validated, posited a sliding seven-point scale from exclusively heterosexual (zero) to exclusively homosexual (six). Kinsey et al., *Sexual Behavior in the Human Male* (Philadelphia: Saunders, 1948), pp. 636–41; *Behavior in the Human Female* (Philadelphia: Saunders, 1953), pp. 468–72.

23. Lawrence Wrenn once wrote, "Here, it would seem is the real problem: the unwillingness of the lower courts to accept the responsibility of doing their own interpreting and supplying. Interpreting and supplying involves a great deal of study and thought and presupposes high maturity and responsible independence" (*Annulments*, 2d ed. [Hartford, Conn.: Canon Law Society of America, 1972], p. 5).

24. *Matrimonial Jurisprudence, United States 1975–1976* (summaries of selected cases published by the Canon Law Society of America), pp. 74, 75, 77. A Judge, who sifts psychiatric contributions through juridic principles, must always be careful not to make medical judgments but only legal ones. (In the same summarized case, the Auditor—who is required to assess a person's credibility—added an unnecessary description of the gay Respondent's "interesting appearance . . . three rings . . . hair styled . . . ," p. 76.)

25. Clara Henning, "Lesbianism and the Canon Law on Marriage," *Homilectic and Pastoral Review* 69, no. 9 (1969): 693. Henning argued in 1969 that homosexuality does not lend itself to the legal provisions of a proposed canonical impediment to matrimony, because the orientation establishes itself differently in females than in males, possibly for women even long after the day of marriage.

26. Lawrence Wrenn, *Annulments*, 3rd ed. (Toledo, Ohio: Canon Law Society of America), p. 6.

27. Donald Webster Cory, op. cit., p. 261.

28. John Cavanagh, "Latent Homosexuality as a Cause of Marital Discord," *Linacre Quarterly* 43, no. 3 (1976): 145. Regrettably, Dr. Cavanagh, a practicing Catholic psychiatrist, added that "permissible exceptions (i.e., for homosexual men) are marriages of convenience with a woman who is either totally anhedonic, or a Lesbian herself, or considerably older."

29. Radclyffe Hall, *The Well of Loneliness* (first published 1928), chapter 15.

30. In some cities there are support groups—such as Gay Married Men's Association (GAMMA), Straight Partners (for their spouses), and Gay Parents (if they have children)—through which individuals help each other to deal with the conflicts in their marital situation.

31. Some appealing qualities of gay people's lives even benefit heterosexual wedded couples (!), "for example, in marriage counseling, where quite a few of the problems which heterosexual men and women have with each other are best solved by what has been gleaned from Lesbian relationships" (C. A. Tripp, *The Homosexual Matrix* New York: McGraw, 1975, p. 274).

32. Heterosexuality or homosexuality should not be a factor in determining the custody of children (if any). No causal connection has been demonstrated between an individual's ability to be a good parent and his or her affectional orientation. Likewise, absolutely no evidence has been found that children appropriate the sexual preference of the custodial mother or father.

33. Richard Woods, *Another Kind of Love: Homosexuality and Spirituality,* rev. ed. (Garden City, N.Y.: Doubleday, Image, 1978), p. 112.

34. John McNeill, *The Church and the Homosexual* (Kansas City: Sheed, Andrews and McMeel, 1976), p. 180.

35. Bishop Francis Mugavero, *Sexuality—God's Gift* (11 February 1976), a pastoral letter to the Diocese of Brooklyn.

APPENDIX: CANONICAL JURISPRUDENCE
ON HOMOSEXUALITY AND MARRIAGE

Preliminary Note: The "Sacred Roman Rota," the ecclesiastical tribunal of Rome, becomes the court of final appeal for many marriage cases. By reason of its unique position, the Rota constitutes the chief source of canonical jurisprudence for diocesan tribunals throughout the world.

In the past, canonical jurisprudence generally did not consider homosexuality by itself as an invalidating force with regard to marriage. Instead, the Roman Rota and other Church courts invoked the traditional grounds for nullity, which included "underlying mental illness," since same-sex orientation was supposedly symptomatic of deeper disturbances. Other standard grounds, likewise not unique to the circumstances of lesbian and gay persons, are briefly summarized as follows and can still be used (rarely) when applicable.

Total Simulation—if the (homosexual) man or woman wedded, for example, solely to create an artificial facade of respectability.

Intention Against Perpetuity—if the individual merely intended a trial marriage, for instance, to escape family pressures toward matrimony.

Intention Against Children—if the person, being apprehensive about a successful relationship, positively planned a childless union.

Intention Against Fidelity—if the wife or husband definitely excluded sexual conjugal commitment (although jurists questioned whether homosexual affairs were equivalent to "canonical" infidelity).

Psychic Impotence—if the spouse, though physically capable, were unable to have heterosexual intercourse for psychic reasons (though canonists disputed the impossibility of a "cure," since invalidating impotence must be "perpetual").

Condition—if the heterosexual party, perhaps suspicious of the other's sexual orientation (prior to the wedding), made heterosexuality an absolute condition of marital validity.

Error—if the nongay partner, having later learned about the mate's affectional preference (after the marriage), alleged a substantial error about the person intended as a spouse.

Nonconsummation—if in fact the conjugal bond were never physically consummated through genital union (strictly speaking, cause for "dissolution" by the Holy See, rather than a basis for "nullity" by a Church court).

Recent canonical jurisprudence—as explained in the essay itself—has increasingly recognized that homosexuality, by its very nature, can render a person unable to enter a valid union. Several important Rotal decisions, in particular, have looked upon same-sex orientation as relatively autonomous grounds for nullity. Although the Judges frequently quote at length from traditional psychiatric data (written prior to 1974), their differently nuanced conclusions can nevertheless stand independent of outdated medical opinion.

Charles Lefebvre, in an affirmative Rotal decision, declared the homosexual partner incapable of valid marriage due to "lack of sufficient discretion" as well as "lack of necessary competence" to assume conjugal obligations (2 December 1967).

Heinrich Ewers, in another affirmative decision, placed homosexuality among the causes of personal inability to undertake heterosexual rights and responsibilities (22 June 1968).

Lucien Anné, in a well-known negative decision pertaining to lesbianism, nevertheless affirmed that the marriages of homosexual persons can be invalid because of "lack of essential object"—the essential object understood (in the light of Vatican II) *not only* as "the right to the body" *but also* as "the right to a community of life" (25 February 1969).

Nicola Ferraro, when granting an affirmative decision, held that homosexuality rendered a marriage null because of lack of object, that is, lack of capacity to hand over and accept nuptial responsibilities (14 March 1969).

Mario Pompedda, in upholding Lefebvre's earlier decision, based his opinion not on "lack of due discretion" but on "lack of due competence" to assume conjugal obligations as the "essential object of marital consent" (6 October 1969).

Dorio-Marie Huot stated that homosexuality suppresses the object of the matrimonial covenant, because the party lacks a radical competence to enter nuptial union and undertake its essential commitments (28 January 1974).

José Serrano affirmed that homosexuality places under question the ability of the individual with regard to "the interpersonal relationship" of marriage (30 April 1974).

Like any other discipline, canonical jurisprudence is loyally dynamic and conscientiously evolving. Through the decades, by utilizing up-to-date information from the behavioral sciences as well as ongoing theological insights into the nature of marriage, jurisprudence has found fresh applications for old laws and expanded its principles to include newly understood situations. Accordingly, although gay women and men can form *enduring same-sex relationships* (contrary to prevalent stereotypes and despite adverse pressures from clergy and laity), the Church has come to declare *marriage itself* as invalid for those whose orientation is genuinely homosexual.

> "Lord, you have probed me and you know men. . . . From afar you understand all my thoughts. . . . Truly you have formed my inmost being. . . . Guide me in ways that are everlasting."
>
> (Psalm 139: 1, 2, 13, 24)

BIBLIOGRAPHY: CANONICAL WRITINGS ON HOMOSEXUALITY AND MARRIAGE

Cautionary Note: None of the published articles refers to homosexuality without invoking the old medical literature. Even the most recent contribution by Thomas Green in 1976 uses phrases such as "character disorder," "affective disturbance," and "irresistible impulses," despite the widely known assertion by the American Psychiatric Association in 1973 that "homosexuality per se implies no impairment in judgment, stability, reliability, or general social or vocational capabilities."

Bordeleau, Jean-Marc. "Homosexualité et Nullité du Marriage." *Studia Canonica* 2, no. 2 (1968): 223–46.

Cavanagh, John. "Latent Homosexuality as a Cause of Marital Discord." *Linacre Quarterly* 43, no. 3 (1976): 138–46.

Coburn, Vincent. "Homosexuality and the Invalidation of Marriage." *Jurist* 20, no. 4 (1969): 441–59.

Green, Thomas. "Homosexuality and the Validity of Marriage—The Developing Jurisprudence." *Linacre Quarterly* 43, no. 3 (1976): 196–207.

Henning, Clara. "Lesbianism and the Canon Law on Marriage." *Homiletic and Pastoral Review* 69, no. 9 (1969): 691–98.

Kenny, Walter. "Homosexuality and Nullity—Developing Jurisprudence." *Catholic Lawyer* 17, no. 2 (1971): 110–22.

Menard, Pierre. "The Invalidating Force of Homosexuality." *Studia Canonica* 3, no. 1 (1969): 5–21.

Ritty, Charles. "Possible Invalidity of Marriage by Reason of Sexual Anomalies." *Jurist* 23, no. 4 (1963), 394–422.

Schmidt, John. "Homosexuality and Validity of Matrimony"—three articles in *Catholic Lawyer*: 19, nos. 2 & 3 (1973): 84–101, 169–99; 21, no. 2 (1975): 85–121. The first two articles first appear in *Jurist* 32, nos. 3 & 4 (1972) 381–99, 494–530.

In additional to the listed articles, canonists refer to two well-known dissertations: William Tobin's *Homosexuality and Marriage* (Rome: Catholic Book Agency, 1964), which surveyed all of the prior jurisprudence, and John Keating's *The Bearing of Mental Impairment on the Validity of Marriage* (Rome: Gregorian University Press, 1964), pages 196–200, which foreshadowed present-day emphasis on the homosexual person's incapacity to fulfill the requirements of a heterosexual relationship.

Finally, tribunal personnel make use of standard reference texts such as Germain Lesage and Francis Morrisey's *Documentation on Marriage Nullity Cases* (Ottawa: Saint Paul University, 1973), pages 182–94; Lawrence Wrenn's *Annulments*, 3d ed. (Toledo, 1978), pages 50–52; J. Edward Hudson's *Documentation II on Marriage Nullity Cases* Ottawa, 1979), pages 326–48; and J. Edward Hudson's *Handbook for Marriage Nullity Cases*, 2d ed. (Ottawa, 1980), pages 224–25. Only the Wrenn book, published in the United States, refers to homosexuality in nonnegative terms and simply defines it as a same-sex "strong preferential erotic attraction."

M. BASIL PENNINGTON

Vocation Discernment and the Homosexual

This is not meant to be a magisterial essay, by any means. I want, rather, to use the opportunity this forum affords me to raise some questions and share some ideas. I was going to say, ". . . to open out further the dialogue between the Church and the gay community." But who is "the Church"? The way we speak of "Church" at times gives the impression of its being something out there: a body of doctrine, perhaps, or the hierarchy, or all those who are 100 percent yes to every word of the pope, or all who disagree or agree with certain theological positions, or . . . or . . . or . . . The fact is, I am Church, and, since I presume most of the readers of this particular book wil be baptized Christians, you are Church—all of us who have been baptized into Christ are his Church. Our degree of participation, our roles vary—there are many mansions in our Father's home, many parts in our one Body. And so I see this primarily as an intra-Church dialogue. If others wish to join in, they are welcome, but I will be working with presuppositions that pertain to our faith community.

I am speaking in the context of vocation within the Church, albeit, as every Christian vocation must be, in service of the whole human family. More specifically, I am speaking of vocation here in that narrow sense in which Catholics have commonly employed it: the call to a committed life in the priesthood and/or religious institute which involves a commitment to celibacy. However, I do not want in the least to give the impression that I am in any way sympathetic to a concept of vocation that fails to recognize that the call to marriage or to the single life is also a vocation. At this point I do not know if I am ready to do anything more than say that some should, if they are consistent with the position they hold, also raise the question of vocation to a homosexual union.

Another limitation of the considerations here is that I am writing in the context of the male homosexual. What I say may well be applicable to the lesbian. But I prefer to speak out of lived experience. My experience as a vocation father has been almost exclusively with men.

I would define a homosexual as one whose erotic orientation is for his or her own sex. By erotic I mean the desire to communicate with the other in a way that involves the genitals. In our vocation counseling I think it is important to be able to distinguish between homosexuality and homophilia. It is natural that men who live in all-male communities, especially over a long period of time, are most comfortable with men and find their closest friends among them. A candidate, especially if he has been oriented toward religious or priestly life since his youth, might also largely restrict his social contacts to men and feel most comfortable among them. This may have nothing to do with homosexuality in the strict sense, though I think a wider socialization is certainly to be encouraged. All candidates, gay or straight, can profit by a wide and deep social experience with both sexes.

My concern here, then, is with the vocation of homosexual men to the religious life, primarily, and to the priestly life insofar as some religious are called to priesthood and insofar as most priests, by present Church law, are expected to have also a vocation to celibacy for the Kingdom. It goes without saying, of course, that it is of supreme importance for the candidate to have a right grasp of what the celibate life will demand of him. This may devolve in large part upon the vocation father and his way of receiving and guiding the candidate.

First of all, I would like to expose some positions or attitudes which I believe are not acceptable. Many gay men have spoken to me of finding priests, religious, and seminarians in the bars and baths. They are not objecting to their presence in the bars to socialize, agreeing that it is a good thing if priests and religious, in fraternity and love, can bring a Christ presence into bars—gay or otherwise. The fact that there is a certain amount of cruising going on there does not make this unfitting any more than the seduction going on in other bars precludes a priestly or religious presence. But what is seen as unfitting is for men committed to celibacy to be cruising and actively engaging in sex. The rationalization that their commitment only excludes heterosexual or marital sex or a permanent liaison does not strike most gays as very honest or creditable. I do feel a certain compassion for the priest or religious who is searching to understand himself and his sexuality. Some have entered the seminary or religious life with little or no sexual experience, and with little thought given to the significance of sexuality in their lives. Vocation directors and spiritual guides did nothing to explore the matter with them. Their sexual awakening was delayed until suddenly, perhaps in their thirties or at mid-life, they were confronted with their own mysterious forces, with new attractions and nagging questionings. The bar or the bath, entering the scene and acting out is not the best way for them to seek to come to sexual maturity and equilibrium, but oftentimes they see no other way, knowing no one who they feel can walk with them in their quest for self-understanding and acceptance. I feel compassion for such men. I hope today's vocation fathers see that every candidate has faced and substantially settled these questions before he moves ahead in priestly or religious life.

I feel much less compassion or sympathy with the religious or priest who holds that "the vow of chastity only excludes marriage and sins against chastity, and since the expression of one's affection genitally is not sinful, it is not precluded by a commitment to celibacy for the Kingdom." Or for the religious who speaks of "progressive chastity" and feels free to indulge himself so long as he is aiming at eventually practicing complete chastity. We all have our weaknesses; it is one thing to admit them humbly and struggle with them; another, to excuse them glibly and indulge them freely. I think few gay men can stomach such rationalizations. As one put it to me: He wants his cake and to eat it, too. I think it goes without argument that the common sense of the faithful (*sensus fidelium*), gay and straight alike, is that a commitment to celibacy for the Kingdom, whether by vow or priestly state, precludes genital activity.

At a somewhat different level, there is a position taken by an active leader of Dignity which I find also unacceptable. This dedicated young man holds that gay men should not enter religious life because by so doing they are capitulating to the position—unacceptable to him—that celibacy is the only legitimate course for a gay Catholic. Besides failing to see the strict logic of this reasoning, I would not like to see gay men deprived of a right which belongs to all Catholics, whatever their sexual orientation, to follow the call of the Lord into any true vocation. If a gay person discerns that he can best live out his life of love in a committed celibate community—and that judgment is the fundamental one in vocational discernment—then he should feel completely free to pursue such a way of life, no matter how his action might be judged or interpreted by others.

Let me say a word about the vocation counselor himself. I think it is very important that a man in vocation ministry have a good grasp of his own sexual identity and be fully comfortable with it. He should know whether he is homosexual, heterosexual, or bisexual. If he is heterosexual he should be in touch with his homosexual side, well aware that it is a rare man who is exclusively oriented in one direction. If his macho image is such that he cannot tolerate seeing any homosexual tendencies in himself, he is hardly apt to be able to understand or welcome sympathetically a candidate who is in touch with his homosexuality or to help a man who needs to get in touch with it. The vocation father should be very comfortable with his own body, feelings, emotions, and attractions. He should not be afraid of erections or emissions. He should be able to speak freely and openly, albeit reverentially, of sex and sexual activity. He should be able to embrace another man and hold him when he needs to be held. He should be free from that false mind-set that immediately relates all tactility to genitality. He needs to be a free man who fully appreciates and reverences his own male body and all other human bodies, male and female.

If the vocation father is himself a homosexual or bisexual, it is important that he be aware of it and fully accept it. He should be watchful in regard to the attraction candidates can arouse in him and be careful that the way he reaches out and responds to them is dictated by their genuine need and not by his own desires and needs. This may call for a lot of prayer and self-control and a real striving for purity of heart. More than one young man has related to me how a trusted counselor or vocation director has tried to engage him in genital activity. Such a mode of action is a real betrayal of confidence and of a ministry accepted in the Church.

When the vocation father is fully comfortable and controlled in the area of sexuality, he creates the climate within which the candidate or inquirer can be comfortably open about his own sexuality and his sexual history. Obviously this is evoking an ideal to which few of us fully attain. It is important that we strive toward it. But even this is not yet enough. "The just person lives by faith." A natural understanding of ourselves, a conformity to an order of nature, falls short of the reality. The human person has not been left in natural state. We have been called to share in the divine nature, to be truly sons of God. The use of our sexuality, our love, must conform to our exalted status. Like the love of the Son, it must always be open to life, be life-giving. What all the practical implications of this are I am not prepared to spell out. The important thing is that in understanding ourselves and in helping others to understand themselves, we do not neglect this important dimension of our reality. It seems to me that all too many theologians, who should know better, tend to do this in their consideration of sexuality and their postulation of the demands of nature.

In order to be able to touch this divine dimension of our being and that of our candidates, it is essential that we have a living faith, and a deep faith, one that is deep enough to be in touch with the roots and source of our being. This calls for a serious prayer life that goes beneath the surface, beyond reason, to the level of experience, under the action of the

Holy Spirit, through those gifts we received at baptism: knowledge, understanding, wisdom, and counsel. The vocation father who is not functioning at this level will not really know himself, nor be able to understand the candidate and the working of the Spirit in him or help him to such an understanding.

The keynote of this essay is that fundamental, beautiful, and very characteristic Christian virtue: compassion—in the fullest sense of the word: seeking to be one with our brother in the fullness of his experience. Looked at objectively, the lot of the gay person is not an easy one. First there is the "question" of who is to "blame" for one's being gay: God, parents, society, environment, upbringing . . . If one gets beyond that and is able to accept peacefully the reality of one's gayness, then there is the question of acceptance on the part of others. Any decent person wants to be open and authentic, to be freely himself and accepted as such. Yet the gay person knows that much of what he legitimately wants in life may well elude him if he is open about his gayness: acceptance in society and Church, job position, even parental and fraternal love, acceptance, pride, and satisfaction.

Finally, there is for the gay person the question of what to do with his life. A fully human and permanent commitment in love to another person is man's way to happiness and fulfillment. The possibilities for a successful permanent homosexual union are seen to be increasing, but such unions still have the odds greatly against them. The possibilities for a gay man to develop his heterosexual side—which in his experience may be virtually nonexistent—and to find a woman who in love will accept a gay husband and join with him in the challenge to be faithful and to make a successful marriage are not great.

It may seem to the gay man that the easiest and best option for him is the way of consecrated celibacy, choosing for his lover the ever-faithful and fully accepting Lord. But is this so and is this option open to all? Celibacy for the Kingdom is a mystery of grace. To live out this mystery in a single life in the world is certainly not a common or easy vocation. It is at this point the gay man may come to encounter us, the vocation fathers, in the quest to embrace consecrated celibacy within a religious community or the presbyterate.

Sexuality is important because it is intimately bound up with our love. It is meant to undergird a human love relationship powerfully. When someone chooses celibacy for the Kingdom he chooses as the focusing love of his life God in Christ, and he wants to sublimate the power of his sexuality in support of this love. Masturbation undergirds our self-love, love of our false self, and that is the last thing we want to do. That is why the choice of this truncated genital expression is undesirable and destructive of the true human growth. I realize that some would take a different position in regard to this last point, but it is my conviction.

Because of the intimate connection of sexuality with what is absolutely central in life and vocation—love—it is important that the vocation father or counselor explore this area thoroughly with the candidate or inquirer and help him come to a strong position of self-understanding, acceptance, and freedom. I find that most candidates are eager to have an opportunity to speak openly and freely about this dimension of their lives—an opportunity which perhaps they have never been able to find. While every person must be respected as a unique individual and my response to each must be geared to him, in general I prefer to provide such an opportunity in the course of an initial interview, provided the time and the atmosphere are such that they will support the climate of openness. After the candidate and I have gotten reasonably comfortable and I feel he has received the message that I do love him and am with him in his concerns, I might first ask (if it is appropriate—the question may have already been answered) if he has given serious thought to marriage, and then ask rather bluntly and matter-of-factly if he identifies himself as homosexual, heterosexual, or bisexual. I think most are a little surprised by the question, but find its bluntness an invitation to speak frankly and openly. If the man expresses or shows hesitation to go into the matter, I respect this and leave the question to another time, merely stating the importance of his sexuality in relation to his life as a lover and to his vocation. At some point in the discernment of his vocation the candidate must come to where he can freely discuss his sexuality; for if he is unable to talk freely and comfortably about it, he can hardly live with it in freedom and comfort.

The man's statement of his orientation should not go unexplored or unchallenged. If he asserts a heterosexual orientation it is important to see that he is comfortably aware of his homosexual side. Otherwise he might be profoundly shaken if at some future time when he is immersed in a male community with limited female contacts he experiences an attraction towards one of his fellows or becomes aware that one is attracted to him. In the case of an asserted homosexual orientation, the vocation counselor wants to explore if this is not a pseudohomosexuality. If in a particular case a man's estimation of his orientation arises from a lack of maturation which has held him back from venturing forth into heterosexual society, the candidate might—maturing in the religious or priestly life—discover that he can and does love women and question his choice of a celibate vocation made when marriage was not seen as a real option. The candidate should have experience of healthy social relations with both sexes.

For one who is opting for celibacy for the Kingdom, in a certain sense it matters little if he be homosexual or heterosexual. What is important is that he have a mature grasp of his sexuality, know his orientation, and fully accept himself and his sexuality as something good. If this is lacking he can never really give himself in love to God nor to anyone else. If he cannot accept himself, he cannot accept the fact that God or anyone else really accepts and loves him. This can be very difficult for a gay person. His self-image is often very poor indeed. The message he has received from society, from his Church, and frequently even from his own parents and family is that he or at least his gayness is bad. A lack of self-acceptance and an inability to accept true affirming love are, I think, the greatest obstacles I run into in regard to gay candidates. These are heightened by the fact that most religious communities and seminaries are not yet ready to accept a homosexual who is fully out of the closet. Many will now accept a homosexual candidate, especially if they have first got to know him as a person before they become aware of his sexual orientation, so long as he is quiet about it and doesn't "embarrass" them by taking a public stand.

It takes a very significant level of maturity and self-affirmation for a homosexual person to hold himself in honor and peacefully accept the fact that some of those with whom he lives and with whom he has thrown in his lot, whom he loves and respects, would have difficulty accepting him if they knew his sexual orientation. He has need of that self-confidence that assures him that when he is really known, he is loved and accepted, that his sexual orientation is not central to who he is, and that a relationship that leaves this out, while incomplete, can still be sufficiently meaningful.

The vocation father can play a very decisive role in developing this maturity, especially if he is the first straight or first significant person to whom the candidate has revealed his gayness, or the first who fully accepts him with his gayness revealed. The vocation father's full acceptance, with respect and affection, with the assurance that one's sexual orientation is not a bar to his being accepted as a brother, can help the gay man to accept himself as equal to the straight man, as fully acceptable as the straight man. The vocation father should be able to show the same marks of fraternal affection to the gay man as he shows to the straight, and to help the gay to be able to accept them and show them in return. The gay candidate, as much as the straight, needs to be comfortable with his own body, his feelings and emotions and physiological reactions, comfortably aware that different things set him off. He needs to be fully in touch with the legitimacy of the normal tactile expressions of fraternal love which need imply no genital orientation, even if in his case there are physical reactions. Healthy, satisfying, affectionate relations among the brethren are one of the best safeguards for chastity, as well as a powerful maturing and integrating force. Each community has its own ways and modes of expression. The candidate needs to be able to be comfortable with them. This is not to say that there is not plenty of room for growth and development in this area in very many communities. But if a man is choosing a particular community, he has to be able to accept it comfortably where it is, not barring realistic hope for the future.

With great patience and tact the vocation father has to help the candidate to see where the community stands. He has to see if the candidate can really accept this—compassionately accept the limitations and prejudices of the members and live peacefully with them. Most gay men have learned to live at least partially in the closet. Their ideals with regard to religious life may be such that they will find it hard to accept that this may still be necessary even within the religious community. On the other hand, they should not be left with any naive idea as to how easy or difficult this may be. The closeness in the community may make this something much more difficult to live with than it was in the office, at school, or in military service.

It will not be enough if the vocation father alone accepts the gay candidate. It seems to me it is minimally necessary that the novice master and major superior and anyone else with whom the man will have to work in a close, personal way in his formation should also be ready to accept a homosexual person fully as a good candidate and work comfortably with him. Not to be able to be open with someone who is going to have a significant role in his formation is to place an insupportable burden on the candidate.

Some vocation directors undoubtedly will have to refuse gay applicants because their communities are not ready even in a minimal way to accept them. If such is the case, the vocation director should make it very clear to the candidate that he is not being rejected because of his gayness but because of the lack of understanding within the community. To allow the candidates to feel that there is a fault on his part in such a case would be a grave injustice. Obviously I am speaking of a case where the candidate is otherwise fully acceptable. If the candidate has some real lacks, whether these be in relation to the homosexuality or not, they should be honestly brought to his attention. As I have said above, often gay applicants cannot be accepted because they do not accept themselves. But such men are apt to be so defensive that they cannot see this, and will interpret the rejection as a rejection of them because they are gay. The vocation father should make every effort to help such a man to see the facts, but he must be prepared to face failure at times and be branded as prejudiced and homophobic. This can hurt, especially if the vocation father is perhaps being misunderstood by some of his own community because of his true respect and acceptance of gay men.

The vocation father may have to face the fact that a deep-seated prejudice against homosexual persons was bred into him and remnants of it remain in spite of his acquired understanding and respect. If he is aware that such is the case, it is well to discuss it openly with the candidate. This will help to further dissipate the remnants of such an attitude and allay the fears of the candidate, as well as perfect their communication in the case where the candidate was sensing some of the underlying negativity. The father may also be aware of some fears or attractions in himself. These will be more difficult to own up to, and if brought out too early in the relation, could frighten or scandalize the candidate. A very prudent weighing of time and manner is called for, but openness again will ultimately be best if the relationship with the candidate is to be ongoing.

It frequently seems to happen that once a candidate has definitely decided to enter the religious life and a date has been set, there are emotional upheavals. This often enough involves falling in love. I think it is good when this happens. It gives the candidate a real opportunity to test his option of celibacy. Sometimes there is a naive idea that once one opts for celibacy or enters a religious institute or seminary he will no longer experience any attractions, crushes, or love affairs. It is good for the gay man to realize he may still fall in love with a man in the community and this can be especially difficult because of the continual intimacy within which they live. He needs practical advice on how to handle such a situation: the importance of complete openness with a spiritual father; respect for the other person, and that person's right to the freedom of celibacy; the means of letting go of feelings and emotions and finding freedom within himself for his own celibate love.

Some gay persons argue for the legitimacy of playful or recreational sex or genital activity, just for fun, pleasure, or relaxation. Straight persons, by the way they act, often seem to hold for this, too. But I do not think, given the human makeup, that in fact it is possible to use one's genital power in a way that is divorced from love without it being disintegrative of the person and a use or misuse, albeit willing, of the other person. Be that as it may, such activity is wholly imcompatible with the respect a religious or priest should have for his own body as a temple of the Spirit, especially consecrated to God through vow or unction.

It goes without saying that in the process of vocational discernment, many other areas of life besides sexuality need to be explored. Some of these may be influenced by one's homosexuality or others' perception of it. We are, thank God, moving beyond the mythological stereotype of the effeminate homosexual. But if the individual gay man is not a "jock," he may have to work through some negative feelings and associations in regard to his lack of gifts, whether it be in athletics or in other areas, while rejoicing in the gifts he has.

An important part of achieving maturity is breaking away from a dependent relation towards one's parents and establishing a new, responsible relationship with them. The gay person may have particular difficulty here if he has suffered a good bit of rejection on the part of a macho father, or one who was negative or defensive because of insecurity in regard to his own male identity; or on the part of a mother too affected by what others think, and so on. He will need to achieve a deep spirit of forgiveness and compassionate understanding towards them while retaining a loving gratitude for the fundamental gift of life.

Provided, of course, that the particular individual is psychologically healthy and truly opting for celibacy for the Kingdom, I think a gay man who knows and accepts himself can become an excellent religious and/or priest. All men must be lovers. The celibate chooses as the focal love of his life God in Christ Jesus. The gay person has a special ability to bring a strong, tender, affective love to Christ-God. And he can bring the same to his brothers in Christ. Saint Benedict calls upon monks to love each other with a tender and chaste love. The early Cistercians, in their effort to live the Rule fully, so emphasized this that one of their fathers, Saint Aelred of Rievaulx, who wrote a beautiful treatise on spiritual friendship, has often been looked to as a special patron saint for gay men. He may not be a model for vocation fathers, as he and his community suffered much from his notoriously lax admission policy, but if the vocation father brings to his ministry that tender love and deep understanding that marked Aelred, he will do much to help the gay aspirant to experience that self-acceptance and respect that will give him the freedom to choose the way of love that is best for him, his true vocation.

MARGUERITE KROPINAK

Homosexuality
and Religious Life

A recent article about homosexuality in religious life suggested that a person's sexuality, if directed toward another person of the same sex, indicates an inadequacy in *all* personal relationships (Kraft, 1981). As a result homosexual persons are unable to sustain any kind of personal commitments and may have difficulty living out a religious commitment.

This essay will present another perspective in order to show that the homosexual person can be a mentally healthy person, that this person can live a life-style no less stable than that of a heterosexual person, and that there is no reason to exclude the homosexual person from religious life. A major premise of this essay is that a separation between a person and his or her sexuality is not possible.

As Mary Mendola states:

> I am a human being. I am a woman. I am a lesbian. Like other lesbians and homosexuals, I am tired of being defined in terms of my sexual behavior because sexuality is but a part of my emotional life, is but a part of my humanity. Like other human beings, I am a whole person: I hope, I laugh, I pray, I work. (Mendola 1980)

NOTE: This essay is the result of discussions and research conducted by Karen J. Evanczuk, M.S.N.; Marguerite Kropinak, M.S.W.; R. J. Meenihan, Ph.D.; James R. Wolfe, M.F.A.; and two other members who are not able to have their names included because of personal and professional reasons. The group's professional experience includes elementary and secondary education; psychiatric nursing; academic counseling; counseling with children, adolescents, juvenile offenders, adults, gay couples, married couples, and families; drug counseling; rehabilitation counseling; pastoral ministry; formation work; spiritual direction; university administration; and industrial administration.

Psychological Perspective

Before exploring homosexuality in religious life, some exploration of homosexuality in general is appropriate. In relationship to gay/lesbian religious, two questions seem to be crucial: (1) Can a homosexually oriented person be psychologically healthy; and (2) What is the effect of a homosexual orientation on the development of one's personality?

The gay/lesbian person is capable of personal maturity and personality integration. Knowledge about homosexuality, like knowledge of every other aspect of human development and behavior, is an ongoing process, a continuing evolution. Views among many mental health specialists have changed with the acquisition of more information and the completion of more recent studies of gay/lesbian persons.

The psychoanalytic model of sexuality (the first comprehensive theory of intrapsychic functioning written by Sigmund Freud in the early 1900s) took the position that homosexuality is a form of arrested development. This theory was prominent for many years until sufficient clinical and research data produced another model. A new view, for example, has been stated by the distinguished psychoanalyst, Judd Marmor, as follows:

> Surely the time has come for psychiatry to give up the archaic practice of classifying the millions of men and women who accept or prefer homosexual object choices as being, by virtue of that fact alone, mentally ill. The fact that their alternative lifestyle happens to be out of favor with current cultural conventions must not be a basis in itself for a diagnosis of pathology. (Marmor 1973)

This revision of thought is due in part to greater consideration being given to the role of biology in sexual behavior. Interestingly, Freud himself was aware that theories of sexuality would require revision as new data was yielded by biological and psychological investigations. We should

> . . . bear in mind that someday all our provisional formulations in psychology will have to be based on an organic foundation. . . . It will then probably be seen that it is special chemical substances and processes which achieve the effects of sexuality. (Freud 1905)

Research on lesbians conducted by Freedman (1975) reported that they scored higher than a heterosexual control group in autonomy, spontaneity, and orientation toward the present. Oberstone (1976) found no major differences in psychological adjustment between women with a preferred homosexual orientation or heterosexual orientation. In Brown (1977), lesbians were not found to be more "pathological" than heterosexual women, nor to have poorer self-concepts or lesser satisfaction with interpersonal relationships.

Bell and Weinberg (1978) found no significant differences between heterosexual and homosexual men in tendencies related to good physical health, feelings of happiness at the time of the interview, and feelings of happiness related to those feelings five years earlier. Homosexual men did appear to be somewhat less self-accepting and more tense than their heterosexual counterparts, but on the other hand they were found to be more exuberant.

In their most recent work on the development of homosexuality in men and women, Bell, Weinberg, and Hammersmith (1981) reported significant differences between homosexuals "ever in treatment" and "never in treatment." Respondents "ever in treatment" tended to have family constellations which clinicians traditionally described as typical for homosexuals (e.g., detached/hostile fathers for males and rejecting/detached mothers for females). However, for homosexual persons "never in treatment" the stereotyped parental variables did not appear. The clear suggestion here is that clinical descriptions of homosexual persons have been based on the study of only those persons in treatment, rather than on a more representative sample.

Finally, gay/lesbian persons do not all have a stereotyped personality. Bell and Weinberg (1978) have found a wide diversity among homosexual persons, leading them to conclude that it is difficult to make generalizations about lesbians and gay men, since "most are indistinguishable from the heterosexual majority with respect to most of the nonsexual aspects of their lives. . . ."

In summary, this literature supports the notion that homosexual persons are capable of psychological health.

A second significant question involves the effect of society's attitudes toward a homosexual orientation in the development of one's personality. According to C. A. Tripp (1975) in *The Homosexual Matrix*, the causes for both heterosexuality and homosexuality are much alike and cannot be understood apart from each other. Whatever the reasons for developing a homosexual orientation, homosexual individuals must begin to consciously consider the implications for their own self-concept, as well as their attitudes toward other homosexual persons, their families, society, and particularly the implications for the quality of their own lives.

A major discovery for gay/lesbian persons in Western culture is a recognition of the phenomenon of homophobia, a term coined by psychotherapist George Weinberg (1972) in his classic book *Society and the Healthy Homosexual*, and described as being the irrational fear of homosexuality. In American society both heterosexual and homosexual people are affected by homophobia.

In summary, current research seems to conclude that homosexual persons are not necessarily less healthy than are heterosexual persons, but that a homosexual person's self-concept and attitudes about others are strongly influenced by the society in which the homosexually oriented person lives.

Sociological Perspective

Another question confronting gay/lesbian religious is the capacity of a gay/lesbian person to make any kind of commitment. In fact, such commitment is possible both in marriage-type situations and in religious communities.

Before exploring the existence of committed relationships among gay men and lesbians, two difficulties must be addressed: the difficulty involved in researching a representative sample of the homosexual population, and the lack of support systems for gay/lesbian relationships.

Regarding the difficulty in researching the homosexual population, one must recognize that it is impossible to obtain a random sample of lesbians and gay men because of the reluctance of some to admit their homosexuality due to fears of social, legal, and/or employment consequences. In the past most research was conducted with lesbians and gay men who were in treatment for adjustment or emotional problems. Currently, more healthy lesbians and gay men are willing to "come out" to discuss various aspects of their lives with researchers.

As for the lack of support systems, one evident, even glaring explanation for the difficulty homosexually oriented persons have had in sustaining long-term relationships is society's condemnation of them. Given the legal, employment, and religious sanctions that lesbians and gay men experience when considering a committed relationship with a lover of the same sex, it is not surprising that serious obstacles are present from the start. There are no family, societal, or cultural supports or incentives for maintaining the relationship. Society, the Church, and the legal system, in fact, work to destroy it.

This absence of support can be exemplified by the attitude of the Church itself. In *Human Sexuality: New Directions in American Catholic Thought*, the authors state:

Given the fact that their friendships and relationships are not sustained by the normal approval and supports that society provides for heterosexual relations, homosexuals tend to suffer the very real temptation of promiscuity. Inadvertently, Catholic pastoral practice has promoted the incidence of promiscuity among homosexuals precisely by advising them against forming intimate or exclusive friendships. Homosexuals living together have been regarded as living in proximate occasion of sin; they were counseled to desist or else be denied absolution. . . . (Kosnik et al. 1977)

Society at large states the same principle in its own sphere by ridicule and denial of human and civil rights such as jobs and housing.

Heterosexuals have the benefit of most public support systems, including the family, Church, state, and the economic system. Yet statistics from the United States Department of Health and Human Services indicate that there were 2,178,367 marriages in the United States in 1977, and 1,091,000 divorces, a ratio of two to one. Can one truthfully say that heterosexual persons are more capable of committed relationships than are gay/lesbian people? Do these statistics means that it is time to seriously question the ability of heterosexual persons to commit themselves to long-term relationships?

The common stereotype that homosexual persons, particularly gay men, are incapable of commitment to a long-term relationship must be considered when these persons present themselves as candidates for religious life. If it is truly impossible for them to commit themselves to a person, how can it be possible to commit themselves to a spiritual ideal, vow or promises, or to a community of persons?

It has been noted by counselors of lesbians or gay men (Jones 1974; Kraft 1981) that many of their clients express a yearning for permanence and growth in a love relationship. One study reported that both heterosexual and homosexual persons can and do find love and satisfaction in intimate relationships (Peplau 1981). Mary Mendola (1980) studies 405 homosexual men and women: 67 percent defined themselves as permanently committed or married to their partners, and 17 percent had been living with their partners for ten or more years. Quite simply, the common stereotype can no longer claim validity. Many gay men and lesbians are capable of long and stable relationships.*

In conclusion, gay and lesbian persons are capable of deep and long-term relationships even without the support systems and encourage-

---

* In some cases, the lesbian and gay relationships which have survived have been those which have been "invisible" to society. Recently, public health nurses in New York City have discovered many elderly gay men and lesbians who have lived in coupled relationships for forty or more years.

ment—institutional and personal—which are given to most heterosexual persons. But statistics and psychological theory do not explain, let alone express, what being a homosexual individual is really like. Only by knowing individual homosexual persons can one begin to understand the real problems that homosexual individuals encounter.

Perspective on Religious Life

Self-Acceptance

Self-acceptance is a crucial task for anyone, particularly for a gay/lesbian religious. Society has represented homosexual persons as "sick" and "sinful," causing them to feel unworthy and guilty. Some persons feel sinful even though they have never acted out their feelings, somehow sensing that it is sinful even to have a homosexual orientation. Every time a sexual feeling arises, they feel that they are guilty. They doubt that God could love them as gay, yet they deeply know that that is an essential part of their personhood. For true self-acceptance, gay and lesbian persons must come to know themselves as holy persons created and redeemed by God within this sexual context. They must come to know themselves as lovable—not in spite of their gayness—but within, and through, that gayness.

Unfortunately, even after accepting their sexuality, gay or lesbian persons in religious life are often led to continue a deception—to "wear a mask" of heterosexuality before others. They must endure jokes, sarcastic remarks, negative comments, and stereotyping of males and females, and at the same time pretend to be unaffected by them. Lesbians in particular experience a "nonexistence." Other women religious speak and act as if the reality of a lesbian Sister could not exist. There is perhaps no greater hurt than the assumption of a person's nonexistence.

Potential Problems

Acceptance and integration of sexuality with the total person is essential to healthy life. Lack of such integration can lead to serious problems in all areas of the person's life. Basic to all other areas is a lack of self-acceptance—a sense that no matter what the person achieves or accomplishes, no matter who the person helps, it is not sufficient to achieve acceptability as a person. There is the constant, unconscious feeling that: "If they knew who I really am, they would reject me and my work." Often gay/lesbian religious, even those who have never been involved in any overt sexual contact, will feel sinful because of their sexuality. They might fight this fear by overwork in an attempt to gain affirmation through professional excellence. In other cases, they might yield to the fear by despairing of any possibility of acceptance and by giving into depression and apathy in work. For some, work can become a burden; they might be constantly tired. The emotional energy used in "covering up" in both community life and in the ministry can leave little energy for work, prayer, recreation, or social activities.

In personal relationships and affective life, gay/lesbian religious might have a tendency to suppress all feelings and attempts to relate as a protection against recognizing sexual feelings. They may well withdraw because of the inability to deal with affectionate feelings and begin to fear their own self. Attempts to control feelings could lead to their becoming very structured or highly organized, or overflow into high expectations or regimentation of students (if a teacher) or co-workers. In some cases, this denial of feelings, coupled with the constant anxiety associated with this fear and attempt to control, can lead to alcohol or drug abuse as a means of relieving the anxiety.

Spiritually, gay/lesbian religious might find solitude and prayer to be unbearable. They may seek external stimuli (television, music, constant involvement with people) as a means of avoiding being alone with the self and its feelings of unworthiness. The religious might begin to avoid prayer, especially if sexual thoughts or feelings have come up at that time, and experience guilt or shame. If they are unable to talk about the experience with a spiritual director, or if the director reacts negatively, they might attempt to suppress the experience and simply avoid prayer altogether.

Affection in Religious Life

The experience of friendship can cause concern for the gay/lesbian religious. Realizing their sexuality, they might have concern about the warm and affectionate feelings—and perhaps even the sexual feelings—expressed toward a friend of the same sex. But God gifts a person with friends so that both may grow in deeper human love and in deeper love of God. If every person is allowed to really experience affection, liking, love, and sexual attraction, and yet to know the limits of the physical expression of those feelings, then they can grow in a deeper knowledge of their self as lovable and as loving, and in a deeper gratitude for the God who is love.

Healthy religious will not withdraw from the experience, but rather use it as a means of mutual growth. In talking together and sharing thoughts and feelings, both can begin to realize the beauty of an intimate and loving relationship. They may come to realize that God has given the relationship as a gift to both persons so that each can come to know how much God loves each of them. God's love can become more tangible and visible through the "growth" of love in each other. Each can say, "My friend represents the deep and intimate love that God has for me." Being lovable and being in love take on new dimensions—dimensions beyond the love of friends. The religious can grow beyond seeing just this person to seeing God's action in affirming, and in "bringing out the best" in the other.

Practical Difficulties

There are practical difficulties involved in the process of falling in love. Among these are the problems of a relationship affecting community life and the potential threat to celibacy.

In a community, the amount of time and energy invested in a relationship may detract from the two persons' entering into a more total experience of community. Spending time together will detract from time spent with other members of the community or with total community functions. Community members may resent the "coupling" of individuals which excludes others. Close sharing with one person may lead to avoidance of sharing feelings, events, and experiences with other community members. The primary focus of the religious may shift from community interests and a God-centered life to an almost exclusive concern for the friend and the friend's interests. Yet, with proper encouragement and support, a relationship which is truly God-centered and Christian can overflow into the wider community as the two individuals experience joy, lovableness, self-confidence, and self-celebration.

A second difficulty is a threat to celibacy. The experience of a strong attraction and affection may lead to a desire and perhaps to an occasional actualization or physical expression of love. This experience may lead to guilt and feelings of being lowly and disgusting for having given into a sexual act. But this too can be an occasion of grace. The person may realize his/her human weakness—as well as his/her total dependence on and need for God—in order to fulfill the vow of celibacy. Reflection of the feelings and experience can lead to a renewed decision and commitment to celibacy as a response to God's love—a love now experienced, and known in a profound and personal way.

Finally, the experience of falling in love can lead to the experience of being in love. Being in love is the growth experience which continues to occur when the intense feelings and the amount of time spent together lessens. This experience can lead to a deepening in prayer life and in the relationship with God. Love takes on the experience of knowing hurt from another; of sharing suffering with another; of experiencing both closeness and distance, as well as togetherness and separation; of knowing deepened joy and deepened appreciation; of knowing boredom with another and a willingness to just be with another. All of these experiences can lead to a deepening revelation of the God who is love.

However, as in the case of sexually active heterosexual persons, community members with a history of continual sexual activity should be challenged to celibacy. They should be asked to examine their reasons for remaining in religious life. A religious makes a free choice in responding to God. If the religious has freely and publicly committed himself/herself to celibacy, that commitment must be fulfilled. There are other ways of serving God for the person who feels unable to live a celibate life.

In addition to the lack of living out the commitment, noncelibate religious offend their community. If they are involved in an exclusive relationship—either with another community member or with someone outside of the community—that exclusiveness is destructive to community. Persons who are actively soliciting other community members are creating uneasiness and an uncomfortableness which is also destructive to communal life and growth. Charity demands that the group not be so damaged.

While it may be true that men and women of homosexual orientation would experience a temptation to engage members of their religious community in some form of genital experience, and that these community members should be challenged to the reality of their life-style, i.e., celibacy, this experience is not necessarily indigenous to homosexual members only. To assume that simply because a member is of homosexual orientation, that person would be looking for some type of sexual relationship within the community is overstating the case. It would be hoped that by the time of admission a candidate has successfully demonstrated a psychological and spiritual maturity that will control sexual desires.

Candidates

A more germane topic must be examined here—the reality of call. Those who seek some type of a formalized spiritual life are responding to that same voice that speaks to all people of goodwill. The number of homosexual men and women who are successfully performing ministerial functions, both as ordained clergy and lay religious, would indicate that the powers of the Spirit transcend the range of sexual experiences. In responding to a call, candidates bring with them all of the talents and abilities, strengths and weaknesses with which they have been blessed.

Part of the initial formation process is the introduction of the candidate into an understanding of and a first living out of the vows of poverty, chastity, and obedience. A freedom to explore the strengths and weaknesses of how each candidate uniquely faces and embraces the call is necessary. A candidate seeking to live a religious commitment may come to the congregation from a variety of backgrounds: executives and blue-collar workers, poor and rich, virgins and the sexually experienced. Executives will find obedience a challenge. The rich will struggle with poverty, while the poor will see religious communities oftentimes as too affluent. Widowed persons may find the celibate life-style a real challenge. In responding to the variety of candidates who are called to religious life, superiors or formation directors need to not be overly sensitive to gay/lesbian candidates.

Often in considering gay/lesbian candidates for religious life, the community (whether subtly or overtly) presumes an unhealthiness in them merely by reason of sexual orientation. To impose a closer scrutiny, more intense psychological testing and constant reassessment of gay/lesbian candidates implies a mistrust and a misunderstanding. To think that they will have more personal problems or less ability than heterosexual candidates to live celibately is false. A director or superior would not ordinarily require candidates from a materially rich background to undergo more intense testing or evaluation, or question their ability to live a vow of poverty without hoarding material goods. Yet the prejudice that gay/lesbian persons must have greater psychological problems and will have a greater difficulty in being celibate does exist. In reality, it is perhaps easier for some gay/lesbian persons to live in a religious community. Since they prefer relationships and involvement with members of the same sex, they may experience more personal satisfaction and enjoyment in a community than heterosexual persons. This might lead to greater involvement with community and greater appreciation of community members.

The gay or lesbian candidates experience the same problems that heterosexual candidates experience. How can they transfer the close friends and relationships from outside the community to inside the community? How can they learn to relate to all community members—regardless of ages, jobs, and personalities? How can they learn to relate to members of both the same and the opposite sex? How can they learn to minister to God's people? How can they grow into a deep and loving relationship with God?

Spirituality

Given the importance of these questions, the role of the spiritual (formation) director and superior is of great importance in the development of healthy and holy gay and lesbian religious. These questions cannot be answered in a vacuum. Individuals cannot begin to grow as persons if they disregard their sexuality as an important aspect of their personhood. If they grow in friendships, community living, relationship with others, ministry, and spirituality, it will be as sexual persons. Otherwise, the total integration of these aspects within the candidate's personhood is not possible. The unfolding of one's sexuality needs the support and guidance of others. A director or superior who offers direction based on ignorance or prejudice may be destructive of the candidate's formation.

Unfortunately, it will probably be necessary for gay/lesbian candidates to be cautious in talking about their sexuality. They should probably limit sharing about sexuality to those persons who are able to be accepting toward it, and who can help them grow spiritually as gay/lesbian persons. They may not help themselves if they risk being hurt or misjudged in this extremely personal and sensitive area.

In acknowledging their homosexual orientation, such persons have been through a long soul-searching task. They are acutely aware of who they are, who they are becoming, and what they have to share. When people are ill, they turn to a specialist, someone who has studied a particular field in depth. The healer heals from both his/her academic and life experience. So too, homosexuals who are specialists in self-healing will minister with their total being, with all the texture and dynamics of their personalities. Homosexuality is not a clinical condition, but a lived experience.

Spiritual directors often encourage a person to pray about all that he/she is—to pray "what and who you are—how you view life—how you relate to people." Such persons are encouraged to pray about their joy, affection, anger, sorrow, or hurt, but how often are they encouraged to pray about their sexual feelings? When a feeling arises in prayer, even a sexual feeling, it might be the Spirit at work—the Spirit praying through the person "in sighs too deep for words" (Rom 8:26), leading into an area that needs to be made whole and holy. A person is asked only to abandon his/her feeling to God, allowing God to lead and create new life which will blossom in love and service.

Do we really want the responsibility of denying admission to men or women who are truly called, who are truly responding with their total person, who are responding to a life of self-surrender? Do we want to reject vowed members of communities and force them to live a dichotomous life-style rather than celebrating their total gift of sexual personhood?

The Spirit speaks to each of us at different times and in different ways. Trying to explain in natural reasons the actions of the supernatural would be no more successful than explaining the purpose of the moon.

REFERENCES

Bell, A. P., and Weinberg, M. S. 1978. *Homosexualities: a study of diversity among men and women.* New York: Simon & Schuster.

Bell, A. P.; Weinberg, M. S.; and Hammersmith, S. K. 1981. *Sexual preference: its development in men and women.* Bloomington: Indiana University Press.

Brown, L. 1977. A comparison of some personality variables in lesbian and heterosexual women. (Cited by Sang, B. Lesbian research: a critical evaluation. In Vida, G., ed. 1978. *Our right to love: a lesbian resource book.* Englewood Cliffs, N.J.: Prentice-Hall.)

Freedman, M. 1975. Homosexuals may be healthier than straights. *Psychology Today* (March): 28–32.

Freud, S. 1962. *Three essays on the theory of sexuality.* London: The Hogarth Press.

Jones, C. R. 1974. *Homosexuality and counseling.* Philadelphia: Fortress.

Kosnik, A.; Carroll, W.; Cunningham, A.; Modras, R.; and Schulte, J. 1977. *Human sexuality: new directions in American Catholic thought.* New York: Paulist Press.

Kraft, W. F. 1981. Homosexuality and religious life. *Review for Religious* 40: 370–81.

Marmor, J. 1973. Homosexuality and cultural value systems. *American Journal of Psychiatry* 130: 31–40.

Mendola, M. 1980. *The mendola report.* New York: Crown.

Oberstone, A., and Sukeneck, H. 1976. Psychological adjustment and life style of single lesbians and single heterosexual women. *Psychology of Women Quarterly* 2: 172–88.

Peplau, L. A. 1981. What homosexuals want in relationships. *Psychology Today* (March): 28–38.

Tripp, C. A. 1975. *The homosexual matrix.* New York: McGraw.

Weinberg, G. 1972. *Society and the healthy homosexual.* New York: St. Martin.

United States Department of Health and Human Services. 1977. Volume III, Marriage and Divorce. *Vital statistics of the United States* (PHS 81-1121).

ROBERT NUGENT

Priest, Celibate and Gay: You Are Not Alone

The National Federation of Priests' Councils devoted their 1981 Memphis meeting to the theme, "Priest as Person." Father Thomas Kane, director of the Whitinsville (Massachusetts) House of Affirmation, urged the group to address the pressing need "that the significant number of priests with a homosexual orientation join and be encouraged to join support groups of other homosexual priests," and that "new structures . . . be implemented for the pastoral support and care of the priest who is homosexual" (Kane 1981, p. 18).

At the same meeting another priest shared part of a letter from a gay priest: "I'm a priest who has gone from self-hatred because I'm gay to self-acceptance and celebration of who I am. One definite problem is the isolation I felt from other priests. This is surprising since so many of the clergy are gay, but it was never talked about or acknowledged and so I felt myself one of a kind and lived in a private hell. For a while there was a group of us priests meeting for mutual support . . . and it helped me to realize that I wasn't the only one struggling to reconcile ministry with being gay. Somehow we have to get the word out to gay priests. you are not alone" (White 1981, p. 2).

A letter from a priest reader appeared in the February 1981 issue of a clerical journal asking, in response to Kane's recommendation of support groups, "Are we faced with the possibility of a Sodom and Gomorrah rising in the clerical ranks?" (Van Bergan 1982, p. 3). His alarm was based on what he called his own "spiritual formation," which would judge groups of gay priests as an "occasion of sin."

Few people challenge the assumption that the percentage of gay clergy and male religious is somewhat higher than that of the population at large. The reasons for this, however, are not always clear or compelling. There is much less agreement in answering the question of how the

Church should respond to gay clergy, or what kind of "support" is called for today. Some object to support groups, for example, because they might be interpreted as Church encouragement for an "alternate life-style" which is rejected by Church teaching. Others are concerned about scandal or the "image of the priesthood."

The bottom line for many people, especially ecclesiastical authorities, is the question of sexual activity among gay clergy who are already committed to a life of celibacy. Leaders of religious orders are articulating their own concerns about homosexually active clergy. Lay people are equally outspoken—even in public. Arthur Jones, in the pages of the *National Catholic Reporter*, openly voiced his fears about active gay clergy: "Do not discount the possibility of major scandals. The percentage of homosexual seminarians and priests increases; the pattern of the times is that homosexuals are more likely to be active than passive. Who will be scandalized? Not the homosexuals. They may be mortified, but they know the risks. Not all bishops, they may be acutely embarrassed, but they cannot be completely unaware of the problem. . . . No, the ordinary priests and religious, the ordinary Catholic parishioner, the ordinary member of the public, these will feel hurt and betrayed" (Jones 1981, p. 28).

In the past five years several cases involving gay priests have come to national attention. In none of them, however, was the issue of sexual activity *per se* a reason for conflict with Church authorities. Theologian John McNeill, S.J., author of *The Church and the Homosexual* (1976), was silenced by the Sacred Congregation for the Doctrine of the Faith for his views on homosexuality challenging traditional Church teachings and pastoral practices. Ecclesiastical permission to publish his book was withdrawn in 1977 although McNeill was never formally required to retract any of the opinions propounded in the popular and best-selling work (Sacred Congregation for the Doctrine of the Faith 1978).

Richard Wagner, O.M.I., was dismissed from his order after refusing to accept several conditions outlined by his provincial regarding his ministry, life-style, and public statements on celibacy and homosexuality (Kenkelen 1981). Wagner's doctoral study, *Gay Catholic Priests: A Study of Cognitive and Affective Dissonance* (Wagner, 1980a), was an interview with fifty gay Roman Catholic priests, 26 percent of whom had a current lover. Although the release of the study in San Francisco, and the subsequent media event, caused some of Wagner's problems, what brought him to the attention of Rome was a 1980 article in the *National Catholic Reporter* (Wagner 1980b) in which he suggested that for many priests celibacy was exhausting, debilitating, and a privation which makes them less healthy, less creative, and less giving. In discussing sexually active gay priests, Wagner also intimated that while there might be cases of morally disintegrating behavior where a priest leads a "double life" of public morality and private vice, not all cases of sexually active priests or religious can be so characterized.

In 1979, Father Robert Hummel, a priest of the diocese of Richmond (Virginia), was suspended by Bishop Walter Sullivan after the priest gave an interview to the *Washington Star* where he identified himself as being homosexual (*Catholic Review* 1979). Although he had previously done exactly the same thing in two other newspapers in Washington including a gay paper and a campus paper, he had been warned by Sullivan that he would be suspended if he went ahead with a public disclosure in the *Star*. Ironically, the bishop in this case is one of the least homophobic among the U.S. hierarchy. Sullivan has established a Human Sexuality Task Force for the diocese which provides educational and pastoral resources for homosexual people and others ministering to them, and has encouraged the formation of local chapters of Dignity, a Catholic homosexual organization.

In 1982, a Miami diocesan priest gave an extensive interview complete with photographs to the *Fort Lauderdale News and Sun Sentinel* (Cox 1981) after his local paper refused the offer. Father Philip Scheiding said he felt compelled to take the step to announce his homosexual orientation publicly to avoid what he called being "inherently dishonest" (Cox 1981, p. 1), and to identify with other Catholic homosexual people in the Church. As a result of the publicity he was removed from his parish assignment. According to Bishop Edward A. McCarthy, Scheiding's actions had "made it impossible to trust you with a pastoral assignment involving the care of souls" (Overman 1981, p. 2). The chancellor of the diocese, however, put his finger on the real issue when he said that by speaking out about his homosexuality, Scheiding had created "grave scandal and confusion among many of the faithful and has greatly jeopardized the effectiveness of his priestly ministry" (p. 2). The priest's declarations, said the diocesan official, "are not sensitive to the difficulty of the average parishioner in distinguishing between homosexual orientation and immoral sexual activity" (p. 2).

John Boswell, in his massive and scholarly work, *Christianity, Social Tolerance and Homosexuality* (Boswell 1980), has documented the presence of gay clergy and religious, including bishops, in some periods of Church history, although Boswell's use of the word *gay* in its present-day meaning to describe intense, same-sex friendships and writings among some monastic figures has been questioned. Boswell shows that moral and ecclesiastical opposition to homosexuality were far from uniform in use of Scripture, the severity of opposition, and even methods of argumentation.

The new element, however, which has entered the picture today is not only a widespread awareness of gay priests and religious in contemporary Church life, but also public declarations involving names, faces, and case histories. In 1976, the *National Catholic Reporter* (Rashke 1976) ran a five-part series on homosexuality and the Catholic Church which included interviews with a number of gay priests. In one of the lead articles, titled "I Am a Gay Priest with a Community Role" (p. 29), an anonymous priest described in some detail and, with obvious deep feeling, his own gradual awareness and eventual acceptance of his homosexuality. Unlike many priests before him, however, he decided not to leave the active ministry. Today, even the thin veil of anonymity has begun to fall. This has created new problems and new challenges both for bishops and religious superiors as well as for individual gay priests.

There are several issues that inevitably arise in discussions of homosexuality and the clergy. I would like to single out three for discussion which I believe are crucial for a balanced and productive dialogue on homosexual clergy in the Roman Catholic community. These issues are: (1) educaton of the general Church public (including leadership) on the topic of homosexuality; (2) definitions and contemporary experiences of celibacy/chastity; (3) ministry to gay clergy and the male religious.

Education

Since 1969, at least in the United States, we have been flooded with a steady stream of information on the topic of homosexuality from the gay community and from other individuals and groups who are supportive of the homosexual liberation movement in one way or another. The quality of the information varies considerably and includes everything from detailed and reputable scientific studies to outright propaganda. Although the subject continues to receive increased attention, even from the entertainment media in such films as *Making Love* and *Personal Best*, Catholics generally, despite some minimal exposure in the Catholic press, lag far behind the larger society in both awareness of the issue and social acceptance of gay and lesbian people, Even support of civil rights for homosexual people is weak among the majority of Catholics. Most Catholics remain unaware of the most basic information that is available which would help them eliminate many of the fears, myths, and stereotypes that continue to inhibit any kind of Church outreach, and which cause many unnecessary problems for gay clergy and religious.

A good example of the confusion among Catholics concerning this topic is the common assumption that a homosexual *orientation* is equivalent to homosexual *behavior*. Church documents have already endorsed this vital distinction (NCCB 1976; Sacred Congregation for the Doctrine of the Faith 1976; Quinn 1980; Weakland 1980; Roman Catholic Church of Baltimore 1981), yet the Catholic public remains, for the most part, unaware of its import. In 1979, when New Ways Ministry announced a weekend retreat for "gay women religious," reactions were swift and sharp (Nugent 1979). The Sacred Congregation for Religious intervened and attempted to halt the retreat (Winiarski 1979). Many Church leaders in this country strongly objected to the use of the word *gay* in conjunction with *women religious*. What the retreat organizers later learned was that many people had simply assumed that *gay* implied sexual activity. Several diocesan papers ran notices of the event and were deluged with calls and letters from shocked and angry Catholics who were upset not only that the retreat was to take place, but that the Catholic press should even acknowledge the existence of "gay women religious." Even people who were generally open and sympathetic to gay ministry and the need for such a gathering raised objections because they felt that the image of women religious would be damaged, that vocations to the sisterhood would suffer, and that some would use the event as a weapon against other women religious who were in the forefront of the struggle for equality and justice for women in the Church. The Episcopal Church had already witnessed accusations of "lesbianism" directed by male clergy against those women who wanted to be ordained. Others thought that the work of women religious among young people would also be damaged by publicity about "lesbian nuns," even though it was in the context of a spiritual event like a retreat.

Despite ensuing tensions and conflicts surrounding the event, it was truly a teachable moment for all of those involved. People came to understand the distinction between behavior and orientation. They came to see that although most people come to an awareness of their sexual identity through some kind of behavior, it is still possible to arrive at a free and mature decision to forgo all sexual-genital activity entirely for a variety of reasons. Not all of these reasons are necessarily linked with religious or vocational motives. There are, in other words, people who are fully comfortable with the identities "homosexual" and "celibate."

Although official Church counseling for homosexual Christians is celibacy or total sexual abstinence, some Church authorities seem to doubt its possibility. This became apparent from a paper originating with the Sacred Congregation for Religious as an official response to the proposed retreat for gay women religious. The paper's anonymous author suggested that public support for homosexual organizations and causes was "more delicate" for priests and sisters than for lay persons, and that such support, unless accompanied by a clear affirmation of Church teaching on the morality of homosexuality, "cannot but help be perceived by the public at large as support and sharing in the aims of the homosexual culture" (Sacred Congregation for Religious, p. 2). This is especially true "when the priest or religious 'comes out' or openly declared himself or herself to be 'gay' or homosexual *even when such a declaration is accompanied by a slogan* such as 'gay and celibate' to imply that the homosexuality in question is a matter of orientation and not of activity" (p. 2, emphasis added). The use of the word *slogan* seems to indicate an unwillingness to concede that gay clergy can, in fact, live celibate lives.

According to many gay clergy and religious, public identification as homosexual is a vital part of the whole educational process that has to occur in a diocese, parish, religious order, or any ministry where there is a desire or need to clarify issues and help people deal with homosexuality in an honest and nonthreatening way. This process, it is thought, will not only help Church people accept the validity of a gay celibate commitment, but will also aid the Church in ministering more honestly and realistically to homosexual people. Celibate gay persons can also provide strong role models for those in the Church who are attempting to live out the Church's teaching in all its fullness. Those who attempt to do this now do it without the benefit of either private support groups or public figures who have successfully integrated their homosexual identities into the lived reality of a healthy "celibacy for the Kingdom."

Yet, Church leadership is still very uncomfortable and often punitive in face of priests who, for whatever reason, decide to go public on the issue of a homosexual orientation. The motivating factors for priests to "come out" are as varied as the individuals who take this option. Undoubtedly, some of these decisions involve sensationalism, personal self-seeking, unresolved authority conflicts, institutional anger, and other immature behavior. But there are also other instances where a priest has come to this decision after careful prayer, discernment, and support from others. Generally, the "coming out" process is a slow one involving at first only close friends and colleagues and, eventually, extending to bishop, religious superior, or even to a group to whom one ministers. The exhilarating sense of personal freedom and integrity that most individuals describe after they have taken that step is impossible to deny or discount. Nor can its import for both personal growth and mental health be gainsaid or ignored. In the face of the very real possibility of rejection, alienation, isolation, loss of esteem or position, trust or friends, "coming out" is a great risk that should not be taken lightly.

The analogy of homosexuality with alcoholism is one that many vehemently reject. Yet, there are similarities in the way that Church leaders have responded to both chemically dependent and homosexual priests. For a long time Church leadership refused to admit, especially in public, the presence of alcoholics or other chemically dependent clergy and religious. Excesses were either readily excused or "problem people" were repeatedly moved from one assignment to another. Today there are Church-funded studies, congregational policies, residential treatment facilities, outpatient programs, support groups, and specialized ministries to people dealing with alcohol and drug problems. Understanding, study, and much more honesty in dealing with individuals struggling in these areas have replaced the silence and embarrassment which had previously isolated them. It is unfortunate that prior to this change in attitude persons grappling with drug-related problems were encouraged with pious exhortations to "do better" or threatened with punitive measures designed to make the individual "shape up or ship out."

Gay clergy and religious who have a positive understanding of their homosexuality and who have come to terms with it in a conflict-free manner will obviously not respond to offers of "rehabilitation" or "reorientation." Unlike the drug or alcohol abuser, gay clergy many times feel that their most effective ministerial gifts and talents flow from or are dirctly related to their unique experience of being homosexually oriented. What they look for is a willingness among Church leadership to acknowledge their presence, reverence their gifts, and help create an atmosphere for open discussion and sharing at all levels. Gay clergy also want recognition in ways which will promote their human and spiritual growth and that will help Catholics accept their presence in the Church community, including official ministry and leadership positions. Precisely how this is to be done, however, is impossible to determine at the present time. Much more groundwork has to precede this kind of recognition and support.

The crux of the seeming impasse between demanding total sexual abstinence from gay Catholics on the one hand, while refusing public acknowledgment of celibate gay clergy on the other, is the fundamental value judgment about homosexuality *as an orientation*. This basic judgment, whether made individually or communally, has a great impact on the structures and procedures of Church life. Many people are opposed to public disclosures of homosexuality among celibates simply because they disvalue not only homosexual behavior on moral grounds, but they also disvalue the orientation on psychological, social, and other grounds. Despite talk about respect for the dignity of each unique person as the USCC guidelines for sex education (USCC 1981) stress again and again, these people believe that there is basically something wrong, or least incomplete and lacking, with a homosexual orientation. For them, there is, indeed, something a little "queer" about being gay. They might admit that a homosexual orientation (and all that this notion implies in terms of affectivity, emotional responses, etc.) is part of the individual psychic given; that a homosexual orientation is established (through, as yet, not completely known factors) at a rather early age; that the homosexual orientation is morally neutral. But they are unwilling to concede that this is also socially, biologically, or even psychologically "neutral." Nor do they believe that a homosexual orientation can fulfill the real meaning of human sexuality in the same way that heterosexuality does. Heterosexuality remains "normative," and, as Bishop Mugavero has stated, "any other orientation respects less adequately the full spectrum of human relationships" (Mugavero 1976). And so if a person believes that a homosexual orientation is "morally neutral," but still deficient in other essential ways (lack of procreative possibilities, lack of complementarity, violation of the fundamental sexual differences and symbolism, etc.) he or she will not want to give the impression that a homosexual orientation is as acceptable *as a sexual identity*, apart from actual behavior, as a heterosexual orientation. The entire issue of the relationship and dynamics between orientation and behavior needs greater study. We must avoid either confusing them so much that we deny the possibility of celibacy or separating them so much that we render meaningless all talk of the "body-person" and negate the teaching of the *Declaration on Sexual Ethics*, which states that "the human person is so profoundly affected by sexuality that it must be considered as one of the factors which give to each individual's life the principal traits that distinguish it" (Sacred Congregation for the Doctrine of the Faith 1976, p. 3). People, then, who disvalue a homosexual orientation will avoid focusing any undue attention on homosexual clergy especially in the public arena, where such recognition might be interpreted, explicitly or implicitly, as supportive of a positive role model. I think this is the position of most Catholics today and certainly those in leadership roles.

On the other hand, if one believes that a homosexual orientation contains basically all the humanizing and Christian elements and interpretations of *agape* (trust, self-sacrifice, vulnerability, loyalty, fidelity, suffering, etc.), then one is more comfortable in the face of full and honest affirmations of gay celibates, which can be seen as promoting their human growth and spiritual development. Although this position still fails to throw light on the orientation/behavior discussion, at least it broadens the consideration of homosexuality beyond the area of sexual gymnastics and bedroom sociology. This view also helps people develop their thinking on the full meaning of "orientation" and its implications for one's stance toward ministry, life, religious experience, faith, prayer, and a host of other issues. Archbishop Joseph Bernadin stressed the centrality of human sexual identity when he wrote: "Human sexuality is part of our God-given natural power or capacity for relating to others in a loving, caring way. From it flow the qualities of sensitivity, warmth, openness and mutual respect in interpersonal relationships. To deny or altogether repress these qualities thus inevitably lessens one's ability to relate to others and truly love them. Such a denial or repression can warp our personality and turn us into frightened, threatened or bitter men" (Bernadin 1981, p. 212).

Despite differences in evaluating homosexuality as orientation, some people advise clergy against coming out at this period in the Church for many reasons. Some are genuinely concerned that the priest or religious be able to cope with the confusion, alienation, or even rejection that could result from disclosing his sexual orientation. Others see the serious consequences for even gay celibates in the face of an attitude expressed by one American bishop, who stated that the "sick must recognize the sickness, renounce it and seek needed help to get well or he gets sicker. We're ready to help any one of them who are willing to come back to a normal attitude" (Harris 1981, p. B6). Another group would advise that celibate homosexual persons share their sexual orientation only with superiors and, perhaps, with a few close friends on an individual basis, especially when such sharing is seen as an aid to strengthening a celibate commitment with a counselor or spiritual director. Any public sharing would be counterproductive, limiting the individuals to a "gay identity" which might have adverse effects on their public ministry.

A more generally shared concern, however, is that many times the claim to celibacy by some gay clergy is less than the full truth. Heterosexual celibates do not have to publicly identify themselves in any way since it is assumed that priests are heterosexual and celibate. Therefore, the condition of lived celibacy is not questioned as frequently in the context of heterosexual celibates, although recent writing on the actual state of heterosexual celibacy in the clergy is beginning to change the picture in this area as well (Farrell 1982). If celibate gay clergy, it can be argued, plan to have some part in the educational process of the Church in the issue of homosexuality as publicly identified gay persons, their credibility level has to be, perhaps, even much higher than usual. If they wish to speak from their own experiences in relating homosexuality to a celibate priesthood, the dialogue has to be based on a strong mutual trust that both parties are being honest about their claims and ulterior motives. This means, for example, that a celibate gay priest has to be honest about the degree of his involvement in a gay "life-style," including association with other gay individuals or groups. A gay priest's social life often includes gay bars and other aspects of the gay subculture (religious, political) that are not in conflict with celibacy, ministry, or community commitments, although these interests can precipitate problems. This is not meant to imply that the gay priest must first have attained some near perfect state of celibacy. It simply means that he is not fooling himself—or others—and that he is striving, in a generally successful way, to live out a mature and healthy celibacy as a gay person. It also means that this endeavor has not impaired his ability to relate warmly to all people, to minister to heterosexual people, or to have intimate friendships that do not include an ongoing genital relationship. This brings us to the second issue: celibacy and chastity.

Chastity/Celibacy

Celibacy has traditionally been defined as a "gift and a call from God whereby one freely decides to renounce the human values of marriage and genital sex for the sake of devoting oneself totally to Christ and the extension of His kingdom" (Pable 1981, p. 60). As such, it is distinct from the Christian virtue of chastity whereby "one guards against all irresponsible uses of sexual power, whether inside or outside of marriage" (Pable 1981, p. 60). Consecrated (vowed or otherwise) chastity is essentially the same as celibacy. Both exclude genital expression. For single, nonvowed people, chastity does not exclude those interpersonal dynamics and relationships that lead to marriage as it does for celibates. But those who voluntarily forgo those kinds of courting procedures, however, do not forgo either intimacy or deep personal relationships with both men and women, as Donald Goergen has stressed in his groundbreaking work, *The Sexual Celibate* (Goergen 1974). The "limits" of these relationships have already been discussed elsewhere (Fourez 1973).

In the last twenty years, though, writings on celibacy and chastity for priests and religious have prompted new definitions to surface from the lived experiences and reflections of men and women in religious life and ordained priesthood. A recent document from the U.S. Bishops' Committee on Priestly Life and Ministry has cautiously noted that "the theology of celibacy itself has found less compelling articulation in recent years" (Bishops' Committee on Priestly Life and Ministry 1981, p. 6) when it discusses some contemporary causes of stress in the priesthood. Some people are questioning, for example, whether celibacy necessarily excludes all possibility of committed love relationships including sexual (and even genital) expression. Shared celibacy, excluding genital expression but including deep love, has become known as "The Third Way." Homosexual religious and priests have contributed, perhaps even more than other people, to taking this discussion even further, and are catalysts for others to reflect on and respond to the evolution which is seen to be taking place especially among younger clergy and religious in relation to concepts of celibacy and vowed chastity.

Public consideration of chastity and celibacy is nothing new in Church history. Movements for optional celibacy have appeared at different times in the Church's life and seem to be again gaining ground in the Church today. Talk of celibacy and chastity for gay clergy, then, has to be seen in light of the larger discussion in the universal Church.

Edward Schillebeeckx, in his recent book, *Ministry* (Schillebeeckx 1981), says that the law of celibacy is essentially a law of sexual abstinence but, historically, a connection has come to be established between complete abstinence and an easier, undivided love of God which is not directly concerned with the presence or absence of the love of a man or woman. Speaking of the statement of the 1980 Dutch Synod and its references to "The Third Way," Schillebeeckx also says that if the synod's treatment of celibacy means not only the exclusion of genital love, but also the love of a woman for a man or vice versa, then we have a completely new pronouncement from the Church on celibacy which is not in keeping with the Second Vatican Council and which differs radically from any other Church pronouncement on the nature of the charism of celibacy. What is really at stake in this whole question, says Schillebeeckx, is the "anthropologically inner relationship between sexuality and love" (p. 95). We are faced with a dilemma, he claims, that priests and religious are coming more and more to experience in their own personal lives. Clerical celibacy involves either a law of abstinence or a question of some degree of competition between love of God and love for another person. In the first case we can ask the question: ". . . does physical abstinence as such of itself ever have a religious value?" (p. 96).

For Schillebeeckx, this is hard to affirm if we want to avoid a negative attitude which is opposed to sexuality. The second option, the competition quandry, is theologically unjustifiable. Schillebeeckx believes that it is impossible to separate these two problems unless one wants to dehumanize sexuality and make it purely a physical phenomenon. Although he sees celibacy as a kind of radical and religious protest against both sexual consumerism and sex as power, as well as against liberalism in all forms of subjugation and objectification, he maintains that we cannot determine *a priori* anthropologically whether such forms of celibate protest "can through complete abstinence, finally be turned into a realistic and truly human possibility" (p. 96). Commenting on the contemporary scene, he says that experiments are being carried on all over the world which will eventually give us better information about this issue. He warns, however, that "naivety is not the best teacher, far less anxiety and strictness . . . in my view the debate about celibacy is not closed; it has hardly been open" (p. 96).

Several years ago Luke Salm (1977) outlined four basic approaches to the issue of chastity which I believe are still valid today, at least for discussion purposes, to which I will append another position from a feminist perspective.

1. The first approach accepts the traditional norms of the past in which vowed religious and celibate clergy must abstain from all genital sexual experiences regardless of any new interpretations of chastity or celibacy, even chastity for single, unmarried people (Kosnik, et al. 1977). This is the view which continues to dominate Catholic life, religious formation and common expectations of laity and hierarchy. While upholding and enforcing the traditional norms of chastity and celibacy, proponents of this approach are also open to encouraging the development of more positive values such as mature sexual awareness, respect and care for the body, and a healthy, affective life through friendships and community support.

2. A second approach preserves the older, traditional norms, but allows for a relaxation and variation in certain limited situations. Proponents of this view admit that while genital acts outside marriage may not always be objectively sinful, they remain inappropriate especially for vowed religious, and ought to be limited, exceptional, and, eventually, terminated altogether. A homosexual priest who finds himself involved in a genital relationship that is characterized by friendship and love is a good example. For many gay clergy, the process of self-discovery and self-acceptance often includes some overt homosexual behavior, usually combined with a strong affectivity, especially when this process has been bypassed in the usual course of sexual development. This approach would support his gradual growth to full and complete sexual abstinence, while trying to preserve the values of the friendship and mutual care and support.

3. The third approach manifests a clear break with tradition and holds that genital sexual activity is morally justified and compatible even with chastity as long as it is exercised with responsibility according to the

individual circumstances. This approach distinguishes several purposes of genital sexuality, from total commitment and exclusive love for another to sex for pleasure and recreation where neither physical nor emotional harm can result. Salm believes that religious orders should give serious consideration to this approach and to formulating some response to it since it seems to prevail among younger people today, the population from which orders and dioceses recruit future membership. This approach (or a variation of it) is often heard from gay clergy or religious who say, for instance, that celibacy is a commitment "to put my sexuality in line with the person-oriented and love-oriented directives of the gospel" (Wagner 1980*a*, p. 57) or that "Chastity means learning how to love people properly . . . there are clearly numerous occasions when genital expression would be proper and appropriate" (Wagner, p. 57). Another priest says that he understands his promise to be celibate as a way of being "free emotionally and psychologically to be a witness and a minister of God's love in the world. My understanding of these virtues does not preclude genital sex" (Wagner, p. 57). A common understanding of celibacy for many people like these is simply that it is a promise not to marry heterosexually or to have a committed homosexual relationship, but neither of these understandings necessarily precludes genital relationships. Some priests, who have been involved in a lover relationship, claim that the experience has affected them positively in both their personal growth and ministerial efforts. Others feel that they were never really committed to celibacy; or were so but are no longer; or continue to want ministry, but do not want a celibate life-style. In some cases, an obvious choice becomes necessary for personal survival, but in other cases some priests seem able to avoid the choice with no apparent psychological damage.

4. Although there is no one feminist perspective of celibacy, some feminists, rather than simply considering the concept irrelevant, have attempted to redefine it. The feminist approach moves away from a patriarchal model (celibacy in *genital* terms) and toward an understanding in *relational* and *communal* terms. Celibacy, in the patriarchal model, is understood like every other sexually based definition, i.e., married women sleep with men, divorced women used to, single women do not, separated women might again, lesbian women do not, and celibates generally do not talk about it. From a feminist viewpoint, the understanding of celibacy leaves aside the *private* (who sleeps with whom) and focuses on the *personal,* which is also *political.* Relationships between women as well as between women and conscious men are valuable for community. Celibacy then is seen in terms of those responsible committed relation-

ships which are conducive of community. Whether or not they involve sexual expression is not crucial, since this area is private rather than personal, and it is, therefore, not political either. Underlying this idea is the notion that healthy, integrated people make for healthy, integrated communities.

5. A fifth approach is the least useful because it does nothing at all about the present situation. One simply continues to deny, repress, or sidestep actual cases involving peoples' lives and ministerial careers hoping that the "problem" will either disappear, resolve itself naturally, or, at the very least, not reach the public's attention. The bishop or superior who simply continues to reassign individuals struggling with obvious sexual issues (including arrests, blackmail, complaints from parents or other clergy); who provides no supportive counseling or direction for individuals involved in affective/genital sexual relationships; or who refuses even to address the situation when it has been called to his attention with substantial evidence, embodies this approach. In the same way, those who view sexuality and celibacy issues solely in terms of confession, spiritual direction, or therapy with little or no appreciation of the social and political implications, let alone the need for open, honest discussion in formation programs, clergy retreats, and renewal experiences, adopt a policy of benign neglect. Salm remarks that this attitude exaggerates the gap which exists between some older and newer approaches, generates tensions over scandalous situations, and promotes an unhealthy attitude towards sexuality. "Old and young alike," he writes, "are left to resolve their deep sexual problems in isolation and without community support. Recruitment and formation of new members becomes increasingly difficult when the specific demand and full Christian meaning of chastity are left ambiguous and confused. Thus the continued unwillingness of religious orders to bring contemporary theological reflections to bear on the vow of chastity means that they are willing to sacrifice their very existence on the altar of the status quo" (Salm 1977, p. 24). Dr. Michael Peterson's observation to the American bishops at their workshop on human sexuality in 1981 could easily be applied to the present situation of gay clergy in their attempts to relate to Church leadership: "It is the considerable experience of many committed Christian psychiatrists and psychologists that there is an ever widening gap between the sexual practices and scientific explanation of those practices in human sexuality on the one hand, and the theological reflection of the Christian church, including the Roman Catholic Church on the other. The fact that the authoritative teachers of the Roman Catholic Church would even request a conference to examine the complex issues in this area of human sexuality is a major step toward closing that gap" (Peterson 1981, p. 108).

Ministry to Gay Clergy and Religious

The first stage in a ministry for gay clergy and religious is to validate the topic as an area of serious concern, discussion, and some concrete and public pastoral initiatives. Conversations on the private level are always intense, strongly emotional, and very honest, especially where there is a deep level of trust. Informal groups of clergy can be very open about their sexual lives. In workshops, however, and on priests' retreats and other more institutional levels, the atmosphere is much different and the topic of homosexual clergy, if addressed at all, is handled with much more delicacy. Several recent attempts to deal with the issue provide some hope that the American Catholic community is moving from the totally private and personal to the more communal and public approach to homosexual clergy.

The National Federation of Priests' Councils is considering the formation of a group of experts and consultants for a study of sexuality and American priests. Part of this study will consider the way homosexuality is dealt with in the priesthood. An *ad hoc* committee of the NCCB under the direction of Bishop William Hughes is in the process of preparing a study guide for priests and bishops which will include a treatment of homosexuality as part of the larger consideration of human sexuality and the American clergy. The objectives of the guide are to facilitate genuine discussion among priests and bishops; help them face the questions with honesty, scholarship, and prayer; and to stimulate them to familiarize themselves with the latest body of knowledge published on the subject. The guide will also present materials on topics such as relationships, cultural impact and expectations, loneliness, self-esteem, spirituality, and "other concerns in the area of sexuality which have an influence on the lives of priests today" (National Conference of Catholic Bishops 1981, pp. 6–7).

The Spring 1981 issue of *Chicago Studies* (1981) published a series of papers on sexuality originally commissioned as part of the bishops' committee's general background. In the area of homosexuality, the contributions of two writers are encouraging; provided they find their way into the final draft of the guide. "Within the priesthood there are homosexual as well as heterosexual males who choose to express themselves in genital sexual activity. It should be clear that such behavior is not automatically a problem for a therapist to handle, and that a priest who is sexually active may be choosing to be so without having any psychological disturbance. In such cases, the observable behavior of the priest demands a clearcut administrative decision from the appropriate authority and is not the therapist's responsibility. Although therapeutic assistance can be offered, encouraged or advised, it is not a panacea for a change of behavior or sex object preference" (Breckel and Murphy 1981, pp. 47–48).

This attitude is in marked contrast to that of several Jesuit psychiatrists who, in 1978, stated in a widely read policy paper on homosexuality and religious life that they regarded homosexual behavior itself as sexually disordered and generally representing impaired personality development (Gill 1980). According to these priests, since "homosexual behavior in a religious person frequently manifests serious emotional disturbance" (Gill, p. 25), it ought to receive psychological or psychiatric evaluation and a vocation decision should await the outcome of professional evaluation and treatment. Undoubtedly, there are some priests and religious whose homosexual acting out indicates a variety of other related issues and problems and those cases which come to the attention of concerned leaders can be evaluated and judged as such. Of growing concern and interest, though, is the number of individuals engaged in some form of homosexual behavior who do *not* manifest serious emotional problems, and who are often among the the finest members in a diocese or religious community holding offices of great responsibility. Too often the only individual who comes to the attention of authorities is the one involved in a public scandal, seduction, or a brush with the law. Every diocese and community has some of these "skeletons in the closet," so to speak, and many times they appear in the media as scandals in homes for boys or arrests for solicitation. As disturbing as these incidences always are, they should be faced with as much honesty and realism as possible by all of those involved and should also serve as some indicator of the need to look seriously at the whole issue of celibacy. Fortunately, there are a number of competent resources for dealing with those individual cases which involve identity, behavioral, or vocational problems and decisions.

Gay clergy who get into trouble with ecclesiastical or civil authorities, however, are only the tip of the proverbial iceberg. The majority of gay clergy are able to function well in social relationships and ministry although almost all of them struggle with issues of "coming out," personal relationships, support systems (or lack of same), isolation, and some inner dissonance generated by conflicts between appearances and reality or ideals and tensions especially related to the celibacy/chastity issue. If the atmosphere in a particular diocese, community, or geographical region (rural areas for instance) is such that hiding, pretending, and evading are the order of the day, then this increases the pressure on gay priests, which, in itself, may contribute to periodic outbreaks of erratic, irresponsible, or compulsive sexual behavior and some personal disintegration. If bishops, religious superiors, and colleagues adopted more open and trusting approaches to gay clergy and the entire issue of homosexuality, I think the incidences of such behavior would show a marked decrease. If a priest who is coping with homosexuality on any level is able to seek and find individual and group sources of support and guidance without fear of reprisals, recriminations, or suspicion from authorities or other priests, we, as Church, might create a more healthy and growth-producing atmosphere in which priests can learn to handle tensions that are related to being gay and celibate in both Church and society. In most dioceses and religious orders there is still a strong taboo against open and honest discussion of homosexuality, due, in part, to the real dangers associated with giving one's self away. At the same time, there is always a strong undercurrent of gay humor and interest lurking just below the surface of almost every clerical gathering, especially when the gay priests congregate rather obviously, at least to the discerning onlooker. Contributing to the taboo atmosphere is the fact that most gay clergy do not feel comfortable in acknowledging their homosexual orientation or difficulties. This is especially true in a large group where responses are quite unpredictable or where, from previous experience, some individuals are known to react with nervous silence or defensive distancing if not with outright hostility and condemnation.

There are few organized and structured ministries to gay clergy and religious, although support groups of gay priests joining together for discussion and socializing are beginning to develop in many parts of the country. Despite the apparent risks associated with such a gathering, the results, thus far, seem to have been most encouraging, especially in terms of personal healing. In some cases these groups meet with the full support of a particular provincial, but in most cases they are very informal and loosely organized along geographical lines with an acute realization of the absolute need for each member in the group to respect the privacy of the others. In one Midwestern diocese a support group of both diocesan clergy and religious priests meets on a regular basis to socialize and dialogue about common experiences and concerns about being gay. In some cases priests have been accompanied by individuals with whom they are (or were) involved in relationships. The group experience has enabled many priests to continue in or return to a life of celibacy devoid of genital-sexual expression. One individual who had been arrested for solicitation was able to survive that traumatic and painful event and come to a satisfying resolution about his future in ministry with the local bishop through the ongoing concern of the peer support group.

In both the United States and Canada there are communication networks of gay clergy and religious whose main purpose is to share, through a monthly publication, areas of general interest and concern. These groups have provided a strong link for many people who live and minister in isolated rural parts of the country and whose only contact with other like persons is a monthly newsletter. The moving excerpts from letters provide eloquent testimony to the powerful and effective ministry being carried on by those unofficial groups. Days of reflection and weekend retreats have also been provided by the networks even though widespread publicity is impossible since an obvious need for anonymity dominates this form of support and pastoral concern.

A more widely known and official ministry, titled "Rest, Renewal, and Re-creation," is directed by Father John Harvey, O.S.F.S., and headquartered in Arlington, Virginia. Harvey's work long predates that of others, and his clear articulation of official Church teaching has earned him both moral and financial support from a number of American bishops. Harvey's approach to homosexuality and especially to active gay clergy is based on the AA program of therapy and group support. While he does not actually attempt to reorient priests and brothers who participate in his week-long program, he does attempt to provide at least the beginnings of support (psychological, spiritual, etc.) in helping priests return to a completely celibate life. Harvey's approach includes the formation of local support groups of priests who have gone through his program. It is hoped that frequent group meetings or even contact with one or two others will help sustain the resolutions that are a crucial part of the process. One of the main differences between Harvey's approach and that of others is his belief that a homosexual orientation itself always involves some kind of emotional or psychological disorder. He would caution against priests "coming out" other than in purely private ways to friends and counselors. He also holds that the only option possible for gay and lesbian Catholics is a life of total sexual abstinence and has developed a spiritual plan of life to that end. Since the initiation of his retreat program, Harvey has ministered to many priests and brothers, many of whom discovered the program through his weekly ad for priests and perpetually professed brothers "with homosexual difficulties" in the "Ad Random" section of the National Catholic Reporter. Harvey has published a rather complete description of his principles and the retreat program in Linacre Quarterly, a Catholic journal for physicians (Harvey 1979). In the past several years he has also given talks and workshops on homosexuality for diocesan clergy and religious communities and presently runs a support group called Courage for gay celibates in the Archdiocese of New York.

We have come to a point in the life of the Church where the shock or scandal of realizing, through extensive media coverage or personal contact with gay clergy, that not only are there homosexual priests and religious, but that some of them are sexually active, can no longer paralyze us from dealing honestly and openly with this reality. We are finally able to admit that many of the priests who have served as models of compassion, faithfulness, and dedication are homosexually oriented. The argument that one often hears against public discussion or study of the emotional issue of homosexuality, especially in relation to clerical life, is that the "simple faithful" are not ready for such disclosures or that the information will "disturb the laity." "The use of the laity as an inkblot into which to project one's own fears, anxieties, and doubts," says Andrew Greeley, "has gone far enough. . . . This posture of concern about the naifs is demeaning, patronizing, insulting and dishonest. It fails to recognize the fact that the Catholic laity are educated, responsible and quite capable of making decisions for themselves without being shocked, troubled or disturbed. People . . . are trying to intimidate some of us into silence, not because we are doing things they don't like, but because we are shocking the innocent, they say. . . . At a time when three-quarters to nine-tenths of the faithful reject the principle elements in the Church's sexual ethic, it is a little ridiculous to pretend the Catholic laity are innocents who must be protected from shock or dismay" (Greeley 1982, p. A6).

Those who seem to be most upset are those who are basically unwilling to face up to the presence of gay clergy and religious in a public and responsible manner, and to respond in ways that reflect both Gospel fidelity to Christian principles of sexuality and recent papal calls to value the human dignity and personhood of each unique individual. If we can begin to create a more trusting atmosphere for the growth of gay clergy and religious in whatever situations they find themselves; if we can give serious study to related issues of chastity and celibacy, intimacy and ministry; if we can provide sound education on homosexuality in all its multiple dimensions, then we might be able to reduce, if not eliminate, some of the pain associated with loneliness, isolation, and tension generated by conflicts of value systems and experiences of life. We can provide strong support systems for gay clergy who struggle for a life of sexual maturity, affective growth and fulfillment, and celibacy for the Kingdom. Their struggles are similar to those of nongay clergy, although the stresses and strains of coping mechanisms differ in some significant ways. If the Church in the next few decades can conquer innate fears and anxieties about homosexuality in general and gay clergy and religious in particular, we can improve the quality of clerical life, enhance the ministerial gifts of many priests, make celibacy itself more credible and compelling, and help other priests come to the experience that one priest recently shared: "I have been out with my superiors since I was a novice, and, aware of my gayness, they have approved me for vows and now for ordination. . . . I have witnessed an evolution in myself in terms of my relationship to my own gay identity that has come to a crucial stage. When I entered religious life, I was certain that religion was my only bid for a life of human dignity and morality. Homosexuality was a curse to be escaped. Later on, I felt it was a cross, gratuitously given, to be nobly borne. Then I began to discover that my sexuality was the source of most of my personality traits that I valued and found effective in ministry. Now it is clear to me that my gayness is a key for growth and health and relationship. . . . I do know for certain that I must find ways of replacing the cycle of repression and depression that I have inflicted on myself as a mode of 'reconciling' my sexuality and my vows with some as yet undiscovered pattern of expression and celebration" (Anonymous 1979).

REFERENCES

Anonymous 1979: personal correspondence.

Bernadin, J. In W. Sullivan, The priesthood seminarians prepare for. *Origins,* 17 September 1981, pp. 210–15.

Bishops' Committee on Priestly Life and Ministry 1981. *The priest and stress.* Washington, D.C.: United States Catholic Conference.

Boswell, J. 1980. *Christianity, social tolerance and homosexuality.* Chicago: Univ. of Chicago Press.

Breckel, S. and Murphy, N. M. 1981. Psychosexual development. *Chicago Studies* 20: 41–58.

Catholic Review. Va bishop censures homosexual priest. *Catholic Review,* 14 March 1979, p. A-8.

Cox, C. He dedicated his life to honesty but telling the truth may hurt. *Fort Lauderdale News and Sun-Sentinel,* 4 October 1981, pp. 1, 3D.

Farrell, M. Secret lives of the almost celibate. *National Catholic Reporter,* 16 April 1982, p. 18.

Farrell, M. Celibacy remark sparks flame of controversy. *National Catholic Reporter,* 16 April 1982, p. 16.

Fourez, G. 1973. *A light grasp on life.* New Jersey: Dimension Press.

Gill, J. 1980. Homosexuality today. *Human Development* 3: 16–25.

Goergen, D. 1974. *The sexual celibate.* New York: Seabury.

Greeley, A. Inkblot laity. *The Catholic Review,* 12 March 1982, p. A-6.

Harris, H. Church leaders differ on homosexual groups. *Greensboro Daily News/Record,* 1 February 1981, p. B6.

Harvey, J. 1979. Reflections on a retreat for clerics with homosexual tendencies. *Linacre Quarterly* 46: 136–40.

Jones, A. Play and stay priests. *National Catholic Reporter,* 16 October 1981, p. 28.

Kane, T. 1982. The priest: An affirmation of human sexuality. *The Priest* 38: 13–18.

Kenkelen, W. Priest faces ouster; views on gays cited. *National Catholic Reporter,* 31 July 1981, pp. 3–4.

Kosnik, A. et al. 1977. *Human sexuality: new directions in American Catholic thought.* New York: Paulist Press.

McNeill, J. 1976. *The church and the homosexual.* Kansas City: Sheed, Ward and McMeel.

Mugavero, F. 1976. Sexuality–God's gift. Brooklyn, N.Y.: Chancery Office.

National Conference of Catholic Bishops Documentation. 1981. Washington, D.C.: USCC.

Nugent, R. Silencing of gay issues in the christian churches. *Insight,* Summer, 1979, pp. 7–9.

Overman, S. Miami archdiocese reassigns homosexual priest from parish to research. *National Catholic News Service,* 3 December 1981, p. 2.

Pable, M. Priesthood and celibacy. 1981. *Chicago studies* 20: 59–77.

Peterson, M. 1981. Psychological aspects of human sexual behavior. In *Human sexuality and personhood.* St. Louis: Pope John Center.

Quinn, J. Pastoral letter on homosexuality. *The monitor,* 15 May 1980, pp. 7–8.

Rashke, R. Homosexuality and the church of today. Kansas City: *National Catholic Reporter,* 1976.

Roman Catholic Church of Baltimore. 1981. *A ministry to lesbian and gay catholic persons.* Baltimore: Catholic Center.

Sacred Congregation for the Doctrine of the Faith. 1976. *Declaration on certain questions concerning sexual ethics.* Washington, D.C.: USCC.

Sacred Congregation for the Doctrine of the Faith. Vatican directive regarding priest author of book on homosexuality. *Origins,* 16 March 1978, pp. 612–15.

Sacred Congregation for Religious and Secular Institutes. Observations. Rome: SCDFSI, n.d., 2.

Salm, L. 1977. The vow of chastity and moral theology today. In M. Heldorffer, ed. *Sexuality and brotherhood.* Illinois: National Assembly of Religious Brothers.

Schillebeeckx, E. 1981. *Ministry leadership in the church of Jesus Christ.* New York: Crossroad.

United States Catholic Conference. 1981. *Education in human sexuality for Christians.* Washington, D.C.: United States Catholic Conference.

Van Bergan, L. 1982. Alarming statement. *The Priest* 38: 3.

Wagner, R. Being gay and celibate—another view. *National Catholic Reporter,* 21 November 1980a, p. 16.

Wagner, R. 1980b. *Gay Catholic priests: a study of cognitive and affective dissonance.* San Francisco: The Institute for Advanced Study of Human Sexuality.

Weakland, R. Who is my neighbor? *Catholic Herald,* 19 July 1980, p. 3.

White, J. Remarks of Jack White to house of delegates, observers and guests in reaction to the National Federation of Priests' Councils' 1981 convention on priest as person. Private notes, n.d.

Winiarski, M. Vatican ban on gay retreat sidestepped. *National Catholic Reporter* 18 May 1979, pp. 1, 5.

Bibliography

Books

Bailey, Derrick, S. *Homosexuality and the Western Christian Tradition.* Shoe String Press, 1975.

Barnhouse, Ruth Tiffany. *Homosexuality: A Symbolic Confusion.* New York: Seabury Press, 1977.

Batchelor, Edward, ed. *Homosexuality and Ethics.* New York: Pilgrim Press, 1980.

Boswell, John. *Christianity, Social Tolerance and Homosexuality.* Chicago: University of Chicago Press, 1980.

Coleman, Gerald. *Homosexuality—An Appraisal.* Chicago: Franciscan Herald Press, 1978.

Coleman, Peter. *Christian Attitudes to Homosexuality.* London: SPCK, 1980.

Doherty, Dennis, ed. *Dimensions of Human Sexuality.* Garden City, N.Y.: Doubleday, 1979.

Fortunato, John. *Embracing the Exile.* New York: Seabury Press, 1982.

Gearhart, Sally, and Johnson, William R., ed. *Loving Women/Loving Men: Gay Liberation and the Church.* San Francisco: Glide Publications, 1974.

General Synod Board for Social Responsibility. *Homosexual Relationships: A Contribution to Discussion.* Kent, England: Wickham Press, 1979.

Guindon, Andrew. *The Sexual Language.* Ottawa: University of Ottawa Press, 1977.

Harvey, John F. *Pastoral Care and the Homosexual.* New Haven, Conn.: Knights of Columbus, n.d.

Horner, Thomas. *Jonathan Loved David: Homosexuality in Biblical Times.* Philadelphia: Westminster Press, 1978.

Jones, Kimball. *Toward a Christian Understanding of the Homosexual.* New York: Association Press, 1966.

Keane, Philip. *Sexual Mortality: A Catholic Perspective.* New York: Paulist Press, 1977.

Kosnik, Anthony, et al. *Human Sexuality: New Directions in American Catholic Thought.* New York: Paulist Press, 1977.

McCaffrey, Joseph, ed. *The Homosexual Dialectic.* Englewood Cliffs, N.J.: Prentice-Hall, 1972.

McNaught, Brian. *A Disturbed Peace.* Washington, D.C.: Dignity, 1981.

McNeill, John. *The Church and the Homosexual.* Kansas City: Sheed, Andrews and McMeel, 1976.

Malloy, Edward. *Homosexuality and the Christian Way of Life.* Washington, D.C.: University Press of America, 1981.

Nelson, James. *Embodiment: An Approach to Sexuality and Christian Theology.* Minneapolis: Augsburg Publishing House, 1978.

Nugent, Robert, and Gramick, Jeannine, eds. *A Time to Speak.* Mt. Rainier, Md.: New Ways Ministry, 1982.

Nugent, Robert; Gramick, Jeannine; and Oddo, Thomas. *Homosexual Catholics: A Primer for Discussion.* Washington, D.C.: Dignity, 1982.

Oberholtzer, W. Dwight. *Is Gay Good? Ethics, Theology and Homosexuality.* Philadelphia: Westminster Press, 1971.

Oraison, Marc. *The Homosexual Question.* New York: Harper and Row, 1977.

Pittinger, W. Norman. *Time for Consent.* London: SCM Press, 1976.

Scanzoni, Letha, and Mollenkott, Virginia Ramey. *Is the Homosexual My Neighbor?* New York: Harper and Row, 1978.

United Church of Christ. *Human Sexuality: A Preliminary Study.* New York: United Church Press, 1977.

United Presbyterian Church. *The Church and Homosexuality.* San Diego, Calif.: The General Assembly of the United Presbyterian Church in the United States of America, 1978.

Valente, Michael. *Sex: The Radical View of a Catholic Theologian.* New York: Bruce Publishing Company, 1960.

Weltge, Ralph W., ed. *The Same Sex: An Appraisal of Homosexuality.* Philadelphia: Pilgrim Press, 1969.

Woods, Richard. *Another Kind of Love: Homosexuality and Spirituality.* Chicago: Thomas More Press, 1977.

Documents

Baltimore Archdiocesan Task Force. *A Ministry to Lesbian and Gay Catholic Persons.* Baltimore: Catholic Center, 1981. An official statement on gay and lesbian ministry in the Archdiocese of Baltimore.

Catholic Social Welfare Commission. *An Introduction to the Pastoral Care of Homosexual Catholics.* Mt. Rainier, Md.: New Ways Ministry, 1980. Guidelines for the pastoral care of homosexual people from the Bishops of England and Wales. This document includes a discussion of human relationships, causes, the Christian tradition, and sixteen pastoral guidelines.

Committee on Pastoral Research and Practices. *Principles to Guide Confessors in Questions of Homosexuality.* Washington, D.C.: National Conference of Catholic Bishops, 1973. This is the official statement of the U.S. Catholic hierarchy on homosexuality and pastoral ministry. The booklet discusses Church teaching, objective and subjective morality, permanent and temporary homosexuality, pastoral issues, and sacramental practice. It also includes remarks on homosexuality among priests, religious, and seminarians.

Dutch Catholic Council for Church and Society. *Homosexual People in Society.* Mt. Rainier, Md.: New Ways Ministry, 1980. A discussion document authorized by the hierarchy of the Netherlands. It is intended as a contribution to the dialogue within the faith community and covers questions of human dignity, discrimination, homosexuality and the Scriptures, and homosexual behavior and Church teaching.

Mugavero, Francis J. *Sexuality—God's Gift.* Brooklyn, N.Y.: The Chancery Office, 1976. This is a pastoral letter in response to the Vatican *Declaration on Sexual Ethics* and contains a small section on homosexuality. Its overall positive approach to human sexuality makes it one of the best statements on the topic from a U.S. Catholic source.

National Conference of Catholic Bishops. *To Live in Christ Jesus.* Washington, D.C.: United States Catholic Conference, 1976. A pastoral letter of the American hierarchy dealing with many contemporary moral issues including one paragraph on homosexuality which calls for protection of the civil rights of homosexual persons and a special degree of pastoral understanding and care, and enumerates the rights of homosexual Catholics.

Sacred Congregation for the Doctrine of the Faith. *Declaration on Sexual Ethics.* Washington, D.C.: United States Catholic Conference, 1976. A statement of traditional principles of Catholic sexual ethics as applied to four contemporary sexual issues including homosexuality. This document, while condemning homosexual behavior, officially recognizes the phenomenon of a homosexual *orientation*.

New Ways Ministry. *Catholic Coalition for Gay Civil Rights*. Mt. Rainier, Md.: New Ways Ministry, 1978. A statement supporting education, gay ministry, and social justice for homosexual people and endorsed by individual Catholics, religious communities, diocesan institutions, Catholic organizations, theologians, and other Catholic leaders.

Quinn, John R. *Pastoral Letter on Homosexuality*. San Francisco: The Chancery Office, 1980. A pastoral statement by the Archbishop of San Francisco which discusses the contemporary situation of homosexuality and Church life, conclusions from Scripture, cultural notations, moral and ethical considerations, and sacramental practice.

Task Force on Gay/Lesbian Issues. *Homosexuality and Social Justice*. San Francisco: Commission on Social Justice, 1982. A 150-page report on homosexuality and the Church prepared for the Archdiocesan Commission on Social Justice. The report is the work of a task force of fourteen persons and covers a wide range of issues including violence against homosexual people, the moral and political dimensions of language, the Latino community, the family, the spiritual lives of homosexual persons, education, homosexual people in priesthood and religious life, the disabled, youth, and the aged. The report also includes fifty-four action recommendations.

Weakland, Rembert. *Who Is My Neighbor?* Milwaukee: The Chancery Office, 1980. A brief but clear statement from the Archibishop of Milwaukee calling for dialogue on the issue of homosexuality among all groups in the Church and touching on Scripture, pastoral ministry, relationships, and social justice.

Contributors

Gregory Baum teaches in the Department of Religious Studies of St. Michael's College, University of Toronto. He is a theologian and sociologist, editor of *The Ecumenist* and member of the editorial board of *Concilium*. Among his many books are *Man Becoming, Religion and Alienation,* and, most recently, *The Priority of Labor.*

Lisa Sowle Cahill is Associate Professor of Theology at Boston College. She holds a doctorate from the Chicago University Divinity School and specializes in Christian theological ethics, medical ethics, and sexual morality. She is the ethics editor of *Religious Studies Review* and associate editor of *The Journal of Religious Ethics.* Her articles and reviews have appeared in *The Journal of Medicine and Philosophy, Theological Studies, Journal of Ecumenical Studies, America,* and *Theology Today.*

Margaret A. Farley, R.S.M., is currently Associate Professor of Christian Ethics at Yale Divinity School. She holds a master's degree in philosophy from the University of Detroit and a doctorate in religious studies from Yale University. She has published articles on medical ethics, sexual ethics, women's studies, and social ethics in *Theological Studies, The Journal of Religious Ethics,* and *The Journal of Religion.* She is coauthor of *A Metaphysics of Being and God.*

Matthew Fox is a Dominican priest and director of the Institute in Creation-Centered Spirituality at Mundelein College, Chicago. He holds a doctorate from the Catholic Institute in Paris and is the author of eight books on spirituality. He is a popular teacher and lecturer and has been the featured speaker at numerous conferences, conventions, and other religious gatherings. He is also editor of *Bear & Co.,* a journal devoted to creation spirituality.

Jeannine Gramick, Ph.D., is co-founder and co-director of New Ways Ministry, a social justice organization working for the reconciliation of gay and lesbian persons within the Catholic Church. She directed an extensive sociological research project on the coming-out process of lesbian women and coordinated the First National Symposium on Homosexuality and the Catholic Church. A member of the School Sisters of Notre Dame, she has been involved in pastoral work with lesbian and gay people since 1971.

Michael D. Guinan, a Franciscan priest, is Professor of Old Testament and Semitic Languages at the Franciscan School of Theology, Berkeley, and Adjunct Professor of Semitic Languages at the University of California at Berkeley. He is the author of *Gospel Poverty: Witness to the Risen Christ.*

Mary E. Hunt is a Roman Catholic theologian with a doctorate from Berkeley. Her dissertation was titled "Feminist Liberation Theology." In 1982 she completed a two-year assignment as a Frontier Intern in Buenos Aires, where she was Visiting Professor of Systematic Theology at ISEDT, an ecumenical seminary, and was active in women's and human rights groups.

Marguerite Kropinak is a member of the Sisters of St. Joseph of Baden, Pennsylvania. She has a master's degree in social work from the University of Pittsburgh and a master's degree in theology from Duquesne University. She is a member of the Academy of Certified Social Workers and presently works as a parish family-life minister. She is also involved with Dignity/Pittsburgh and is the Eastern representative for Sisters in Gay Ministry Associated (SIGMA).

John McNeill is a Jesuit priest and psychotherapist in private practice in New York City. He has a doctorate in philosophy from Louvain and was previously Professor of Christian Ethics at Woodstock College and Union Theological Seminary. He currently teaches in a pastoral counseling program at the Institutes of Religion and Health and conducts workshops on gay-related topics. He is the author of *The Church and the Homosexual.*

Daniel Maguire is an internationally renowned ethicist who teaches at Marquette University. He is president of the Society of Christian Ethics and co-founder of Moral Alternatives. His books include *Death by Choice, Moral Choice,* and *The New Subversives.*

Edward A. Malloy is a priest of the Congregation of the Holy Cross and a member of the faculty of the Department of Theology at the University of Notre Dame, where he also holds the post of Associate Provost. He is the author of *Homosexuality and the Christian Way of Life* and has published several articles on sexual morality, bio-medical ethics, war and peace, and ethical methodology.

Gabriel Moran is Assistant Professor of Religious Education at New York University. He is the author of numerous books and articles dealing with religion and education. His most recent book is *Interplay: A Theory of Religion and Education.*

Robert Nugent is a Salvatorian priest and co-founder and co-director of New Ways Ministry. He holds a master's degree in library science from Villanova University and is currently on leave studying for a master's degree in theology at Yale Divinity School. He has lectured and written widely on the Church's pastoral ministry for gay and lesbian Catholics. His articles have appeared in *America, Ministries, Catholic Digest,* and *The Priest.*

M. Basil Pennington is a Cistercian priest at St. Joseph's Abbey, Spencer, Massachusetts. He holds a doctorate in church law from the Pontifical Gregorian University. He was a peritus at the Second Vatican Council and has taught moral theology and directed novices at St. Joseph's Abbey. He has published several books, including *Centering Prayer, Monastic Journey to India,* and *Jubilee: A Monk's Journey.* His articles on contemporary spirituality have appeared in *Emmanuel, America, Pastoral Life,* and *Review for Religious.*

Paul K. Thomas is a priest of the Archdiocese of Baltimore, where he serves as Procurator-Advocate for Annulment Cases and as Judge-Delegate on the Archdiocesan Tribunal. He was ordained in Rome in 1963 and has pastoral experience in both urban and suburban parishes. He is a member of the archdiocesan team outreach ministry for gay and lesbian Catholics established by Archbishop William Borders, and is on the board of directors of Communications Ministry, Inc., a support group for gay clergy and religious.

Evelyn Eaton Whitehead is a development psychologist with a doctorate from the University of Chicago. She writes and lectures on adult development, aging, and social analysis of community and parish. Among the books she has written with James Whitehead are *Christian Life Patterns* and *Community of Faith*.

James D. Whitehead is a pastoral theologian and historian of religion with a doctorate from Harvard University. He is concerned with questions of contemporary spirituality and theological method in ministry. Among the books he has written with Evelyn Whitehead are *Method in Ministry* and *Marrying Well*.

Bruce A. Williams, O.P., is on the faculty of St. John's University in New York. He has also taught at the Pontifical University of St. Thomas Aquinas in Rome, where he recently received a doctorate in theology with a dissertation on the topic of homosexuality.

James R. Zullo, F.S.C., is founder and director of the Christian Brothers Counseling and Consultation Center in Westchester, Illinois. He holds a doctorate in clinical psychology from Northwestern University and is a registered psychologist in the state of Illinois. Since 1972 he has been Adjunct Professor in the Institute of Pastoral Studies at Loyola University of Chicago and has written and spoken on the psychology of adolescence and the psychology of mid-years. His articles have appeared in *Human Development* and *Chicago Studies*.

Index